Twilight of the Literary

Twilight of the Literary

Figures of Thought in the Age of Print

Terry Cochran

HARVARD UNIVERSITY PRESS

Cambridge, Massachusetts

London, England

2001

To Hervée

Library of Congress Cataloging-in-Publication Data

Cochran, Terry, 1955–
   Twilight of the literary : figures of thought in the age of print /
Terry Cochran.
      p.   cm.
   Includes bibliographical references and index.
   ISBN 0-674-00454-X
   1. Printing—Social aspects—History.   2. Books—Social aspects—History.
3. Written communication—History.   4. Intellectual life—History.
5. Globalization.   I. Title.

Z124.C66 2001
302.2'244—dc21   00-054013

Contents

Acknowledgments

Limited portions of the introduction appeared in "The Linguistic Economy of the Cosmopolitical," *boundary 2* 26, no. X (1999), and portions of chapter 8 appeared in "The Matter of Language," *boundary 2* 25, no. 2 (1998). Early versions of chapters 3, 6, and 7 appeared as follows: "History and the Collapse of Eternity," *boundary 2* 22, no. 3 (1995); "The Emergence of Global Contemporaneity," *Diaspora* 5, no. 1 (1996); "Culture in Its Sociohistorical Dimension," *boundary 2* 21, no. 2 (1994).

The research resulting in this book has been funded by the Social Sciences and Humanities Research Council of Canada.

Twilight of the Literary

Introduction

Efforts to characterize modernity have splashed barrels of ink over countless pages. In a particular, very limited sense, this book falls into that seemingly endless series of attempts to reiterate aspects of modernity. Most frequently, reference to modernity does little more than inscribe a narrative technique that claims supremacy for the modern period; assertions of modernity permit the illusion of a seamless historical unfolding from a premodern, to a modern, and perhaps even to a "postmodern" moment. Unfortunately, awareness of this narrative mechanism does not dispel its necessity, for it rests on the conceptual needs of secularization, on the need to show that human beings largely control their own fate. This confrontation between modern and premodern, which translates into a precise vision of historical understanding, belongs to modernity as it is mentioned in this book. In attempting to take a less immediate view of history, I use the term *modernity* to describe the West's (and, ultimately, the globe's) relative disengagement from a theologically grounded view of human history.

This supposed break between a theologically ordered universe and a terrestrial, humanized understanding has often been equated with the Renaissance, with the rise of the vernacular state, or with some other historical or conceptual phenomenon. But this book follows no chronological impulse. Rather than presuming modernity to reside on this side of a vast chasm separating it from a superseded historical understanding, I consider the schemas of modernity more as a meandering out of the past that follows no simple temporal succession, even if from today's perspective certain tendencies may seem clear. In this larger framework, the book plots a shifting configuration of ideas and attempts to come to terms with key assumptions or preconceived notions in a secular generated world, notions I have called figures of thought. What this expression entails will be more concretely rendered in what immediately follows.

In this encompassing landscape of modernity, the twentieth century —or, rather, the transformations it signals—has had an overwhelming role to play, both implicitly and explicitly. The multiplicity of media, whether cinema, video, audio recording, or software, involves new ways of transcribing human thought for posterity and alters understandings of historical continuity. In this context, many aspects of cultural production have become visible for the first time, and the notion of culture, including its dynamics of circulation, has become a privileged object of reflection. More importantly, however, these twentieth-century transformations have occasioned unprecedented consideration of how thought is inscribed, materially registered in the world, and of its role in producing historical understanding. In a general and tentative way, reference to "figuration" in this book names this process of inscribing human thought, which includes the interpretations that might be read into such inscribing. Finding the reasons for this theme's emergence requires little effort. The literary or written foundations of history, which reigned supreme prior to the twentieth century, have been severely undermined by the proliferation of other time-resistant media, ranging from visual to audio reproduction, in which written language takes on a lesser role. At the same time, primary assumptions about how one receives and potentially makes sense of material artifacts, whether a literary inscription, a painting, or some other materialized product of human thought, have been no less destabilized.

Consequently, this book—the presuppositions underlying it, the questions it addresses, and the analyses it advances—resides at a specific historical juncture that enables a new critical perspective on the material bases of modernity. This interrogation of modernity's worldview is both historical and conceptual; it concerns the historical deployment of print as the dominant physical means of inscribing human thinking (or the human spirit or *Geist,* as the nineteenth-century German historians used to say), as well as the conceptual assumptions regarding human thought and its representation that this reproductive medium permitted or encouraged. A specific understanding of the limits and possibilities of producing sense, of moving beyond the visibly explicit to find, invent, or affirm multiple meanings, has been central to the dominance of written culture. Whether in the form of manuscript or print, writing as a mode of inscription and transmission of human thought involves correlative historical views, social formations, and institutions of knowledge. For example, medieval interpretations of religious texts, produced and reproduced according to the logic of the scriptorium, attest to this vision of unfolding meaning that cannot take place in isolation from a correlative organization of society and understanding of history. The epoch of printing, however, which corresponds directly to the emergence and elaboration of global modernity, transmuted and magnified the inscribing powers of writing, creating previously unimaginable possibilities to organize and institutionalize secular knowledge. Moreover, in the epoch of print, the real and ideal constraints implied in bestowing meaning on material artifacts underwent serious transformation, and they form the conceptual and historical backdrop of modern and contemporary thinking. In sum, the shifting conditions of generating and materially inscribing human thought have profound repercussions on the emergence and consolidation of worldviews in the so-called modern age, and this book attempts to bring into focus the fundamental elements of this modern constellation of notions and presuppositions.

A broader panorama renders these issues somewhat less ethereal. Before the advent of linguistic writing, which is so bound to historical understanding that whatever precedes it is relegated to prehistory, inscribing human thought and effort had few possibilities. A favorite prewriting or prehistorical example of how humans leave material traces behind them is the menhir, an upright monumental stone of which there are numerous extant specimens. Before linguistic transcription, the limited means of rendering human thought visible make the menhir a sort of unadorned lowest common denominator of purposeful intellectual inscription. The carvings inscribed in their surfaces, often indicating elements of some human figure, offer no meaning to decipher in the sense so customary for a world governed by linguistic transcription, by writing as linguistic record. The interpreter after the advent of writing can try to make sense of it, can invent an elaborate interpretation, but any search for sense remains for the most part supposition; there is simply not enough correlative material to corroborate any meaning definitively. Though difficult to imagine in the perspective of the contemporary world, the figure's incisions *say* nothing about its meaning and highlight only its necessary material aspect: it is a physical object, a stone bearing the marks of human intervention, and its continued existence in time transcends the here and now of the act producing it. In effect, the figure is constituted by this disjuncture between the material that historically endures and the here and now that is immediately lost. While the menhir's figurer may have launched, knowingly or unknowingly, a temporal message in a bottle to whoever might stumble across it, only succeeding history could write that message *for the first time.* This seeming paradox, unavoidably present in the historical relationship to the menhir's presumed meaning, constitutes the temporal quandary inherent in any attempt to appropriate the past. In this sense, this paradox lies at the heart of all historical interpretation.

For today's world, this aspect of the figure has lost its sense of urgency, and the temporal understanding belonging to the menhir makers is inconceivable. Contemporary society is built on material and, to a much greater extent, immaterial elaborations that include strategies of interpretation and attributed meanings zealously guarded by interrelated institutions of knowledge. Just as modern technology moves the demands of daily life farther and farther from the empirical—for example, heat is more and more controlled by manipulating a thermostat rather than by poking logs in a fireplace—secular worldviews have rendered presuppositions and figures of understanding more and more abstract. Instead of being stalemated by the menhir's material barriers, immaterial figures—such as ideas of the human spirit, the auteur, or collective consciousness, all of which have been historically elaborated on the basis of specific historical needs—provide the basis for producing the effect of historical continuity and for bestowing meaning.

In contrast with the world surrounding a simple menhir standing in some corner of a forgotten countryside, today's material and conceptual complexity is incalculable. Moreover, one cannot slough off centuries of interpretive elaboration running through the very fabric of thought; nor would one want to. Caught up in this spectrum of concerns, this book explores the idealizing constellation of the self-styled modern age, the figures of thought that emerge to anchor modernity. In moving to interrogate this constellation of notions, it gives a particular weight to the material aspect of the process of inscription. Unlike the menhir, which came to exist in what could almost be called a historical vacuum, modern inscription spans multiple material possibilities of reiterating tradition, culture, and civilization (all terms with a problematic history) and includes painting, architecture, sculpture, tools, and any other artifact that endures historically. But, above all, modernity's figures of thought—like those of the Middle Ages—find their most forceful expression and duration in writing, to a large extent because writing can easily offer commentaries on the other materials; in contrast with the ages before printing, however, the mass means of reproduction and diffusion dramatically altered the configuration of historical understanding. Writing—and especially in its more hegemonic modern forms of national literature and history—has formed the backbone for interpretation generally, assembling the various expressions of thought or human "spirit" in other media into a coherent, discursive whole. In modernity, itself coextensive with an ever greater proliferation of printed matter, writing still has the last word, so to speak. This last word, which is only provisionally final because it is constantly surpassed by new "last words," takes on another character in print. As Montaigne already remarked in the sixteenth century, *"Nous mettons en dignité nos bêtises quand nous les mettons en moule"* ("We dignifie our fopperies, when we put them to the presse").[1] The dignity—of the word, the name, the inscription, or the figure—is as much its material staying power as what it might express.

Institutional Groundwork

In the mundane world of physical action, clearing the ground to lay the foundation of an architectural structure entails a manual engagement with tangible objects, whether merely found in nature or resulting from human craft. Conceiving the structure, creating a mental image of the physical edifice, occupies a different plane of existence, no matter how important the real terrain might be to the final conception. At a still farther remove from the empirical world of things is reflection on the significance of any given institution, its meaning for human existence, the interests it serves, the possibilities for human action it enables, and the sociopolitical benefits it represents. In modernity, the gradually spreading print culture greatly exceeded the bare fact of technological advances that made printing possible and opened up an unprecedented dimension of historical reflection. Printing—specifically, the mechanical reproduction it signaled—both accompanied and fostered a transformed conception of the world; while irreducible to the simplistic status of "prime mover" of the modern impulse, printing permitted a new investment of the world, a centering of history, along with its transcription and transmission, in human hands.

A number of seventeenth-century thinkers are often cited as instrumental in chiseling out notions that defined the nontheological thrust of modernity. For example, according to the traditional story, Descartes reconceptualized the human subject and fashioned a new theory of scientific knowledge, Spinoza elaborated an immanent vision of history and argued for excising theology from political formation, and Pascal strove to underscore the power of human thought without jettisoning the active complicity of the divine. While swept along in the same current of secular reflection, Leibniz added a modernizing perspective that concerns the institutional ramifications of print technology and how it strengthens the human role in the overall production of history and knowledge. Unlike the other thinkers cited, who enjoyed a (muted) radical or even renegade reputation, Leibniz had explicit links to various secular powers, a fact that gave some of his writings a decidedly more practical and conservative turn. Leibniz's texts on the institutions of knowledge in the wake of printing take the form of projects that require political decision, although these writings contain largely speculative elements designed to convince the powers that be to implement the various projects. Not surprisingly, these diverse plans for localizing, channeling, and governing the production of knowledge concern the existing and potential institutions in Germany, an important early center for thinking out the implications of print.

In fact, the intellectual hegemony of the German book trade, particularly as it concerns issues of transnational flow of ideas, translation, and property rights, has been seriously challenged only in the late twentieth century. Before Leibniz's time, for example, the Frankfurt book fair was already being held; while its role changed over time, with its eventually becoming the foremost site for selling and buying intellectual property, it has for centuries represented the periodic, often yearly summum of print production on a global scale. Leibniz's endeavors to analyze knowledge production in the light of print technology draw their impetus from the book fair, which serves as the concrete basis for his plans to inventory, preserve, foster, and promote human knowledge. In his pro-

posal to establish Mainz as the seat of royal authority over book production—even if for practical reasons he believed that the overseeing
commission should have its offices in Frankfurt (because Frankfurt was
the *"universale emporium literarum"* in Germany)[2]—Leibniz lays bare
the conceptual scaffolding necessary to rethinking the world from the
perspective of print. First of all, the network of concepts and institutions
calls for a protonational or territorial anchor. As he acknowledges, his
efforts involve basing "in Mainz the supreme authority over all that concerns books and *res litteraria* throughout all of Germany" ("Privilege,"
3). From the outset, the reference to *res litteraria* indicates the breadth of
the drive to envision writing as the backbone of human knowledge and
culture. In the vein of the classical *res publica,* which would later become
republic, the term *res litteraria* covers both the concrete object, the book
or the printed page, as well as the conceptual and institutional baggage
that necessarily accompany it. In other words, *res litteraria,* perhaps best
rendered as "literary matters" or "things in the world of writing," has a
material and an immaterial aspect, in the same way that books themselves have a material existence even as reading them generates a series of ideal or immaterial "worlds." But Leibniz is even more specific
in requesting permission to elaborate his plans for institutionalizing
and keeping track of knowledge production: "The commissariat encompasses inspection of all of *res litteraria* to the extent that it appears before
the public in print" ("Privilege," 7). It is a matter of regulating printed
knowledge that goes public; in Leibniz's vision of the human status quo,
the technology of print simultaneously represents dangers to stability
and enormous powers of historical transformation that must be mas-
tered. The so-called commission he recommends is designed to mediate
the forces that print unleashes.

Contrary to passing comments about how such a commission might
"quietly suppress" unseemly or undesirable publications ("Privilege,"
10), the real thrust of his document in support of an administrative
agency lies elsewhere. Rather than concentrating on its powers of executive action—that is, actions of direct censorship or overt physical intervention—this application for privilege stresses over and over the mental
connections that must be forged in thinking the historical and political
significance of this new "technology." Its existence will set in place a network of relations, a sort of economy of producing knowledge, and its
stable operation will permit, "after prior consultation and correspon-

dence with scholars, the realization of all kinds of things, rules, and institutions that are useful and even necessary for the common good, concerning books, authors, booksellers, correctors, printers, and studies" ("Privilege," 11). The passage underscores the bureaucratic aspect of any governmental agency, but most striking is the explicit link between the producers and distributors of the physical object (the book), on the one hand, and the production of knowledge (such as the scholars and the "studies" they generate), on the other. Ultimately, Leibniz remarks, this new situation enables the ideas of scholars to be legitimated by the force of royal authority ("Privilege," 11–12). In sum, in rethinking the production of knowledge along the lines of what print allows, Leibniz places more than a little emphasis on the formation of ideas and their role in the perpetuation of knowledge. While the preeminence of ideas, of scholarly opinion, is not born with print, in the age of print ideas take on a special significance because of the forms of institutionalization that print allows and, to a certain extent, requires.

Print, in particular print as the material backbone of a new world conception, has readily identifiable characteristics that have permeated modernity so deeply as to be inseparable from it. Once again, Leibniz illustrates the basic precepts that printed matter entails; in the context of this regulatory agency that he describes,

> scholars and inquisitive people throughout Germany, following the example of other nations, will be encouraged to correspond and communicate among themselves and with neighboring and distant universities, to reach an understanding and, thereby, to preserve and multiply numerous new and useful thoughts, propositions, inventions, and observations that would otherwise disappear with their authors; this applies to the domains of natural science, mechanics, manufacturing, trade, and mathematics, as well as to those of history, politics, law, and others, opening the way for the youth in universities and elsewhere to become familiar with the occupations in a timely fashion, in a way more useful than when they unsoundly begin reasoning before steeping themselves in sufficiently rigorous studies, a practice more damaging than helpful to the fatherland, hindering even their own advancement. ("Privilege," 12–13)

The single nation, Germany—still not quite yet a "nation" in the modern sense—appears in a global context vis-à-vis others that have already tried to address the organization and reproduction of knowledge. In this sense, Leibniz brings into the picture the institutions of higher learning, the universities, that serve as the nodes of exchange in transforming or building new knowledge. As the document's passing reference to "youth" suggests, the reason the emergence of print provokes a reaction among its contemporaries—scholars and kings alike, even if they sometimes have dissimilar interests—entails precisely the question of reproducing knowledge on a grand scale.

With the advent of print, the relationship between the past, present, and future changes considerably, in part because of the volume of extant writings that continue to pile up, in part because thinking out and sorting through that quantity calls for an unprecedented compartmentalization of knowledge, including reliance on "scholars" or legitimate judges to oversee it. It is no longer a question only of what is going to be passed on but of the criteria for determining which lines of thought are designated to carry the burden of history into the future. Print is a mechanical apparatus of inscription that upsets the traditional relationship between the preservation and multiplication of past knowledge that is destined to outlive the present. The centrality of print affects all disciplines of knowledge, from the practical to the more theoretical, from science to the human sciences, from commerce to the juridical domain. Writing in the seventeenth century, Leibniz necessarily neglects to mention the literary disciplines, including the national literary traditions that since the beginning of the nineteenth century have proven so important to modern history and to the immaterial ideals that channel it. Nevertheless, the basic insight is evoked: based on the preserving and reproductive powers of print, knowledge institutions—attached implicitly or explicitly to the sociopolitical formations—house the past legacy, the diffused scribblings of dead individuals, that extends from wispy thoughts and propositions to more concrete inventions.

Within this framework, Leibniz pursues his goals to create various knowledge institutions and depositories of written and printed material. His various projects hold nothing startling in the eyes of the twenty-first century, which, in the burgeoning mass of material artifacts of every ilk, has seen thousands of such institutions established, the smallest of which would dwarf Leibniz's institutional ambitions. Among his projects, he calls for setting up a governmental archive to create a line of continuity between the past and present with regard to legal or official questions.[3] In addition, he makes a case for establishing and maintaining a princely library to include writings and representations of every imaginable branch of knowledge; this document, entitled "Repraesentanda," contains a multimedia reflection on the role of images for the human spirit, along with the typical discussion of youth education ("To instruct our young men, above all nothing in the world is better than figures"— that is, visual representations).[4] Nevertheless, with regard to the implications of print, to the institutional transformation it demands, Leibniz's most straightforward text is his actual plan for producing a "Semestria literaria" for every Frankfurt book fair. While still not a full-blown *semestria,* that is, a reference work that condenses and represents new knowledge produced each year, the project constitutes a step beyond his separate request for permission to pursue it. This proposal about organizing published knowledge calls for a number of components, including a series of summaries of everything published *("Bibliothecae universalis contractae"),* an analytical index, information about publishers, and a history of things literary (*"Historia rei literariae totius"*: again, things written or, in this context, things printed and published).[5] What he recommends resembles twentieth-century yearbooks that update ongoing knowledge in the epoch of print domination (a form of publication unlikely to prevail against the perpetual incorporation of new knowledge resulting from interconnected computer networks). For Leibniz, the stakes of this yearly summmum of knowledge, combining information with a conceptual roadmap for the year's production, are quite high and concern the very existence of civilization. The task, he argues, needs to be undertaken with dispatch: "The number of books increases to such an extent that if we delay too long the work would ultimately become so desperate as to be impossible. The result would be no less than total confusion, a scorn for all learning, and, finally, the return of ancient barbarism; in such an indescribable mass of books it would no longer be possible to find and recognize the best in the midst of the bad and the insignificant" ("Semestria," 157). In the seventeenth century, the piling up of printed matter was already at the edge of being unmanageable; according to the logic of these remarks, the rate of new publications demanded careful scrutiny to maintain advances of human knowledge. In this sense, Leibniz poses the question—without, however, offering any concrete answers—of the criteria for separating the chaff from genuine knowledge. Leibniz's own tendencies for evaluating authenticity, very much in line with the spirit of the times, favored explicit advances in (scientific or philosophical) knowledge and speculated little about other sorts of literary or so-called aesthetic knowledge. More important regarding the issue of printing's role in human culture, Leibniz's plan sketches out a readily discernible theory of history. Knowledge and its accumulation, which the mechanical inscription of printing stockpiles in ever greater quantities, permits humanity to transcend its "barbarism" by materially laying down a timeline of memory that lets the present build on past knowledge. But overcoming barbarism cannot be reduced to the brute writing down and disseminating of ongoing knowledge; sheer quantity—in this instance, of books—reintroduces the question of historical continuity, the progress it implies, and, ultimately, the potential return of barbarism. Too much knowledge or, more specifically, too much printed matter brings historical chaos and undermines the technological power of print and the leap in human knowledge it prepared. This linear view of human history, in which each present raises itself to a higher lever and propels history forward, also has the potential of decline. In the face of this threat, Leibniz sees no alternative to instituting a novel organization of knowledge; in attempting to think through what he viewed as the technical challenge to ongoing human progress, he unknowingly laid the groundwork for a process of institutionalization that would come to be identified with modernity.

While Leibniz's plan of synoptic knowledge does not address the criteria, presuppositions, ideas, or figures of thought that gradually emerge to anchor modern historical understanding, it traces out the fundamental notions that such an organization of knowledge implies: "Despite the greatly overpowering mass of books, . . . the largest and best part of human knowledge and experience has not yet been put in books; a special effort should be made to overcome this lack, and learned people should find the opportunity and occasion to fill these gaps and to produce things not yet written rather than repeating the old" ("Semestria," 158–159). The goal is to inscribe human knowledge in a material form that will enable it to be passed down to later times. While for Leibniz knowledge remains incomplete, this fragmentariness is not endemic to human existence but rather derives from practical impediments that the material possibility of print can—at least in principle—surmount. The presumption of totality, in this passage specifically evoked as a synchronic notion claiming that the gaps in current knowledge can be filled in, provides a methodological mechanism for understanding the continuity and motivation of human accomplishment. This presupposition gives a clear rendering of the voluntarist undercurrent of modernity; the human mind, which by means of material representation can extend its reach in time and space, has the powers to invest the world in its entirety, to unearth and reflect on data with the intention of completing omissions in knowledge. Moreover, this new vision of human thought, based on the working assumption of total understanding, places a specific burden on any given present: it must seek to differentiate itself and its knowledge from what preceded it. Contrary to the prehistorical world—that is, before writing—in which repetition of past knowledge keeps alive communal thought and understanding, Leibniz's reasoning emphasizes that the present should break with the past and try to avoid reiterating it. Widespread material preservation of the past frees up the present to operate according to a different set of assumptions. Just as with the idea of totality, this transformation in historical understanding draws material support from printing, which early in its development seemed almost to keep pace with human investigation, creating unprecedented objects of reflection as well as the means to disseminate them widely. In this perspective, printing signals a radical change from the historical limitations of scribal copying, which, with its glacial slowness and the singularity of its production, was more closely akin to the oral world than to the technical reproduction of print.

These assumptions—about potentially totalizable human knowledge, about the human ability to grasp the old in order to produce the new—do not belong to the order of truth and validity but *enable* a particular view of historical understanding. In the seventeenth century, the technical mastery of registering thought in printed matter accompanies rather than causes the emergence of these assumptions. The intimate interconnectedness of ideas and the material production of thought belie any effort to determine causal primacy. But print, along with the "yearbooks" that synthesize yearly production, provides a point of departure for Leibniz's historical and epistemological project. The *semestria* or yearbook volumes should be catalogued and cross-referenced to create "a treasury of human knowledge with an inventory so that everything can be correctly and orderly arranged, readily available for whoever seeks to get his hands on it, and, in a word, to use it. On the contrary, in the present-day confusion, we humans don't even know what we have" ("Semestria," 160). As the twentieth century's deluge of knowledge production amply demonstrated, mapping that knowledge takes on massive importance as the quantity of material increases. Leibniz's inventory summarizes but also offers a guide for accessing the totality of extant knowledge. Long before print, writing was itself viewed as an extension of human memory and history, but in Leibniz's proposal, print, by means of its ongoing synthesis and abstraction in *semestria*, becomes more a material prosthesis of human thought. Print becomes the material means of a more efficient rationalization of the products of the human mind. Thoughts become materialized, achieve an external existence, to become in turn the object of subsequent human reflection.

Much like the calculus notations that take mathematical variables to ever-higher levels of abstraction, the *semestria* pile up, adding layer upon layer, commenting, organizing, probing, and—most important—integrating knowledge as it is produced. Documenting the total output of human understanding is not a short-term task, and Leibniz's plans stress the exponential power of these yearly summaries of published knowledge. The *semestria*, having in a few years "brought all human experience [*Erfahrung*: science or knowledge] to paper," will ultimately constitute the material of and lay the groundwork for the principal structure of an *Encyclopaedia perfectae*. In this way, we will have in our hands the possibility of resolving and ordering human thoughts or notions, of proving demonstratively or fundamentally according to mathematical order all primary truths that flow from reason" ("Semestria," 161).

The *semestria*, themselves a continuing reassessment of knowledge produced and published, give rise to their own reassessment and reorganization into an encyclopedic summa of products of thought. No longer simply in the realm of facts, of what is thought, this encyclopedic abstraction mobilizes a higher-level possibility of interrogating human thoughts and their reason supposedly susceptible to mathematical demonstration. This reiterative structure of thought, which builds a historical network of references farther and farther removed from the strictly empirical world, rests squarely on material organizations and refinements that rest on still other printed matter. In this sense, Leibniz's elaborations spin out the mechanism of modernity that relies on the specific character of print culture and on the intertwinement of immaterial thought and its material rendering. It is at this juncture that what I am calling "figures" take on their greatest significance.

The Spirit of Print

For better or for worse, the emergence of modern institutions corresponds to a mutation in the manner of materializing books. These modern institutions run through various planes of thought and range from empirical manifestations, such as university organizations of knowledge and consolidations of statehood, to the more abstract inventions of vernacular grammar, including phenomena necessary for formulating the modern worldview, such as the so-called discovery of the globe, massive urbanization, and new forms of collective consciousness. With the printed book, the mechanical means of materializing, publishing, and distributing efforts of the human spirit permits sociopolitical practices and conceptions of human understanding that have subsequently been identified as "modern"; these novel conceptions are so entrenched in and intertwined with modernity that not even the multiple media of the twentieth century were able to dislodge them. Just as Leibniz's dream of an encyclopedia of human knowledge becomes realized only after a lengthy period of institutional gestation, modernity's conceptual configuration achieves its early coherence only in the eighteenth century, a century in which the book is often explicitly evoked as the cornerstone of an emergent secular understanding. The most eloquent and succinct formulation of modernity's coordinates is Diderot and d'Alembert's *Encyclopédie,* which simultaneously incarnates a centuries-old intellectual project (which also inspired Leibniz), summarizes the status of human knowledges in every domain imaginable, and codifies an interpretive grid that will be enlarged on in elaborating the national and historical conceptions of the nineteenth century.

In situating the beginning of critical history in the midfifteenth century, the *Encyclopédie* article "History" emphasizes the confluence of various areas, including those of politics, the arts, technology, and knowledge generally. More to the point, in this broad landscape of knowledge transformation, it indicates a close relationship between history or historical understanding and the medium that records it. Although in the late twentieth century the primary medium of history drew no attention to itself and was wholly taken for granted, the notion of history, which even in its most rudimentary form mobilizes claims of objectivity, requires the fixity of a material inscription. In the eighteenth century, awareness of this link between matter and history still belonged to the active cultural understanding, and the matter or medium in question was the printed word:

> It is at the end of the century [the article refers to the fifteenth century] that a new world is discovered, and soon afterward European politics and the arts take on a new form. The art of printing and the restoration of the sciences finally allow for *histories* that are relatively faithful instead of those ridiculous chronicles that had been locked up in the cloisters since Gregory of Tours. Every nation in Europe soon had its historians. The earlier paucity turns into abundance: there is not a city that doesn't want its own particular *history*. One is buried under the weight of minutia. A man who wants to be instructed . . . grasps in the multitude of revolutions the spirit of the times and the customs of peoples. Above all one must follow the *history* of one's own land [*patrie*], study it, possess it, retain all its details, and look more generally at other nations. Their *history* is interesting only for the links they have with us or for the great things they have accomplished.[6]

While the passage openly espouses a secular view of historical understanding, it is less a critique of the divine than a valorization of human capacities. This revitalized human agent discovers the planet, reconfigures European politics, and transforms the arts—or "cultural production," as one might say today with greater precision. Moreover, the idea of national history emerges, and the homegrown histories establish geographies of the mind, identities narrated in printed texts. According to this eighteenth-century rendering, the technology of reproduction, along with the material diffusion of thought it entails, both transforms the physical means of representing thoughts and creates mental images—what one might be tempted to call "figures"—that take on an existence of their own. In other words, history represents some kind of a nonmaterial spirit, that is, an idea such as that of a nation, a fatherland. In the world of tangible objects, that spirit is linked to a demarcated territory or boundary guarded by uniformed individuals who act in its name, to institutions where judges sit to pronounce in reference to its interests. In addition, however, it is bound up with a collective identity, and with an understanding of how events take place and how they are reported or expressed in language. In sum, history is a key component of a conceptual apparatus, a configuration of presuppositions closely associated with modernity and with the nation-state formation that fosters it. As the passage remarks, this entire configuration rests on the dominance of a particular medium—writing—and its mechanical reproduction in print.

This print economy of modernity, along with the concepts that mobilize it, hinges on the concept of the book. Once again, I refer to the *Encyclopédie,* this time to the article "Book":

> [A book in general is] a writing composed by some intelligent person about some issue of knowledge [*science*], for the instruction and amusement of the reader. One can still define a *book* as a composition by a man of letters, realized to communicate to the public and to posterity something that he has invented, seen, experienced, and assembled, and that must be long enough to make a volume . . . The uses of *books* are no less numerous nor less varied; it is by means of them that we acquire our knowledge: they are the repository of laws, memory, events, usages, mores, customs, etc., the vehicle of all the sciences; even the establishment and preservation of religion is in part owed to them.[7]

In the view of the eighteenth-century Encyclopedists, the book was responsible not only for history but for all knowledge, specifically, for its temporal continuity. The book is *the* means of access to knowledge, at least before the twentieth century and the unpredictable proliferation of other technologies of reproduction. The book is the mediation between the human (what the text calls "us") and knowledge, the guardian or repository of all productions of the spirit capable of being in some way recorded, and the vehicle of all disciplines of knowledge (that is, of all *sciences,* or knowledges). The list of the domains determined and channeled by the book is remarkably complete and contains all the branches of intellectual production: the juridical, historical, cultural, scientific, and religious sectors. Once again, this privilege of the book derives from its capacity to materially encode thoughts and effects generated by the human spirit. Print technology exponentially augments the powers of the book, creating a flood of printed matter that transfigures the fundamental notion of materializing the spirit. In other words, it mechanically induces massive transformations that are qualitative as well as quantitative. As the *Encyclopédie* describes it in another article: "Type founding and printing proper collaborated to infinitely multiply the productions of the spirit or, rather, copies of these productions."[8]

The spirit that survives its own death is always materialized; as Leibniz already noted, printing calls for or demands a renewed organization of knowledge specifically conceived to direct and tame its effects. Elevation of the *printed* book (as opposed to the laboriously copied manuscript) to the supreme point of reference for thinking about human intellectual continuity has important consequences for modernity, for the worldview it installs, and for the figures of thought it institutionalizes. In this context, the *Encyclopédie* article "Printing" renders explicit the stakes in the mechanical reproduction of printed matter:

> Thus, with the aid of printing, we come not only to multiply knowledge, but to fix and to transmit throughout the centuries the thoughts of human beings, even as their bodies have become indistinguishable from matter and their souls have flown away to the domain of the spirits.
>
> All the other arts that serve to perpetuate our ideas perish in the long term. Statues, in the end, collapse into dust. Buildings don't subsist as long as statues, and colors last less than buildings. Michelangelo, Fontana, and Raphael are what Phidias, Vitruvius, and Apelles were in sculpture, and the works of these latter no longer exist.
>
> The advantage that authors have over these grand masters comes from the fact that their writings can be endlessly multiplied, reprinted, and renewed in the number of copies desired, without the copies diminishing in value vis-à-vis the originals.
>
> What would one not give for a Virgil, a Horace, a Homer, a Cicero, a Plato, an Aristotle or a Pliny, if their works were restricted to a single place, or in the hands of one person, as is the case of a statue, a building, a painting?
>
> It is therefore thanks to the beautiful art of printing that human beings express their thoughts in works that can last as long as the sun and that will be lost only in the universal upheavals of nature. Only then will the inimitable works of Virgil and Homer perish along with all the worlds spinning overhead.
>
> Since it is true that books pass from one century to another, how could the authors not take great care to use their talents in works aiming to perfect human nature?[9]

The extreme lucidity of these observations deserves careful consideration. The passage aims to characterize the role of printing in producing human continuity; it describes writings in the perspective of their mechanical multiplication. Thoughts outlive the human body that has materially inscribed them and remain behind after the unity of body and mind—a fundamental division of Enlightenment philosophy—has disintegrated, with the constituent elements moving toward their respective spheres. In this sense, thoughts as well as printed knowledge are a sediment if not a fossil of the spirit: these modest remains that continue to exist after the disappearance of the mind creating them necessarily pose the question of history, of matter, and of their entwinement.

The passage's subsequent commentary unfolds in the midst of this bundle of issues. In comparing various "arts," the text is able to pinpoint the specificity of print, that is, of the printed book, even if the book is only vaguely mentioned. The comparison concerns only one aspect of these arts, and the text displays great precision in this respect: they are considered in light of their potential material duration. Instead of employing concepts deriving from fields of knowledge—for example, from the domains of architecture, sculpture, painting, literature—the article limits itself exclusively to empirical objects, that is, it refers only to a building, a painting, a statue. Despite the slight differences separating them with respect to their material duration, these three empirical examples share a number of aspects that contrast with those of a printed artifact: they are not reproducible in mass (given the technology of the epoch), they occupy *one* point in space, and they are concretely perceived by the senses. Print, on the other hand, produces an artifact that occupies a multiplicity of places at the same time; what the article calls "works" (not simply books and certainly not "literature") always exceeds the empirical and requires an imagined or idealizing perspective on two levels. First, the technology of writing itself calls for reading, an intellectual production, so that an "object" comes to be through the mediation of the material; in addition, print technology multiplies the material so that the work becomes even farther removed from empirical books viewed as material objects, as "things." In the very concept of the printed work, figuration, or the ability to produce objects on the basis of material squiggles, acts as a relay between matter and thought. While the interplay between thought and matter characterizes the single-copy parchments emanating from the scriptoria as well as the multiple copies deriving from mechanically produced printing, the idealizing power of printed matter radically exceeds that of the unique manuscript, if only because it simultaneously saturates large swatches of space and time. This mesh of ideal and material factors constitutes the particularity of the printed book as a model of cultural production.

This passage from the *Encyclopédie* comes to a close in referring to historical continuity, on the one hand, and to a specific conception of history, on the other. The multiplicity of print reinforces the power of the human spirit in the face of catastrophes or natural cataclysms; by simultaneously occupying countless places with the help of print technology, intellectual matter progressively escapes the dangers of annihilation. In this perspective, the book's specificity—whether in manuscript or printed form, although the differences between the two are significant—is due not to its linguistic character but to its technologies of materialization, the means of inscribing the effects of thought by leaving a material residue. In this general framework, the article expresses the historical view that seems to be the logical consequence of an infinite accumulation of materialized knowledge. The book, champion of human continuity, lends itself well to historical recuperation and to the idea of progress that is omnipresent in the eighteenth century. The matter of the spirit in book form, which is considered an extension and modification of human nature, grounds the theory and practice of linear history, along with its concomitant notions of progress and decline, which are simply reversed images of the same historical view. That directionality profoundly depends on the transformations that matter provokes in human nature, matter that, with the spread of print, becomes less and less precarious and, at the same time, more and more idealized.

The Global Medium

Contrary to expectations and perceptions in an age conditioned by satellite imaging, the globe is not a twirling object that can be simply grasped and represented in an inert snapshot. Notions of the world, both as a physical entity and as a conceptual space in which humans move and think, that is, as a worldview, have a strong historicity. As the *Encyclopédie* indicates, for example, awareness of the globe as an integral whole accompanied the political and technical changes that help define modern understanding. Prior to space travel, conceiving of the earth's unity required developed powers of visualization to turn the flatness of experience into planetary roundness. In the same vein, thinking the world as a counterpart to its human inhabitants involves a reflection on the medium that potentially links them together. The "world" before writing was immeasurably large, even though the communities that peopled it were extremely limited in number and in extension. At the other end of the spectrum, in an epoch in which writing is itself less and less materialized, the very existence of the global Internet has provoked substantive reflection on the status of human collectivity and the world it literally englobes.[10] In this sense, placing print—specifically, the printed book and its multiple copies—at the center of evolving human knowledge implies a worldview with series of presuppositions and figures of thought, so to speak. Not surprisingly, the question of print and the idealized world it provides leads back to the eighteenth century.

As the first thinker of modernity to ground his sociopolitical philosophy in an explicit understanding of the world at large, what he refers to as the "cosmopolitical," Kant is the obvious reference in this context. In this sense, Kantian thought laid the foundation for modern globalism. Language as such does not constitute a significant theme in Kant's extensive writings, but the matter of language, its medium and the ideal bond it creates between the members of a collectivity, resides at the center of his worldview. Although Kant addresses the cosmopolitical or global question in a number of texts, the issues of language, medium, and cosmopolitical collectivity find their most succinct expression in his much used and abused essay that responds to yet another question, "What Is Enlightenment?" The basic precepts of the Enlightenment form a constellation to project how, in modernity, individuals think reasonably, function as members of a collectivity, organize themselves into states, and interact with each other on a global scale. In plotting the idealizing coordinates of modernity, it is important to sketch briefly the presuppositions that underlie Kant's Enlightenment, particularly how this model of society, grounded in cosmopolitanism, propels itself to ever greater domination by the lights of reason. Kant's description of this sociopolitical mechanism is based on his well-known distinction between public and private reason:

> By the public use of one's reason I understand the use which a person makes of it as a scholar before the entire public of the world of readers [*ganzen Publikum der Leserwelt*]. Private use of reason I call that which a person may make of it in a particular civil post or office that is entrusted to him. Many affairs conducted in the interest of the community require a certain mechanism through which some members of the community must passively conduct themselves with an artificial unanimity, so that the government may direct them to public ends, or at least prevent them from destroying those ends. Here one is not allowed

to use reason freely; one must obey. But so far as this part of the machine regards himself at the same time as a member of the whole community or of a cosmopolitical society [*Weltbürgergesellschaft*], and thus in the capacity of a scholar who addresses the public (in the proper sense of the word) through his writings, he can certainly employ his reason without hurting the affairs for which he is in part responsible as a passive member.[11]

As with any theory of human history, Kant's concerns are two-headed: on the one hand, society requires stability, the conceptual hallmark of all socially conservative thinkers who want to contain the anarchist forces at the heart of any multitude; on the other hand, any historical vision must also account for the transformations necessary for human society to surpass itself and continue to stave off historical exhaustion and decline.

These two categories of historical action have distinct territorial centers of gravity. The scholar—or the educated or learned person, a notion that is anachronistically referred to as the "intellectual"—operates in these two domains, which are, respectively, conservative and transformative. When scholars work for the state, their reason is harnessed to the collective will that is determined by the government in power, which also includes the institutions of civil society. In this sphere of action, scholars do not reason on their own but follow directives; they channel an authority they do not possess but in whose name they act. Kant's text characterizes this ongoing production of stasis as a mechanism of containment in which the person is a cog in the machine. This mechanism is not constitutive but regulative; if the cog does not function properly, the state or institution justifiably removes it, reworks it, or tightens it down. In Kant's text, which concerns primarily the economy of reason and its sociopolitical limits, this state sphere refers to the "private" use of reason, which is private only in the sense of its determined territorial and administrative boundaries. In other words, it is not global.

The contrary of private or state reason, that which Kant calls "public" reason, has a different sphere of circulation; public reason courses through a virtual collectivity, a "whole community" as opposed to simple "community," or what the essay portrays as a "cosmopolitical society." The cosmopolitical needs no homogeneity, no singular collective will or vision, artificially produced to tame the forces of disintegration. This virtual collectivity or, in the words of the essay, the public "in the proper sense of the term," has a peculiar profile: it is constituted by people *who can read,* the *world* of readers. Kant's warning that this public should not be understood figuratively indicates the nature of that public: it is not a particular public, identifiable with specific geographical boundaries or formed around certain themes or objects of interest, in the way, for example, a public is conceived in the twentieth-century world of commerce. Instead, it is formed on the basis of its members' capacity to create links among themselves by reading printed texts, a public formed by an act of rendering public, as in the publication of a book. In other words, for Kant, and for modernity generally, the notion of the cosmopolitical presupposes the dissemination of a certain medium of knowledge, a certain skill to take a material object—a printed text—and produce an idealizing, immaterial "reading."

The public comes together ideally through the mediation of a virtual spirit or "mind." Yet, even if accurate, this way of describing the material phenomenon underlying Kant's vision of global history is far too abstract. In the eighteenth century, print provided the only means of conceiving a "mass" mind linking multitudes spread over large distances. This public, however heterogeneous its members and disparate its tendencies, was of "like mind" in the economy of meaning and collective consciousness; that is the nature of Kant's modernity and of the cosmopolitical worldview that mobilizes it. Print was the only means of mass production in the intellectual sphere, and Kant—in this passage and elsewhere—views the relationship between scholar and public according to a model of communication. Learned persons—solitary individuals acting in their public role—send their discourses to a public formed only by its capacity to receive those discourses, in whatever fashion. That is, through the public use of one's reason, one acts as a "scholar, whose writings speak to his public, the world" (6; 57). Whether conception or realization, the cosmopolitical cannot exist without the medium that creates it. In the constellation of modernity, that medium has been the book, the material object that inscribes a shared virtuality.

As my discussion of the *Encyclopédie* stressed, the question of the book—and the language question it implies—is not a gratuitous side issue in the historical thinking of the Enlightenment. Although it is not widely known, Kant reflected a great deal on the status of the book both as a material and an immaterial entity, that is, as a physical object occupying space and as a material manifestation of what can be produced only ideally, mentally—for example, in a reading. This distinction between the material and the immaterial constitutes the core of all copyright law that developed in Kant's wake; the entire modern economy of what is called "intellectual property," no longer restricted to texts but spanning the gamut of cultural production, depends on this opposition. Kant's definition of a book is simple: "a writing . . . presenting a discourse that someone extends to the public by means of visible linguistic signs."[12] The discourse belongs to the immaterial side of the equation, whereas the written language, visible in essence, occupies the material sphere.

In this communication model, the public—always cosmopolitical—receives the discourse of an individual through the mediation of material, linguistic signs. What is at stake in understanding the global political and linguistic economy of the book turns around the nature of this immaterial discourse. Elsewhere Kant is much more explicit about this discourse, somehow embedded in the "mute instrument" that is the book: "The book is the instrument for diffusing a *discourse* [*Rede*] to the public, not simply thoughts, as is the case for painting, a symbolic representation of an idea or of an event."[13] Ultimately, the book's centrality to historical understanding and to the cosmopolitical sphere derives from its mechanical reproducibility; in the epoch of printing, every publication, every discourse offered in writing to the public, is multiple by definition, a fact that separates the book's *discourse* from its material presence. Before mass production, a painting embodies its representation; burning it destroys its material as well as its immaterial existence. By contrast, a printed book cannot be simply coextensive with the discourse for which it provides the material anchor, partly because its existence in multiple copies allows for no original to which the discourse can be reduced, partly because before the twentieth-century explosion of technological reproduction, the linguistic economy remains distinct from the economy of visual representation.

But in the final analysis, the material aspect furnishes the most decisive ground of comparison. Kant clarifies this facet of discourse in discussing the modalities of dissemination—that is, specifically, art dealers and editors: "The reason that all works of art [*Kunstwerke*] by others can be reproduced for public sale, but not books that already have their appointed editor, resides in the fact that the former are *works* [*Werke*] (op-

era), the latter, *actions [Handlungen] (operae);* works can exist as things existing for themselves, whereas actions can have their existence only in a person *[Person]*" (86; emphasis in original). Objects not subject to mechanical reproduction cannot ever wholly shed their existence as things and cannot be simultaneously present in multiple locations; it is in this sense that, in the eighteenth century, the book—and its discourse—is the means and the medium of the cosmopolitical sphere. Discourse resides on the side of action, of interaction, which, in Kant's vision of the unfolding human spirit, opens the space of historical transformation to counter the stranglehold of the state's regulatory mechanism.

Subsequent interpretations of Kant and of modernity, including the model of knowledge production it sets in place, have put undue emphasis on this voluntarism characterizing human action without acknowledging the material presuppositions on which it rests. A brief reference to Michel Foucault's comments on Kant's "What Is Enlightenment?" indicates the parameters of these presuppositions and offers a backdrop for returning specifically to the language question and to its pertinence for the cosmopolitical sphere. Foucault observes that Kant's essay represents "the first time that a philosopher links in this way, closely and from the inside, his work's significance for knowledge, a reflection on history, and a specific analysis of the single moment when he writes and for which he writes."[14] This historical thinking is bound to the notion of producing a discourse—written, printed, and published—aimed to provoke a public to action. The sphere of mediation is crisscrossed by the book trade, in reality and as an allegory for understanding history—both its documental record and the upheavals that transform it. In this sense, Foucault continues, "the *Aufklärung* is simultaneously a process in which human beings collectively participate and an act of courage to carry out personally. They are simultaneously elements and agents of the same process" (565). Even the notion of subjectivity, so dear to the modern worldview, rests squarely on the materiality of printed ink.

The model of cosmopolitan understanding bequeathed to modernity displays, therefore, a number of characteristics that I am now able to enumerate more precisely. First of all, it entails a notion of the subject who makes a voluntary decision and on that basis attempts to constitute his or her public. Constituting such a public—composed of individuals who are in principle unknown to one another, a public that exists over time and covers an extensive geographical area—requires a medium or a material basis by means of which a mental "unity" can be elaborated. In modernity, at least up until the twentieth century, this medium has been the book. The linchpin of this model is the state, which provides what Kant refers to as the "mechanism" of stability. But, as we have seen, the state monopolizes only a part of the subject's activity; the other pole, the fuzzy domain of the cosmopolitical, both includes the state—that is, the more localized community—and extends beyond it potentially to encompass the globe.

As the model for understanding globalism in modernity, this world-view has had and continues to have political consequences. With respect to language, to the linguistic economy, these consequences are most readily discernible in the link between the state, that is, a single state, and the cosmopolitical, or between what Kant's "Enlightenment" text calls the "private" and "public" uses of reason. These two partially overlapping realms come together only in the subject, what Kant calls the "scholar" or the individual "person." The person broadcasts a discourse, through the medium of print, to a world public. But the notion of discourse employed by Kant had a different inflection than it has today; in fact, in Kant's reflections on the book and on the legitimate means of reproducing it, "discourse" constitutes the fundamental category for determining the status of intellectual property: "Translation in another language cannot be considered a copy [*Nachdruck*] [of some original] because it is not the author's discourse itself [*dieselbe Rede des Verfassers*], even if the thoughts are exactly the same."[15] In other words, the discourse that establishes the cosmopolitical public is the product of one given language, the language of the person writing and publishing.

From the contemporary perspective of intellectual property, this conception of translation rights seems wholly outmoded and irrelevant; in the twentieth century, the conception of the work takes priority over the language of its composition, and, according to international conventions, translation rights legally belong to the creator or owner of the original work. But the real significance of this eighteenth-century notion of intellectual property lies in the model of globalism it engenders. While the cosmopolitical public shares the language of the person or scholar who writes for it, the shared language is not a global language in the way one might understand it today. It is, rather, the language of the individual who has a sort of "split appointment": he works for the state, for a given local or localizable institution, and writes and publishes in the vernacular for a cosmopolitical or global public. To express it succinctly, the modern view of the global sphere has a bipolar logic: language and state are coextensive, and the cosmopolitical economy of language is based on a state language's becoming global. In this model, language is piggybacked on the state, just as the state slips in surreptitiously through imposing its language. We don't have to be reminded of the efficacy of this model, which, as a conceptual counterpart of the European nation-state, has underwritten the colonialism of modernity, the cornerstone of which has been the unbreakable bond between culture, state, language, and education system.

Engaging Anachronism

This modern paradigm of globalization, taken for granted as the product of ongoing technological progress, depends heavily on the medium that anchors it, without which no public would ever be constituted. The modern view of the cosmopolitical is enabled by the hegemony of the printed book, which establishes the view's conceptual limits. Throughout the twentieth century, which has produced a much discussed technological explosion of new global media, the univocal hegemony of print has been gradually diluted until it is on the verge of being dissipated entirely. The media—most of which are global by nature, but according to a different linguistic circulation than that of the book—have played a highly significant role in pushing the question of globalization into the foreground. The issues of this global transformation have been evident since the early part of the century, even if the consequences were not always so readily apparent. In the early 1930s, for example, Gramsci clearly drew the distinction:

> Verbal expression has a strictly national-popular-cultural character: a poem by Goethe, in the original, can be understood and experienced fully only by a German (or by someone who is "Germanized"). Dante can be understood and experienced only by a cultivated Italian, etc. On the other hand, a statue by Michelangelo, a piece of music by Verdi, a Russian ballet, a painting by Raphael, etc., can be understood almost immediately by any world citizen, even by noncosmopolitan minds, even if they haven't moved beyond the narrow confines of their country's provinces.[16]

Writing just at the moment when sound film was being first commercialized, Gramsci's opposition pits the mass-reproduced text against other forms of cultural experience. The cultural artifacts Gramsci mentions, in his analysis all original performances or artworks, no longer escape the economy of mass production that until this century characterized only the book. Today these artifacts are rarely, if ever, experienced in anything resembling an original production, but are omnipresent throughout the globe as transmitted images, whether printed, televised, filmed, or circulated on the Internet.[17] The public "mind" is no longer constituted simply by the capacity to read texts for which it is the addressee, texts in a particular language, carrying a specific discourse, and emanating from a given state subject. This global mind, a virtual public coming to life by virtue of the power of the image and living off of the shared consumption and imagined production of images, no longer requires or even cares about the authentic artifact that characterized nontextual culture. Anyone can possess a Raphael, the same Raphael, which hangs just as well on a wall in Amazonas or Beijing as in New York City.

In this sense, the cosmopolitical is not what it used to be; with the onslaught of the image, which penetrates into every nook and cranny of the globe, the public has become virtually all-inclusive. At the same time, language—and, particularly, printed language—assumes an ever diminishing role in forming the contours of and saturating the cosmopolitical sphere. This shift from text and language to image and other forms of mass cultural production does not signal merely a quantitative change in the virtual global mind. It implies a disengagement of language from the primary production of cultural hegemony and raises questions about cosmopolitical knowledge and about the model of globalization itself, not to mention about the figures of thought that have structured modern historical understanding.

In the model inherited from the Enlightenment and operative in modernity, globalization results from the progressive imposition of a local, state culture on the world. "Culture," cultural artifacts, and culture's reproductive logic, are extended to the globe as part of a political economy that includes commercial domination and straightforward gunboat diplomacy; that economy's medium or "mass media" is the printed word, and the state language is coextensive with the culture for which it serves as the vehicle. In spatial terms, the global is conceived as the irradiation from a center against which the acculturated zones are measured. The prevailing medium of cultural artifacts plays a crucial historical and epistemological role because each medium or configuration of media mobilizes a cultural and political economy that enacts at the same time a process of globalization, however rudimentary it might be. In a world whose collective links are fashioned by multiple visual, audio, and textual media—what is referred to as mass media—cultural production is more explicitly tied to the commercial sector than to narrowly construed ideology, that is, than to the centralizing power of a given state. Nevertheless, the emergence of this new cosmopolitical sphere in no way means that ideology has simply disappeared, nor does it suggest that forces of hegemony are not continually at work to produce and maintain a stability that is as intellectual as it is physical.

While squarely inhabiting the current cosmopolitical situation, which encompasses the newly idealized world and the new media that work to displace print from its solitary pedestal, the chapters that follow are concerned principally with the conceptual and historical parameters of print culture. Specifically, they engage the modern literary understanding, which unfolded over several centuries, that furnishes the historical backbone of modernity. The ascendance of print has anchored a sweeping vision of history, of the way in which the "human spirit," a wispy ghost, becomes a point of reference for establishing virtual links between the past, present, and future. It has created a universalist human subject who undergoes historical transformation and functions as historical protagonist, as the secular motor of progress and decline. This humanoid figure, what I will designate below as the "anthropos," has found its most substantive support in the modern literary tradition, where it has staked claims that are both universal—that is, global or cosmopolitical—and limited to the expression of specific groups or collectivities. The legitimacy of secular literature, which beyond relying on print technology depended on a complex ensemble of factors that include the invention of vernacular grammars, their extension into national languages, and scholars who build and perpetuate its corpus, consolidated the paradigm for the modern organization of knowledge and, in particular, for the historical worldview that gives it coherence.

The printed book, along with the literature and history that are necessarily its immaterial parasites, is no longer alone in its ability to give a mass-produced view of time and space. In the twentieth century, the churning out of cultural phenomena, as well as the growing technological means to inscribe matter, whether on film, audiotape, or in software, not only affected the institutional place of literary thought but also has shaken the edifice of historical understanding. The epistemological problem of literary studies, even if they are revamped as "cultural studies," derives from the unbridgeable gap between the contemporary materializations of human thinking and the concepts and figures of thought that rest on the hegemony of a single materiality, of one technique of inscription: that of print. In terms of their circulation and their materialities, current cultural productions do not obey the precepts so laboriously generated according to the character of printed matter; nor can they be adequately grasped when viewed as simple outgrowths of print logic. As Walter Benjamin pointed out, "Technology is obviously not a purely scientific phenomenon. It is also a historical one."[18] Knowing has its own historicity, and the project of transposing outmoded concepts on new manifestations—as, for example, using the notion of "hypertext," which represents an enriched textuality, more complex and thus more evolved, that at bottom newly reiterates the old presuppositions of literary thinking—only highlights the distance between the contemporary cultural phenomenon of virtual texts and the conceptions available to describe them.

In focusing on the print medium's relationship to the modern organization of knowledge, I have tried in this introduction to sketch the historical context and to lay the groundwork for the reflections elaborated in the chapters that follow. Because of the centrality of literary studies to the establishment of modernity as a worldview, as a mindset and institutional framework in which the notion of worldview plays an important role, the modern literary tradition constitutes a significant touchstone in these investigations. At this juncture, it is not possible to forget or unilaterally to undo the historical privilege of literary studies and their role as guardian of the paradigm of historical understanding. Nevertheless, it seems essential to come to terms with the demise of the hegemony of Literature as the primary reservoir of humanity's historical spirit. Writing in print form, and the literature it spawns, will undoubtedly remain pertinent to thinking because it has the advantage of being a supple medium with low-tech requirements in comparison with other media. But that does not diminish the force unleashed by print's displacement as singular guarantor of the modern configuration of knowledge. A supreme consequence of this shift away from print hegemony concerns the impossibility of adopting without question the customary figures of human consciousness or mind and their presumed temporal unfolding. The current multiplicity of media seems to call for other models of consciousness that give a greater place to images and permit other notions of collective belonging not cordoned off in a territorial and linguistic imaginary.

Any preliminary consideration of these questions entails confronting our own anachronism, which becomes manifest in the inability of our thinking and concepts of historical understanding to grasp the implications of the means of contemporary cultural production. In considering this issue, Gramsci made an observation that has even greater resonance today than when he first formulated it: "One's conception of the world responds to specific problems posed by reality, which are quite specific and 'original' in their immediate relevance. How is it possible to think the present, and a quite specific present, with thinking elaborated for problems of a past that is often remote and superseded? When that happens, it means that we are anachronistic in our own time, fossils and not modern living beings."[19] Being "modern," however, no longer suffices to eliminate the temporal lag and reestablish synchrony. In the whirlwind of contemporary transformation, what is unthought in modernity, its assumptions based on a very specific materialization of human effort, along with an accompanying constellation of knowledge, sociopolitical organization, and historical understanding, takes the notion of anachronism to a new level. Anachronism has become the condition of twenty-first-century modernity. While our necessary anachronism cannot simply be sloughed off, certain of its aspects are not impervious to scrutiny. In this spirit, this book's subsequent chapters tackle the grounds or presuppositions of modernity's intellectual configuration, whose very success has provoked its anachrony.

I

Founding Matters

Hegemony of the Vernacular

Seemingly unleashed at the end of the nineteenth century, and having plowed through the twentieth century, the forces of technological transformation have swept away or disrupted epochs of mental and physical habits. In the realm of culture, or symbolic production, the consequences have been disintegrating, liberating, and unmanageable. From the perspective of literary and historical understanding, which since the onset of modernity has been intertwined with notions of political identity, the twentieth century was not merely a period of transition but constitutes a rupture with past knowledge production. Nowhere is this sense of disjuncture more evident than in examining the workings of hegemony, particularly with regard to its cultural aspects, which up until the century of movies, radio, television, software, and megamall paperbacks had very circumscribed domains and means at its disposal.

Yet in the context of a global discourse and political economy, founded more on proliferating images and immaterial cultural production than on direct or executive intervention, it has become increasingly difficult to grasp the hegemony through the actors—states, corporations, or global institutions—that exercise it. Getting a handle on the workings of cultural or discursive hegemony in a global political economy requires a fundamental questioning of the material and media constraints that underwrite the global space currently under elaboration. In presenting the basic themes and notions that will be developed in greater detail throughout the book as a whole, this chapter begins laying the groundwork for broaching some of the basic presuppositions of modernity. Specifically, it delves into the importance of the matter or material that preserves tradition, the characteristics of the vernacular ideal, and the role of figuration in thinking and historical understanding.

In addressing global views of modernity and the conjunction of cultural and political thought, it is virtually impossible to dispense with a discussion of the Italian peninsula. Italian thinkers have played a fundamental role in Western and, by extension, global political reflections, from Dante's concept of the vernacular, through Machiavelli's analysis of the state, to Gramsci's concept of hegemony. Nonetheless, Italy's contemporary exemplarity is of a different order altogether; in fact, rather than underscoring Italy's specificity, current challenges to Italian unity— challenges that have counterparts in many Western countries—signal the symbolic nature of globalism that does not necessarily act in tandem with the economic and political forces of world order. In this context, the minidrama of "La Padania"—the push to create an autonomous state in northern Italy that would no longer be a part of the Italian republic— transcends whatever purely national meaning it might have. In traditional terms, "La Padania" would be a hegemonic formation under construction. But that formation has a number of peculiarities. As one commentator puts it, the Padania idea, imaginary or not, does not derive from any ethnic or identity-based claim, and its territorial demands are somewhat arbitrary,[1] even if the Swiss mobilized troops to repel a potential Padania invasion.[2] In the absence of "all customary motivations of the great revolts of independence,"[3] Umberto Bossi, the leader of the Padania movement, hit upon a concise way to represent himself and his revolt, placing his struggle in the larger tradition of independence movements. His representation? *"Sono Braveheart,"* "I am Braveheart." He appropriated a cinematographic image that belongs to "world" culture and that consequently his followers could immediately recognize.

Calling oneself Braveheart projects an image that comes with a configuration of other images; as a metaphor, its meaning is obvious: Bossi is to Padania what Braveheart is or William Wallace was to Scotland. But there is no question of referentiality here: Bossi was not expressing a desire to die on the battlefield and usher in 600 more years of "Roman domination." The filmic image has enjoyed a massive distribution and belongs to a global tradition that Bossi and his fellow Padanians share. It is so slightly tied to a referent that even the *Nouvel observateur,* usually attentive to basic historical facts, remarked that Bossi wanted "to represent for Padania what the valiant warrior was for an Ireland fighting for independence" (36). Ireland, Scotland, the Falklands, Hong Kong—it's all the same.

This Braveheart image staked out a topos for Bossi. But it is the representation and its medium that take precedence over whatever referent one might claim for it. In describing what it calls the "Padanian Braveheart," *La Repubblica* noted: "It seems like a film. One already seen. But the voice is not Mel Gibson's and you can't smell the perfume of Scottish Highland thistle."[4] Wholly consonant with this adopted global image, Bossi's speeches included reference to what he called *"l'internazionale indipendentista,"* suggesting a national movement whose primary goal was to become global (Made in Padania).[5] In itself, the Bossi example is perhaps humorous and utterly forgettable. Yet although this story of "Padania-in-the-making" occasionally follows the classic trajectory for building a national social movement, which includes finding and presenting traditional, home-grown images for mobilizing mass support, the example also offers a snapshot of emerging global discourses that operate according to unprecedented hegemony. This tension, if not conflict, inhabits global political and cultural production, just as calls to struggle against the forces of globalization become effective only as they circulate in the global network. This global economy of hegemony, an economy that is itself greater than the actors striving to exercise it, has no isles of seclusion, leaves no havens untouched by its massive effects.

Struggles and debates over Padania may intensify or dissipate entirely, but the movement's real value lies in its dull exemplarity. It signals a new mode of world empire, a new series of conflicts that mark emergent sociopolitical interaction, and a new understanding of hegemony. Antonio Gramsci of course was the first to deal explicitly with what I am calling the "economy of hegemony" in modernity, its circulation, the institutions anchoring it, and the intellectuals charged with maintaining it. In formulating hegemony against the prevailing tendency to limit politics to the realm of state (or executive) action, Gramsci considered it equivalent to "an equilibrium between political society and civil society."[6] Although generally viewed, even in Gramsci's writings, in the nation-state framework, this equilibrium concept suggests the mutual penetration and support of social, political, and civil entities that together constitute a whole. From an analytical perspective, this equilibrium has spatial aspects, yoking the various collective dimensions into a given discursive unity, and historical aspects, discourses that interpret the past and project into the future to underwrite hegemonic visions of historical continuity.

Here, however, I want to focus on aspects of a different order, on the material aspects of this equilibrium of hegemony. But I mean "matter" and "materiality" in a very specific and concrete way. To continue with Italian sources, this material notion can perhaps best be characterized by referring briefly to a text by Machiavelli, who reflected at length about materiality, often in broaching questions of hegemony, although he didn't have the word, and his approach exceeds the hegemony of modernity. In a chapter of his *Discourses* entitled "That the change in sects and languages, together with the mishap of floods or the plague, extinguishes the memories of things," Machiavelli enlarges on how new groups and religions seek to wipe out what preceded them in order to record their own values, traditions, and laws.[7] The primary means for doing this is by introducing a new written language to supplant the old, a procedure which in a short period of time makes the previous culture unusable. He remarks in passing, for example, that the Christian sect was unable to eradicate completely the "pagans" because the Christians could not dispense with Latin to establish their own memory or tradition and write their own laws. With only a slight translation into modern political discourse: political, linguistic, and cultural transformations annihilate memories and build new hegemonies. In the preprint world that is the context for Machiavelli's observations, human memory is tenuous, and, Machiavelli goes on to say, natural disasters are often even more effective than new political powers and possess the force to eliminate centuries of thought in a single moment. This forthright materialism led Machiavelli to the then blasphemous conclusion that because of the material basis of memory or tradition, one cannot even determine whether the world has existed eternally or for only 5,000 years, as claimed in the Bible. Matter or its lack, its ability to accept inscriptions and resist decay, provides the parameters for hegemony and for the equilibrium it consolidates.

To approach the material of hegemony, it is useful to examine the idea of tradition. This banal and often overused notion, which has been bandied about until it has become almost meaningless, was, particularly but not exclusively in preprint society, the mechanism whereby hegemony effected its equilibrium and persisted in time. Reflection on tradition has itself a long tradition that doesn't bear repeating in any detail, largely because it builds on preconceived notions rather than interrogating them. But the basic presuppositions undergirding understandings of tradition (as well as of hegemony), which for historical, political, and technological reasons were utterly insignificant before the twentieth century, have become an impediment for coming to terms with or even recognizing the forces of contemporary globalism. Nevertheless, it is important to understand the nature of this impediment and useful, as a point of departure, to synthesize the often proclaimed classical wisdom of tradition. Plotting out the classical elaborations of the tradition concept (*traditio*), which appears in the works of Cicero, Quintilian, and Tacitus, among others, its range of meaning can be summarized in three categories: (1) handing down; (2) education; (3) narration.[8] In each instance, *traditio* or tradition has to do with selecting and transmitting a body of accumulated knowledge from one generation to another to provide for what Peirce called the "continuity of mind." Thinking of tradition as a "handing down" renders it abstractly, as "education" or "teaching" stresses its institutional aspects, and as "narration" emphasizes the linguistic or historical component of the transmission. These notions are readily familiar to everyone involved in the industries of knowledge production and are deeply ensconced in the restricted worldviews characterizing modernity.

Textual hermeneutics, which in modernity presupposes a certain economy of hegemony and anchors institutionalized knowledge in the human sciences, does little more than expand on these rudimentary notions of tradition. The institutions of knowledge, which police and stabilize knowledge and its relationships to collectivities, provide simultaneously for temporal continuity and historical transformation. This series of dynamics is also expressed in the cliché that tradition "delivers" and "betrays" the past, meanings linked in the etymology of *tradition*. In sum, one can bestow all sorts of dignified descriptions on this model of tradition, which finds expression in groups characterized by "communicative action" or in interpretive communities whose "horizon" of comprehension fuses with that of some past and so on, but it still boils down to the core idea that transmission and betrayal mediated by the institutions of knowledge equal historical continuity and, ultimately, discursive hegemony.

Injecting into this fundamentally idealist vision of human history consideration of the *medium* of tradition, of the way in which tradition is materialized, opens up a wholly different set of issues that relate explicitly to political and discursive economies. For reasons that will shortly become clear, the twentieth century imposed the question of the medium, of the materiality, of tradition and, therefore, of hegemony. What I would like to do now is offer a necessarily rapid and certainly inadequate analysis of tradition that would take into account the material aspects of its temporal continuity. In discussing the material if not materialist aspects of tradition, there is a strong tendency to slip into a pathos-ridden discourse about the frailty of human history. But I want to resist this impulse and limit my remarks to the materiality of this moment of transmission.

In the past fifty years, much attention has been devoted to the presumed workings of tradition before writing.[9] In an oral economy, "matter" has an ephemeral existence. The utterance exists materially only until the sound dissipates; consequently, this mode of transmission relies on extensive repetition both in the life of a single generation and from generation to generation. If the thread is broken, the wheel must be reinvented, so to speak, although a successful outcome is doubtful, for one would have forgotten even what use it might have. But from the perspective of an oral economy, the question of "betrayal" is bereft of sense: since no expression of the tradition definitively survives its being uttered, there is only betrayal because each successive utterance adapts the tradition without awareness of the difference between past knowledge and present reiteration.

Before writing, the *matter* of human tradition that lives beyond its present has no linguistic basis; the artifacts, tools, drawings, and architecture outlast the generations shaping them, but they nonetheless require verbalization to render them compatible with ongoing tradition. In a tradition condemned to an oral economy, verbalization—or as one will call it after writing, interpretation—enjoys an absolute primacy over forms of durable matter, despite its ephemeral nature. Countless studies have demonstrated the institutional forms of social, political, and cultural hegemony that accompany this oral economy of tradition, and reflection on the collective consciousness it represents has been exceedingly important for Western philosophy and literary studies (in this century, for example, one thinks of Bakhtin and Lukács).

In an economy based on writing, on material inscriptions drawn from linguistic practice, a number of differences become immediately apparent. The materialization endures beyond the producer: somebody scribbles something on an object that will deteriorate only at a later date. The life of that object is independent of its producer, who can disappear, run away, or die of old age, while the object and its inscription will continue to subsist. Unlike the utterance in an oral tradition, however, there is no built-in adaptation to successive generations; it is fixed until it disintegrates, and if it is regularly recopied, it can potentially exist in perpetuity. This was the great realization leading to Cassiodorus's understanding of the monastic mission in sixth-century Europe.

While materialization in this sense significantly reinforces a tradition's survival, it permits or even calls for intricate institutionalization. In giving a transhistorical existence to tradition, material inscriptions simultaneously establish an unbridgeable gap between the moment of writing and later moments claiming that tradition as its own. Thus interpretations—also written—emerge to appropriate the matter of tradition, "betray" it, even as they themselves outlive the moment of their production and become subject to the same processes. This describes the workings of tradition and interpretation underlying the necessarily allegorical basis of medieval Christianity, although the textual process had already been analyzed in depth by Philo of Alexandria. In a larger sense, this process requires institutions of knowledge, legitimating structures of authority to monitor cultural production in the interest of the groups or collectivities exercising hegemony. In spite of its secular claims, the hermeneutics of modernity follows the same fundamental precepts.

The real point, however, is that the matter of tradition matters, that the way in which tradition is materialized and disseminated provides material parameters for understanding human knowledge and historical continuity and for the concomitant institutions that produce, legitimate, and guard them. This very broad backdrop places in relief the materialization of tradition in what we have come to call modernity; the "material" characteristics of the twentieth century began producing fodder for a wholly transformed production of hegemony, forcing a new institutionalization of knowledge on a global scale, one in need of radically different critical understandings. In the epoch of printed matter, characterized by mass production and reproduction of ongoing adjustments of tradition, the three categories of classical tradition are closely integrated. Education, narration, and selective transmission belong to each and every institution constituting the knowledge industry.

The hegemonic mechanisms of legitimacy embodied in the modern institutions of knowledge, which of course include the university, have relied exclusively on the written—or, better, the printed—word. The hegemonic character of the print economy characterizes all fields of knowledge, even those that have their own forms of materialization, such as music and painting. Not surprisingly, literature (or, more precisely, literary criticism) and history have been at the (ideological) center of knowledge institutions, along with what one might call the configuration of knowledge that accompanies them. At its most general level, this configuration entails the ideal existence of a number of interwoven concepts: the nation, a given language, a collective spirit that manifests itself in certain material objects (generally written texts) and an understanding of how this spirit becomes a conscious protagonist and gradually evolves through time. These ideas, all of which emerged historically and require certain material supports, including, on the one hand, grammars, encyclopedias, and philosophical concepts and, on the other, massive subventions from states or other collective groups, still constitute the primary assumptions of knowledge, tradition, and hegemony in the human sciences.

Ultimately, however, this elaborate series of apparatuses (the French have a word for this: *dispositifs*) depends more on the supremacy of the printed word, on print as the material continuity of tradition, than on the nation-state and national culture to which it is undeniably linked. The globalism of today is not simply a great economic behemoth that threatens to overtake the planet, nor can it be summarized as some sort of antinational drive toward cultural uniformity. Instead, globalism is bound up in an exponential growth in the materiality of "tradition," of what is transmitted and transmittable: today multiple forms of matter, of materialization, can withstand the ravages of historical deterioration— for example, films, software, and audio recordings, all of which have numerous forms—and can bear extended interpretations and commentaries to compete with the printed word. With the diluted authority of print, the linchpin of the modern discursive economy and knowledge institutions, the entire complex of historical understanding loses its unique cohesiveness and explanatory power. In the knowledge industries, literary fields in general (particularly in North America, but it is a phenomenon that is spreading elsewhere) have attempted to counter literature's waning ideological significance and bolster the position of print vis-à-vis the cultural productions undermining print authority. For example, the introduction of culture and "cultural studies" in university literature departments signals this institutional drive to reposition print (which still plays a central role in determining academic tenure) along with the complex of concepts that fostered its ascendancy. But the material basis of hegemony penetrates to the core of the organization of knowledge itself and cannot be adequately addressed by merely absorbing into the university yet another methodology or field of study.

This transformed matter of hegemony, its political economy and its material existence, is not an abstract problem with simply theoretical implications. In an epoch of print domination—an epoch that is rapidly becoming superseded—hegemonies have been determined by recognizable actors, each vying to dominate the others. This basic characteristic runs through contradictory and even opposing understandings of hegemony of whatever political persuasion. Hegemony or the attribution of hegemony relies on identifying an origin and personifying the actions emanating from it: for example, the hegemony of this state over another, a group's achievement of autonomy to form a historical bloc, or a party's efforts to unify and channel counterhegemonic forces. In this world of binary forces, the ideal existence of these "actors" or "entities" is fostered by institutions and by intellectuals who work in their names. The product of their work, which is never complete, is called culture, tradition, and—sometimes—even history. One consequence of the exponential growth in materiality, in the matter of cultural production, has been to disrupt the carefully constructed package of collective identity, culture, language, and historical tradition.

In this context, it is worthwhile to refer once more to Gramsci, who never ceased rethinking hegemony in every new conjuncture he discerned. In Notebook 13, one of his notebooks on Machiavelli, Gramsci asks himself a series of questions, destined to remain unanswered, in a fragment entitled "Cultural-Political Hegemony." He asks: "In the modern world, is the cultural hegemony of one nation over others still possible? Or is the world already so unified in its socioeconomic structure that one country, even if it can 'chronologically' initiate an innovation, can never keep its 'political monopoly' and thus use the monopoly as the basis for hegemony? Thus what meaning can nationalism have today? Isn't this possible as economic-financial 'imperialism' but no longer as civil 'supremacy' or political-intellectual hegemony?"[10] Even though

Gramsci could not have foreseen the extent to which the economic forces would detach themselves from purely national interests, he readily envisaged the ongoing collapse of national culture and the hegemonic economy it underwrites. And while the economy of hegemony still retains its role of producing equilibrium, it circulates in other venues, becomes materialized in market economies that no longer relinquish the production of knowledge to national institutions, and cannot be readily reduced to identifiable operators.

Ultimately, twentieth-century transformations in *material* existence, as well as in the matter of representation, have created a gap between the institutions of knowledge and the hegemonies they evolved to sustain. This gap is both historical and geographical, both spatial and temporal. It marks a historical transition from a form of empire based on direct hegemony to one anchored in a symbolic economy that derives from no single overpowering state but that traverses them all, even if not uniformly. Simultaneously, no global point—whether European, North American, or Asian—enjoys an absolute, privileged standpoint from which to elaborate a representative global projection. This gap, whose contours can be only partially plotted by referring to notions of hegemony, materiality, and the global circulation of cultural production, marks the implicit edge of contemporary thinking about historical and literary understanding.

Emerging at the end of the nineteenth century, the modern idea of the intellectual, openly engaged in social and political debates about knowledge, does not wholly apply to the Middle Ages. Yet many of the notions that created a context for the modern intellectual can be traced back to the twelfth century, in particular to the groping process of secularized thought. In this process, Dante—or, rather, Dante's work—opens up a dimension of linguistic reflection so closely intertwined with modernity that its radical nature often escapes notice. The figure of Dante occupies a crucial juncture in Western literary consciousness. Viewed in retrospect as anchoring a historical trajectory that leads to national literatures, Dante's work evinces the fundamental elements that nineteenth-century literary history canonizes: the author as a conscious creator of literary artifacts, secular literature as the product of struggling to give a human face to a divine—or transcendental—order, the distinction between poetry and prose as necessary for literary and critical understand-

ing, and so on. But Dante's vision of vernacular language and, more precisely, of figuration serves as the cornerstone for this conceptual edifice
and articulates most clearly the social, political, and linguistic terrain of
modernity. In the remainder of this chapter, I want to focus on this question of the vernacular, on the linguistic and sociopolitical issues it entails, and on its pertinence in the context of a global circulation of discourse.

In attempting to render the specificity of medieval knowledge production, the historian Jacques Le Goff remarked that the Middle Ages' "new
intellectuals are professionals [*des hommes de métier*]. Like the mer-
chants, the 'sellers of time' whom they resemble by being 'sellers of
words' [*vendeurs de mots*], the intellectuals have to overcome the traditional cliché that science is not for sale because it is a gift from God."[11]
Legitimating human knowledge or science as an autonomous, terrestrial
activity required a massive deployment of resources, economic as well as
conceptual and historical. It also involved elaborating new social roles
for the actors in this knowledge production—whether you call them
thinkers, scholars, scientists, or intellectuals—and specifying their relationship with the groups for and to whom they speak, their "public."
Most important, however, it rested on unforeseeable models of linguistic
and cultural understanding. Up through the twentieth century, language
was the privileged medium for cementing collective awareness, and introducing the vernacular as a language bearing knowledge, a process
barely begun in Dante's lifetime, had enormous consequences and implications.

Abetted by Italy's exalted cultural production from the late Middle
Ages to the Renaissance, Dante's linguistic theory, his theory of the collective dimension of language presented in *De vulgari eloquentia,* provided the conceptual and linguistic blueprints for modern vernacular
understanding and the social formations it fosters. Though ostensibly
dealing with language, *De vulgari eloquentia* has often been considered a
"work of cultural politics," to borrow the words of Dante scholar Pier
Mengaldo.[12] As might be expected, Antonio Gramsci's analysis is even
more explicit:

> Dante's *De vulgari eloquentia* should be considered essentially as an act
> of cultural-national politics (in the sense that national had at that time
> and in Dante), just as what goes under the name of the "language ques-

tion" has always been an aspect of political struggle . . . Moreover, Dante's small book has this not insignificant meaning for the time when it was written; not only in deed, but raising deed to theory, the Italian intellectuals during the Communes' most exuberant period "break" with Latin and justify the vernacular, exalting it over against Latinizing "mandarinism," at the same time in which the vernacular has such great artistic manifestations.[13]

As we know today, the "language question" or "languages question" is intensely political, much more so than in the 1930s when Gramsci wrote these lines. But for Dante and medieval Europe generally, the politics of the language question resides on a somewhat different plane than that of today's linguistic or cultural claims against already ensconced literary vernaculars and institutions. Though perhaps difficult to imagine at the edge of the twenty-first century, the medieval political struggle involves wresting cultural production from a linguistic model that maintains an absolute division between the language of knowledge and the language of quotidian local experience—buying bread or talking with one's neighbors.

The power of the vernacular as a basis for social organization will not become evident until the epoch of printing, but Dante's contemporary readers, even if they were unable to grasp the dynamics of a vernacular cultural production, were certainly aware of the immediate implications of an extensive vernacular tradition: increasing the size of the potential public (in modern terms, of the body of producers and consumers) and creating conditions for a more encompassing collectivity. Just as modern Italy's "southern question" becomes paradigmatic for delineating north-south distinctions understood globally, Dante's formulation of the language question, in Italy no more resolved than the southern question itself, furnished a conceptual model for the nation-state that was realized with great efficacy throughout Europe before being exported to circle the globe.

Gramsci's political analysis stresses the fact that reflection or "theory"—as part of the theory and practice tandem—was an integral part of the vernacular project. In this sense, Dante's text proceeds very didactically, building step by step on previous reasoning whose itinerary is traced with great care. Why would one want to elaborate a vernacular tradition, and what is involved in thinking it through? Dante gives the historical background making it necessary to inscribe—in fact, to codify—a vernacular: "All our language [*loquela*]—besides that which God created at the same time as man—is subject to the reworkings of our free will [*beneplacito*], after that confusion which was no more than a forgetting of previous language; since man is the most unstable and variable of all animals, language can be neither enduring nor continuous but, like other human things, such as custom and usage, necessarily varies according to distance in space and time."[14]

This concern with human instability and with its repercussions in preserving the state of language offers a fourteenth-century version of linguistic drift. Only the language that was coextensive with the first humans belongs to a different economy of discourse, and, whether one is religious or not, that situation is not apt to repeat itself. In this description, the problem with language, its inherent characteristic, begins with successive generations. This passage, the substance of which is repeated a number of times in the text, portrays language that has not been given a fixed existence ("*nec stare ullo modo potest,*" IX.10). In other words, it applies most precisely to oral language that has not been materialized, that is, has not been given a material existence in writing; moreover, *loquela,* the word here translated by "language," also means speech. (In other passages in this same chapter, the text refers to *sermo,* that is, discourse.) That is the situation of a vernacular language that has no written tradition: if, hypothetically, a group of people speak a single language at one place and at one given moment in time, their division into separate groups and the passage of time produce inevitable linguistic differences that pass unnoticed in the brief life of a given human being. Linguistic change may be glacially slow, but it exists nonetheless, and this ongoing transformative process stands as an obstacle for a living or vernacular collective language.

As a counter to this thorny problem of linguistic drift, Dante advances the idea of grammar, for which there were of course innumerable classical precedents. Almost two hundred years later, when Nebrija composed a Castilian grammar, the first of a Western vernacular language, he used similar conceptual arguments, although his stated goal was to provide a grammar for a language to accompany empire.[15] In the sense that *De vulgari eloquentia* defines grammar, however, it inhabits a realm of relative abstraction: "Grammar is nothing more than a certain identity of language that does not change in different times and places. This language, regulated by the common consensus of many peoples, is evidently not subject to the will of the individual [*nulli singulari arbitrio*] and consequently cannot be variable" (IX.11). Conceptually, this notion of grammar—and perhaps all notions of grammar—has a peculiar status. On the one hand, as an abstraction, it functions like a collective noun that has no fully empirical existence but that is indicated by empirical manifestations; for example, one does not speak a grammar any more than one can physically touch a "people," although one might be able to shake hands or converse with an individual claiming to represent them. On the other hand, in terms of thought, this grammar resembles a transcendent entity, residing outside of human history, that resists the ravages of time and the ruptures of geographical separation. Regarding language and its potential to project a historical coherence in the face of empirical individuals, these same notions have marked all linguistic thought down to the twentieth century: one need only consider de Saussure's *langue* and *parole*. But grammar in Dante's formulation has an added attribute that further complicates the equation, particularly if the need motivating its conception is historical mutability and the resulting discontinuities. In sum, an oral tradition cannot preserve the necessary abstraction that grammar represents, and it must be written down, as the word *gramma* suggests; it must be given a material basis, otherwise it would be subject to the same forces of arbitrary change it is to counteract.

In pausing to delve into the presuppositions underlying Dante's call for a renewed interpretation of grammar, I wanted to tease out aspects of the "language question" that are today taken for granted, although their emergence and modern hegemony are ineluctably historical. Applying to vernacular experience and language this grammatical conception, which is not at all the same as that of medieval speculative grammar, signaled a real break with prevailing sociopolitical and cultural understanding and constitutes the most important legacy of Dante's philosophical writings. For example, one of Spitzer's essays on the *vulgare illustre*, a chosen vernacular language to be glorified in grammar, attempted to pinpoint the specificity of Dante's mode of idealization by likening it to Max Weber's notion of *Idealtypus* and to some aspects of the Platonic Idea.[16] Yet while Dante's notion of the vernacular undeniably draws on the process of idealization, it manifests characteristics that exceed it, such as its necessary materialization to hold off the arbitrary drift of historical change and the fact that it belongs to a larger configuration of ideas aiming to base collective identity on a common language. It is at the same time a model for producing sociopolitical and cultural unity and a figure of thought that introduces a rupture with medieval discourse and interpretation.

After having established that grammar offers a solution to the inevitable mutability of language, Dante's reasoning leads to a more straightforward empirical question. To conceptualize and inscribe a grammar requires a language. This necessity provides the critical motivation for unearthing the appropriate living language—mentioned in the text as the *vulgare illustre*—that would lend itself to being idealized, frozen in grammar to remain integral in the face of historical change. At this juncture, it is not a question of synthesizing a language from countless overlapping linguistic communities and practices, but of recognizing the most worthy languages to be grammatically rendered: "Since vernacular Italian reverberates in multiple variations, we will seek out the most proper and illustrious language of Italy" (XI.1). Thus begins the allegory of the hunt, which is strung through the text; after surveying the major languages of Italy, and the city-states where they are spoken (among them, Rome, Sicily, and Florence), the hunter returns empty-handed. No living language is illustrious enough to merit selection.

Following the logic of Dante's presentation, the inability to identify an already existing *vulgare illustre* calls for a different mode of reasoning. In lieu of an empirical language, the text appeals to figuration that enables a nonexistent, immaterial vernacular to be thought. The first figure to express the vernacular ostensibly belongs to the allegory of the hunt: "After combing the woods and vales of Italy without coming upon the panther we were chasing, to find it we need to investigate more rationally and try to catch in our snare this prey that leaves its odor all over while appearing nowhere" (XVI.1). As a literary image, the figure of the panther is highly stylized and had widespread currency in the Middle Ages. Aristotle and Pliny portrayed it at length, endowing the panther with the strange characteristics of sleeping three days after every meal and exhaling a perfumed breath that attracted all animals except the dragon.[17]

Spitzer saw in this figure further confirmation of Dante's idealizing: medieval speculation claimed an etymological link between *panthera* and the Greek *pan ther* ("all animals").[18] Therefore, the panther represents an idealized collective figure. In fact, this chapter of *De vulgari eloquentia* proceeds to restate the issue according to the forms of abstract reason. In the Middle Ages, abstract reason means the logical categories of Aristotle's classification of linguistic elements, which is founded on notions of substance, genre, species, quality, quantity, and so on. In a similar vein, Dante's earlier *Vita nova* evoked the Aristotelian category of substance to specify the nature of the figure of love, that is, to demonstrate whether that personified figure repeatedly mentioned in the text was corporeal or conceptual, whether it had real material existence or simply represented a linguistic maneuver.[19] Though much less illustrious than the figure of love, the "panther" projects a figural model for thinking a vernacular language, which has no material or—until that moment—conceptual existence, as well as no grammar to universalize it. This panther image embodies a figure of thought that, as visualization of an immaterial vernacular, assumes the capacity to act on the senses without submitting to the empirical demands of a verifiable presence. The figure asserts that diverse or partial manifestations follow from an entity that exceeds them by being indefinitely absent, just as the sweet smell signals an elusive panther; a language, its grammar; or vernaculars, a *vulgare illustre*.

Thinking requires figures, and this subtle and highly abstract argument creates a figure for understanding collective unity grounded in a vernacular that can exist only ideally, cast by human intellectual labor. As Dante notes in describing aspects of this vernacular, it is as if it were "common to all but belonging exclusively to none" (XVIII.2). The political force of this figuration, far more than simply a rhetorical turn of phrase, becomes most evident in what Dante calls the vernacular's "courtly" (*curiale*) aspect. In the Latin Middle Ages, *curia* designates "the assembly gathered around the ruler that has a political, administrative, and juridical function."[20] In other words, it is coextensive with what we would today call the state. Reflection on political unity has a tradition as ancient as human society itself; in this case, however, political unity is conceived and expressed in conjunction with linguistic unity, and the figural aspect renders more explicit the thinking that serves as a precondition for that unity. As Dante remarks, talking about an Italian court seems to be a joke, because everyone knows that there is none. In fact, the passage does not describe the court but encapsulates it in a figure, furnishing an idealized model to channel thought and action:

[The question of it's being a joke or not] can be easily answered: in fact, although in Italy there is no court understood in the unified sense (as in the court of the king of Germany), the members of such a court are not lacking; and just as the members of Germany's court are unified around a sole prince, members of the Italian court are unified thanks to the light of reason [*gratioso lumine rationis*]. It would be false to say that the Italians lack a court, even if we lack a prince; for in fact we have a court, it is only corporally dispersed [*corporaliter dispersa*]. (XVIII.5)

The prince is a personification, a figure of thought that assembles, by means of the light of reason, its scattered traces. This personified figure has profoundly marked political thought down to the present day, particularly in the form elaborated by Machiavelli, who links the prince figure to the state.[21]

Although Dante's prince—and the mode of understanding it encapsulates—is a political figure, it possesses no direct executive power. Its authority does not emanate from force or physical domination. Instead, it introduces parameters of thought in the guise of a figure, what today might be called a shared imaginary. Yet it is also more than an idea. While a nonexistent vernacular, conceived to bring together a babble of speech, must begin as a figure, as an imaginary project lodged in some corner of the collective mind, it builds on material voices whose discord is collapsed by abstract grammar. To succeed in producing linguistic unity, this tenuous vernacular project requires far-reaching institutional support—in the form of discourses and sanctioned arbiters of knowledge, but also more concretely in universities, governmental administration, and collective spectacles in a managed public sphere. Even if this institutional scaffolding of the vernacular does not come into existence until the diffusion of printing in the sixteenth century, first in Spain and then in France, *De vulgari eloquentia* imprints the figures of thought with its essential characteristics.

Every linguistic theory, because of its built-in collective assumptions, is inevitably a political theory. Machiavelli's reaction to *De vulgari eloquentia*—or, rather, the reaction recorded in the manuscript generally attributed to Machiavelli—exposes the political underpinnings of calls for vernacular grammar. In the form of a conversation between the narrator and Dante, who is addressed in the familiar "you" form (*tu*), this text, "Discourse or Dialogue concerning Our Language," in principle wholly adopts the reasoning of *De vulgari eloquentia:* Italy, which doesn't yet cohere, needs a common written language: "The common speech of Italy would be one containing more elements held in common than elements particular to a given language; similarly, a particular speech would contain more particular elements than those elements in common with any other language."[22] As it turns out, however, this seeming agreement on the level of the figure holds only in the most general terms. A step removed from abstraction, the political rather than the philosophical sphere offers the terrain for specifying the point of contention.

Writing after Spanish unification and the linguistic project undergirding its civil institutions, Machiavelli displays a deeper and somewhat more programmatic understanding of linguistic power. As with Dante, though, the argument is at the outset a logical one: "That the importance of this language in which you, Dante, wrote, and in which others coming before you and after you have written, comes from Florence, is demonstrated by your having been Florentine, born in a country [*patria*] whose speech was, better than any other, suitable for writing in verse and in prose. For which the modes of speech in other parts of Italy were unsuitable" (930). As the text goes on to affirm, only the language's character, its capacity to adopt "such a discipline, which was not present in any other city" (930), could explain why so many writers—including Dante, Petrarch, and Boccaccio—wrote in Florentine. In the words of a French critic, this text advances "a municipal theory of literary language."[23] More specifically, the text does not propose a municipal theory as much as a city-state theory of language, which gives the figure of a unifying vernacular another slant altogether. The figure is linked to a preexistent state, outcome of a converging political and linguistic unity; on a small scale, it already had many of the trappings modernity associates with the state: a demarcated territory, foreign recognition, the beginnings of a domestic militia (one of Machiavelli's principal recommendations in his *Discourses*), and so on.

But for the figure of thought itself, the significance of pleading the case for the Florentine language lies elsewhere. Instead of bestowing the power to unify on an ideal projection, which necessarily precedes its "real" deployment, Machiavelli proposes idealizing (a process that encompasses fixing the language in grammar) a linguistic practice coextensive with political identity and firmly embedded in the "real." This interplay between the "real" and the "ideal," the real that always suggests more than meets the eye and the ideal that resists being relegated to some imaginary realm, has a precedent in Machiavelli's writings. In fact, it is precisely this ideal-real reciprocity that Gramsci appreciated about Machiavelli's prince figure. Although the figure of the prince is an ideal that transcends a given time and place, it had a *real* historical existence in the person of Cesare Borgia. The figure personifies a prince grander than life at the same time that it finds itself embodied in a living person.

Figures of thought build their own framework of political action. Machiavelli's figuration, which incorporates Dante's projection of idealized grammar even while binding it inexorably to a real, living collective language, has become the linguistic model most clearly identified with modernity. While translating this figure of thought into political efficacy, a procedure largely unsuccessful in Italy proper, the model has exuded a hegemonic force in Spain and, with far greater penetration, in France. This figuration's political power derives from the unshakable linguistic bond with a living collectivity that then transcends the moment to stretch across multiple generations. The Machiavellian paradigm turns Dante on his head; expressing the intertwining components of political, cultural, and linguistic power, it entails identifying and elevating into grammar—idealizing—a language weighted down with collective sediment. Just as dependent initially on political might as on its linguistic force, this select collectivity gradually exercises hegemony by overcoming political resistance and by bringing other modes of speech into its orbit.

In this respect, Italy's inability to harness the power of language to political ends sets it off from nations whose drive to nationhood left no room to distinguish the political from the linguistic. Gramsci succinctly characterizes this failure of the Italian Renaissance:

> That literary works, whatever their value, are written in the vernacular is nonetheless a new fact; it is the really important fact. That from among the local vernaculars, one—that of Tuscany—achieves hegemony is yet another fact which, however, should not be overestimated: it is not accompanied by a sociopolitical hegemony and therefore remains confined to a pure literary fact . . . In reality, the emergent bourgeoisie imposes its own dialects but does not succeed in creating a national language.[24]

There are, however, numerous counterexamples. In Spain, Castilian was immortalized in grammar, and its use, backed by the crown, seeped through the rest of the Iberian Peninsula (with the partial exception of Portugal), just as France managed to grant a transhistorical nature to the language of the Île de France, which through the centuries slowly ground its way to the present-day borders of the French state. This logic of incremental territorialization has underwritten modernity's conception of conquest from the so-called epoch of discovery to the massive global conflicts of the twentieth century.

Territorialization, real and ideal, cultural-linguistic and military, intimately inhabits the vernacular figure of thought, rendered operable by the figure of the dispersed prince who needs only to be projected and reassembled, like Osiris of ancient Egyptian theology, to unify a disparate reality. Even historical understanding itself, bound up with the collective consciousness that impels history, partakes of the same figural conception. In Machiavelli's view, the language of the Florentine city-state displaces the question of an ideal, commonly held language because it—that is, the Florentine language—is the "foundation and source" (*"fondamento e fonte,"* 930) of any linguistic commonality one might venture to assert. In other words, that same figure of shared language intertwining the forces of vernacular grammar, political unity, and collective identity projects a coherent vision of experience that necessarily includes both spatial and temporal coordinates—a stable foundation on which to build, from which to launch incursions, and an origin to anchor historical unfolding.

This linguistic understanding, ethereal as it might seem, has bolstered the cultural, political, social, *and* geographical conceptions that merge to form the modern worldview. Furthermore, language's peculiar status as a medium combining a material inscription (the grammar and writing that fixes it for subsequent generations) and an ideal projection (a collective imaginary built on the basis of this materiality) belongs to a specific discursive circulation. The linguistic nationalism of modernity, which realizes one manifestation of Dante's call for a vernacular, simultaneously enacts and diffuses an economy of linguistic meaning that inaugurates modern culture. Within this purview, Benedict Anderson, one of the best known theorists of national community, describes the sociopolitical aspects of modern language: "It is always a mistake to treat languages in the way that certain nationalist ideologues treat them—as *emblems* of nation-ness, like flags, costumes, folk-dances, and the rest. Much the most important thing about language is its capacity for generating imagined communities, building in effect *particular solidarities.* After all, imperial languages are still *vernaculars,* and thus particular vernaculars among many."[25] In other words, language enjoys a status distinct from that of symbols of collectivity, which produce togetherness through their physical presence. A shared language, on the contrary, projects togetherness according to the workings of allegory: departing from a material basis, which Dante described as grammar, the collective idea projects an identity into time, linking past generations, as well as the material residue of their spiritual creations, to the present, heading full into the future. Rather than devolving from an idealized construction, however, the national language of modernity derives from a *particular* language, a vernacular owing more to Machiavelli's view than to that of Dante or, rather, to Machiavelli's interpretation of Dante in a given political context. In following the logic of this conception, a national vernacular would result from the imposition of a particular, living language, from a metropolitan vernacular achieving national hegemony.

Instead of the Esperanto model, a language that, like Dante's, belongs to none and thus potentially to all (within the linguistic constraints marking its invention), empire in Anderson's sense espouses a given particular vernacular that, once idealized and fixed into grammar and cultural institutions, spreads to ever larger geographical areas and therefore conjoins linguistic and political hegemony. But, for modernity, this linguistic model of nationalism, stemming from Machiavelli's vision of Dante's vernacular, relies squarely on the technology that reproduces and disseminates it. As Anderson notes, "Print-language is what invents nationalism, not *a* particular language per se" (134); in speaking of the late twentieth century, he adds that "the very idea of 'nation' is now nestled firmly in virtually all print-languages; and nation-ness is virtually inseparable from political consciousness" (135). Print, the technology of multiple copies that transcend the limits of both space and time, provided the mechanism for implanting Dante's expansive vernacular, even if its point of reference was a real spoken language rather than an ideal construction, a preexistent political power rather than a promised one. More important, though, language—specifically, print-language— served as the touchstone of an entire configuration that encompassed notions of political action, collective consciousness, and national identity. Print-languages, and the vernaculars they embody, produce a mental geography without which modernity would be unthinkable.

Yet disruptions of this placid conceptual landscape loom just over the horizon. Twentieth-century technology offers new ways of inscribing matter, of conquering space and time, and force a reconsideration of Dante's notion of vernacular understanding. Once again, Anderson glimpses this potential destabilization, although *Imagined Communities* mentions it only in passing, without dwelling on its repercussions for the conceptual apparatus of modernity: "[A]dvances in communications technology, especially radio and television, give print allies unavailable a century ago. Multilingual broadcasting can conjure up the imagined community to illiterates and populations with different mother-tongues. (Here there are resemblances to the conjuring up of mediaeval Christendom through visual representations and bilingual literati)" (135). In this rendering, print retains its dominant position and is only buttressed by new forms of communication. But the reference to medieval Christianity is significant and brings to bear another discursive economy more akin to transnationalism or globalization than to city- or nation-states. As has been widely noted, it implies a shift in material inscription (from print to orality or visual images), in time (from slow, relatively laborious reading to the immediacy of perception), in collective participation (from the solitary reception of the book to the mass simultaneity of television and radio), among many other transformations, some of which are contradictory (solitary video viewing, for example). Nonetheless, by far the most striking aspect of this shift or disruption involves the so-called language question, as Anderson seems to recognize in remarking that "nations can now be imagined without linguistic communality" (135). While still at work and gaining increasing power in contemporary consciousness, the collective imaginary is gradually being disengaged from the vernacular and from the configuration of modern historical understanding for which it was the linchpin.

This contemporary landscape presents a new topography for Dante's radical project that asserts, through a figure of thought, a bond between the political prince and the linguistic vernacular. Unhitched from the materiality they were deemed to invest with meaning, vernaculars have exploded into a countless multiplicity. But the hegemony they were to mobilize, support, and perpetuate has slipped into another dimension, a global one irreducible to national imaginaries that themselves already surpass linguistic collectivities. While Machiavelli's municipal vernacular translated Dante's linguistic theory to articulate the modern worldview of political and cultural power, the demise of this modern trajectory seems to be inscribed in the global economy the vernacular set in motion. Already in 1931, Gramsci strove to place Dante's vernacular concept in the context of historically staking out the unity of Italy, which has served since the Middle Ages as a laboratory for sociopolitical understanding. He observed that

> [c]ontemporary history offers a model for understanding the Italian past: there is today a European cultural consciousness and there is a series of manifestations on the part of intellectuals and politicians who assert the necessity of a European union. One can even say that the historical process tends toward this union and that there exist many material forces that can develop only within this union. If in "x" number of years this union is realized, the word "nationalism" will have the same archeological meaning as present-day "municipalism."[26]

In this sense, municipalism (the harnessing of political and linguistic power) and nationalism (the extension of a localized vernacular and political domination to a larger realm) belong to the same economy of discourse, power, culture, and—finally—hegemony. With new forms of political territorialization, channeled by evolving communication technology, the city, the nation, and even the state do not suddenly achieve the status of superseded relics; instead, their anachronism stems from the configuration they share, whose elements no longer cohere into a stable whole.

In effect, language, whether printed, stuttered, or scribbled in the nooks and crannies of postmodern architecture, has been divested of its political role as the glue of the modern world picture. Ironically, the force of Dante's politicolinguistic conception reveals its greatest potential in the contemporary context, precisely when the vernacular can no longer bear the political burden it was destined to carry. The ultimate strength of Dante's political vision, his renewable unorthodoxy, if you will, resides not in the vernacular but in the figuration it incarnated. The figure, introduced by Dante as a mode of thinking the political, will outlive the materiality it was conceived to invest. Casting aside the vernacular as the motor of political action does not mean discarding figuration—an impossible task, since figures are the very matter of thought. It does, however, mean inventing new figures for thinking the political, cultural, and historical dimension of ongoing contemporaneity.

Figural Economy of the Worldview

Since the first critical reflections on visual perspective—traditionally linked to the Italian Renaissance and, specifically, to Brunelleschi and Alberti—visual images have never ceased proliferating in ever greater numbers to saturate the globe. Modernity is, in a certain sense, synonymous with increasing visualization, which describes the sheer quantity of visual images as well as the mode of representation they exemplify. In part, of course, this dominating visualization can be traced, at least in the past 150 years, through photography, film, television, video, and nascent digital imaging—that is, through the technologies that produce and disseminate images. Yet this turn toward visualization marks all of modernity and constitutes a key aspect of modernity's assumptions of historical understanding.

Most fundamentally, the advent of the world picture, with its concomitant perspectivism, signals the fashioning of a secular understanding whose most significant aspect may be the ensuing predominance of the spatial over the temporal, of immediacy over duration, of individual will over the material forces of history. As Erwin Panofsky notes, "Perspective, in transforming the *ousia* (reality) into the *phainomenon* (appearance), seems to reduce the divine to a mere subject matter for human consciousness; but for that very reason, conversely, it expands human consciousness into a vessel for the divine."[1] In what Panofsky refers to as the epoch of "anthropocracy," the human being does not do away with the divine but incorporates it into a terrestrial perspective that endows the human being with the powers to act historically without explicit otherworldly reference and that lays the groundwork for notions of progress, human perfectibility,[2] and technological advance. Time, historical time, becomes a series of synchronous moments succeeding one another only by virtue of the actions of human consciousness. In sum, this worldview or picture implies a very specific understanding of history, theory of human agency, and conception of language.

Although its chronology varies considerably from one discipline of knowledge to another, the historical disjuncture provoking or following from modernity has been subjected to extensive commentary. For art history, as the Panofsky quote suggests, it is tied to the emergence of perspective; Heidegger describes it as the setting into place of the Cartesian subject; Foucault prefers considering it a general epistemic transformation; it has also been characterized as inextricably linked to the epoch of "discovery" or colonialization, to the establishment of the modern state, to printing and the expansion of literacy, and to the Reformation, among other things. Precisely in this context, the work of Erich Auerbach has a profound resonance. For Auerbach, this disjunctive moment, which I have glossed as the advent of modernity, entails the collapse not only of a specific mode of historical understanding but also of an economy of meaning production bound up with a concrete and material figuration. Here I am referring to Auerbach's essay "Figura," which investigates notions that will become an important point of reference for *Mimesis's* historical reflections. In fact, because of the philological nature of the "Figura" essay, the task of indicating the shift in figural economy falls to *Mimesis:* "[I]n the course of the sixteenth century, the Christian-figural schema [*Rahmenvorstellung*] lost its hold in almost all parts of Europe. The issue into the beyond, although it was totally abandoned only in rare instances, lost in certainty and unmistakability [*an Sicherheit und Eindeutigkeit*]."[3] In *Mimesis,* the emergence of the tragic in conjunction with individual experience marks the shift away from the medieval figural economy of meaning.

The loss of certainty, the indefiniteness vis-à-vis the beyond that accompanies the modern view of the tragic, calls for a revised conception of human thought in which the individual plays a crucial role.[4] On this particular issue, a comparison with Heidegger's description of this historical moment proves useful in determining the implications of this shift in discursive economy. Whereas Auerbach's "Figura" essay delin-

eates the bases of historical understanding prior to modernity, Heidegger's essay "The Age of the World Picture" takes the rupture leading to
modernity as its point of departure. In the words of Heidegger's essay:

> The loss of the gods [*Entgötterung*] is the situation of indecision [*Ent-
> scheidunglosigkeit*] regarding God and the gods. Christendom has the
> greatest share in bringing it about. But the loss of the gods is so far
> from excluding religiosity that rather only through that loss is the rela-
> tion to the gods changed into mere "religious experience" [*Erleben*].
> When this occurs, the gods have fled. The resultant void is compen-
> sated for by means of historiographical and psychological investigation
> of myth.[5]

In this context, which Heidegger's essay melodramatically portrays as
the fleeing of the gods, the grid of world interpretation, with its unquestioned series of references, can no longer be taken for granted. The mer-
est doubt as to referential validity calls for reflection and requires an
active decision on the part of individuals whose own thoughts or senti-
ments become the ultimate point of reference. Heidegger characterizes
this moment as one of undecidability, just as Auerbach expresses it as
one of lost unmistakability, a loss that provides the stimulus for the development of modern subjectivity. As Heidegger's text indicates, this
emergent necessity of individual human agents led to elaboration of representational history *(Historie)*, or history that stakes claims on objective truth, which the translation calls "historiography," and of narratives
based on human psychology, discourses that belong to what this text
calls "the age of the world picture." The loss of certitude inevitably creates a situation in which experience, that is, lived experience *(Erlebnis)*,
looms large.

   Projecting back from this side of the rupture, Auerbach's unearthing
of *figura* introduces notions that are not readily graspable on the basis of
representational history. In a sense, Auerbach sketches the historical parameters of a discursive hegemony that has, for a number of reasons, become inoperative, although of course the word *hegemony* never appears
in Auerbach's texts. In discursive terms, however, the general thrust of
the *figura* analysis is unambiguous. As the essay itself states: "The intention of our study was to show how, based on the development of its
meaning, a word can grow into a world-historical situation [*weltge-
schichtliche Lage*] and develop structures that are effective [*wirksam*] for

many centuries."[6] This essay is concerned, then, with the structures of discourse that produce and maintain world-historical effectiveness, that become universal within a specific society and in a specific historical situation. The study moves in two fundamental directions that are mutually reinforcing: it examines the mechanisms of figuration, its elements, and how they articulate with one another, and it depicts the referents or the ultimate otherworldly referent that figural history presupposes.

Although the basic tenets of figuration are relatively easy to state, their implications for understanding are far from evident. The essence of medieval figuration resides in the presumed historicity of the figure: "[F]igura is something real [*Wirkliches*] and historical [*Geschichtliches*] which announces and renders something else that is also real and historical" (29; 65). In other words, figuration in this sense marks a process whereby an event or personage that exists or existed historically displays characteristics that place it in relation with subsequent historical events or personages. This historicity separates the figure from allegory, on the one hand, and symbol, on the other; in contrast, the element that falls out of meaning production in modernity is not simply figural interpretation but historicity itself. Accounts of the modern hermeneutic tradition, such as Gadamer's *Truth and Method,* tend to oppose symbol and allegory as two principal forms of meaning production, without ever broaching the issues of *figura* as outlined by Auerbach.[7] Walter Benjamin's and, later, Paul de Man's rehabilitation of allegory stemmed explicitly from their different but related attempts to reintroduce the question of historicity and its concomitant figurality. In terms of Christian *figura,* Auerbach demonstrates that, contrary to allegory, whose expression is abstract, bears no intrinsic relation to its meaning, and is therefore discardable (54–56; 77–79), or to the symbol, a union of expression and meaning, important for collectivities but without a necessary historical component (56–58; 79–81), the figure cannot be peeled away from the substance it expresses, must be read in its literality, and has a concrete historical meaning as well as a figural one.

In Auerbach's reading, this melding of the concrete historical event with what he calls "providential world-history," a yoking together of terrestrial and universal history through the mediation of the figure, gave Christianity its "tremendous power of persuasion" and paved the way for its domination in the Western Middle Ages (52; 76). While simultaneously a doctrine and a "vision of world history" (52; 77) that severs the biblical writings from their local origins and renders them "universal," the figural notion sustains a method of interpretation that Auerbach designates as the reality-prophecy method (die realprophetische Methode) (52; 76). The real historical event retains its concreteness and pertinence at the same time that it belongs to a historical understanding that surpasses it, projects it into the future, which is also a renewed reading of the past. Linearity has no place here, for there is no unfolding; the relationship between figures comes about indirectly, through the mediation of an asynchronous perspective—for Christianity, the eyes of God.

Nonetheless, this methodology does not propose a conceptual understanding of history, with its human agent or interpreter simply decoding events in the name of a higher power; nor does the human agent in this model of history rely on the aggrandizing naïveté of lived experience that Heidegger so forcefully critiques. A central passage in "Figura" summarizes the complexities of figural interpretation and pinpoints the nature of the human agent's intervention in that process:

> Figural interpretation establishes a connection between two events [Geschehnissen] or persons, the first of which signifies not only itself but also the second, while the second encompasses or fulfills the first. The two poles of the figure are separate in time, but both, being real processes or figures [Gestalten], are within time; they are both, as we have repeatedly stressed, caught up in the stream of historical life. Only the understanding of their connection, the intellectus spiritualis, is a spiritual act [ein geistiger Akt: a mental act]. With regard to each pole, this spiritual act deals with the given or hoped-for material of past, present, or future events [Geschehens], rather than with concepts or abstractions; these are quite secondary, since promise and fulfillment, as real and intrinsically historical events [innergeschichtliche Ereignisse], have either happened in the incarnation of the Word or will happen in the second coming. Of course, purely spiritual elements enter into conceptions [Vorstellungen] of the ultimate fulfillment, since "my kingdom is not of this world"; yet it will be a real kingdom, not an abstract suprasensible form [kein abstrakt unsinnliches Gebilde]. 53; 77)

Although this passage (and the entire essay, for that matter) clearly draws on philosophical vocabulary to describe figuration, the historical understanding it describes is far removed from both Platonic idealism and Aristotle's more earthly notions of underlying essence, two fundamental tendencies of Western philosophy. Connections between past, present, and future occurrences are no less historical than the events they bring together, for making those connections falls to the human agent whose sole intervention is that connecting act of thought. However, although this connection requires active recognition, that is, participation of an agent, the spiritual or mental act accomplishing it does not derive from personal faith or belief. In that historical context, the question of individual faith or belief has no weight, for individuals were only incidental to the historical processes they were to discern. It is for this reason that one can speak of discursive hegemony: interpretation took place in reference to a historical understanding that had no competitors, and all questioning took place within that purview.

Strangely enough for a world that seemingly relies on the transcendental, this absolute necessity to inscribe all interpretation firmly in the historical harbors an unavoidable materialism. Just as the figure must be read literally, must persist in conjunction with whatever deeper significance it might display, so must the historical materiality of events subsist as an integral component of all interpretation. As Auerbach remarks, all real or potential objects of figural interpretation—that is, events, actions, or persons—must meet the conditions of materiality; the mental act, conjoining two or more figures, whether they are historically given or projected into history, presupposes this material aspect. In fact, even the utopian or idealist moment of Christianity, the moment in which it most closely approaches Platonism—a moment exemplified by the projected second coming or final judgment—must meet these criteria; no matter how fantastic or improbable, future events must submit to the demands of "real" material history. This is one of the profound implications of the banal assertion that in figural interpretation both sign and signifier exhibit an inescapable historicity (54; 77). Conceptions of meaning production always have historical consequences, even if they are rarely acknowledged.

This figural conception of history is intertwined with projections into the future that depend neither on the centrality of human consciousness nor on the progress of human knowledge. The future is a structural part of historical understanding, even if the infinite elapsing of historical time does not bring its endpoint any closer to realization. In "Figura," Auerbach juxtaposes this conception of historical process with that of modernity:

Thus history [*das Geschehen*], with all its sensible force [*sinnlichen Kraft*], remains forever a simulacrum [*Gleichnis*], cloaked and needful of interpretation, even if faith provides it with a general orientation. In this way, the world history of no epoch ever arrives at its practical conclusion, which, from both the naive and modern scientific perspectives, resides in the accomplished fact; instead, history remains open and questionable, points to something still concealed, and the living human being's position [*Stellung*] vis-à-vis that concealment is characterized by trials, hope, faith, and expectation. The provisional nature of historical events in the figural perspective is fundamentally different from the modern conception of historical development. In the modern conception, the provisional event undergoes continuous interpretation as part of an unbroken horizontal line of events; in the figural perspective the interpretation is always ascertained from above, along a vertical axis, and events are considered not in their unbroken relation to one another, but torn apart, individually, each in relation to a third that is promised but that has not yet taken place. (58–59; 80–81)

Enmeshed in a proliferation of figures, the historical process, whose primary feature is its open-ended becoming, requires continuous interpretive interventions. However, the historical interpreter's real position in the face of what is cloaked, of what demands interpretation, does not refer to an individual perspective. The trials, hope, faith, and expectation that determine the relationship between interpreter and concealment, between the unpredictable and the sense one might make of it, belong to the very structure of historical understanding. Interpreting individuals, whose act of thought produces a relationship between figures, do not simply choose to hope or to act on faith any more than their belief in God results from personal inclination. This position was given as part of historical understanding itself, a fact that offers a glimpse into the difficulty inherent in discussing any particular discursive hegemony from within the purview of that hegemony.

Modernity—or what we have come to call modernity—does away with figuration as the ground of historical understanding. Instead of considering historical process on the basis of its ongoing unpredictability and necessary fragmentation, modern historical understanding installs the human perspective as the foundation of historical meaning. This historical conception, which Auerbach refers to as history on a horizontal axis, assigns historical agency to the human itself. Human knowledge becomes the motor of history, and historical time thus elapses as the unknown is incrementally conquered. In this vein, Heidegger's essay on the worldview draws the line between the modern position and that of preceding historical epochs; at the advent of modernity, the essay notes,

> Man becomes the representative *(der Repräsentant)* of that which is, in the sense of that which has the character of object.
>
> But the newness in this event by no means consists in the fact that now the position of man in the midst of what is, is an entirely different one in contrast to that of medieval and ancient man. What is decisive is that man himself expressly takes up this position as one constituted by himself, that he intentionally maintains it as that taken up by himself, and that he makes it secure as the solid footing for a possible development of humanity. Now for the first time is there any such thing as a "position" of man. (132; 84)

The ideas presented in this passage are well-known attributes of modernity that were much criticized in the twentieth century. Man or the human being as the focal point for historical understanding has undergirded Western ideas of development and progress, of subjectivity and mastery of nature, and has at the same time guided the elaboration of modern science and technology. First and foremost, however, it sets into place a drastic curtailment of historical understanding by establishing these modern precepts as the prism through which all history must be deciphered. As evidenced in the *figura* essay, Auerbach's work resists that mandate, just as this passage from Heidegger's essay avoids recounting the historical transition to modernity as simply a consequence of the human being's new position. Asserting that shift to be continuous with modern human history ignores the radical disjuncture constituting modernity and refuses to acknowledge the historicity of history itself.

What is at stake in the confrontation between these two historical conceptions, that is, conceptions exemplified by modernity versus the Christian Middle Ages or by a discursive hegemony based on representation as opposed to one based on figuration, has very little to do with debates about theology and secularization. Auerbach's mention of thirdness in the figural discourse suggests a wider range of issues bound up with the material exigencies of figuration—issues ultimately more pertinent to today than to the medieval contemplation of the divine. This thirdness, which in the Middle Ages could not be thought separate from a vertical relationship to an all-knowing deity, has itself reemerged in the twentieth century, stripped of its theological garments. Charles Sanders Peirce, for example, made the notion of thirdness the touchstone of not only his theory of signs and meaning production but also his work on logic, mathematics, and universal history. As defined by Peirce, "Third-ness is the mode of being of that which is such as it is, in bringing a second and third in relation to each other,"[8] a phrase that echoes the tripartite figuration described by Auerbach (for firstness, in Peirce's schema, means what has absolutely no connection with anything else). Peirce's pragmatism introduced the notion of thirdness to reconfigure the understanding of human action that had been reduced to a bipolar vision, which, like the modern theory of knowledge emanating from the relationship between subject and object, flattens out history. As Peirce points out, this dyadic conception, which places agency in the human subject, distorts historical understanding: "I think that great errors of metaphysics are due to looking at the future as something that will have been past" (27). Reading the future as the not-yet-past, as simply the stationary object of subjective knowledge, gives the illusion of historical mastery at the same time that it misreads the history of the present.

In this context, the question of the world picture emerges once again. Just as advent of modernity does not signal a new position of the human being but the emergence of human positionality itself, the world picture of modernity does not betoken a modern world picture succeeding an outdated medieval one. As Heidegger remarks, "[W]orld picture, when understood essentially, does not mean a picture of the world but the world conceived and grasped as a picture" (129; 82). Localizing historical agency in the human being, redrawing the map of the world according to the subject staring at its objects, constitutes the world as tableau, as a landscape in which the subject moves at will. In describing figuration, Auerbach also draws upon the picture, but in a very different sense: in discussing the Middle Ages, he affirms that figuration gives "a picture of reality," of "history" (*Wirklichkeits- und Geschichtsbildes*), and of "sensibility in general" (*Sinnlichkeit überhaupt*) (53; 77). Figuration, precisely because of its thirdness, as refusal to relinquish the material historicity of figures, cannot exceed the provisional and endorses the fragmentary nature of historical experience. It pictures the world, creating a space for action, without even the minimal possibility of painting a world picture.

The early twenty-first century is far removed from the mythical face-off between medieval figuration and modernity's world picture. Technological transformations—including changes in the media of communication, modes and systems of transport, the demographic explosion in the wake of medical advances—have disturbed the naive historical certainty underlying the modern world picture. In contrast, Auerbach's meticulous study of medieval economies of knowledge and history describes a closed world dominated by a sacred text, a restricted class of interpreters, and a network of knowledge production that depended on a long-term stability—even rigidity—scarcely imaginable in modernity. The emergence of the modern picture, whose seeds were already sown in medieval Christianity (in Heidegger's account and in Western narratives generally), signaled a change in historical understanding; the rupture with the medieval theory of figuration, which provided a means to integrate and reintegrate the changing present into an ongoing past that refused to be overcome, ushered in a vision of the world as a picture, as a representation. Not by happenstance is modernity also the epoch of massive topographic exploration and of the geographic and stellar mapping that results from it.

Heidegger's essay describes the discursive and conceptual elements that achieved dominance in what he calls the age of the world picture, that is, the epoch of representation, just as Auerbach's elaboration of the medieval *figura* foregrounds a complex temporal schema that resists spatial representation, for the past increasingly intervenes in the present to point to the future, and the actors have no ready-made positions to render time spatial. The picture, bringing a totalizing overview within human grasp, gives priority to the spatial and assigns the temporal a derivative role in the march of history. That is why the vast majority of modern theories of history—whether deriving from Hegelian philosophy, positivism, or Darwinian evolution—view history as a linear progression. This spatial priority, which accompanies the ascendancy of human perspective, has profound implications for theories of language, meaning, and reality, in addition to its more immediate consequences in the domain of history, the actors producing it, and the narrative discourses interpreting it. In the so-called epoch of representation, however, figures do not disappear, they simply diminish in significance; they become no more than meanderings between the proper meaning and the figurative meaning, what the French have formally institutionalized as the difference between *"le sens propre"* and *"le sens figuré."* The assumption of the proper meaning projects a reality, a representation of reality, that is by definition exempt from the vagaries of figuration. The correctness of this representation is what goes under the name of truth, just as representations judged to be unfaithful are called erroneous. From the perspective of the modern world picture, it is difficult to ask whether the representation has a role in producing what it represents.

The world picture of modernity, rapidly becoming planetary after its initial articulation in Europe, requires a substantial network of military, political, and civil institutions to sustain it. In a very mediated way, difficult to grasp and represent with objective precision, these institutions, the authoritative discourses they emit and the mindset they foster, are part and parcel of a discursive economy of hegemonic force. In contrast with the discursive hegemony of the Middle Ages, which could respond only obliquely and sluggishly to contemporary change, the secular discursive hegemony of modernity permits a rapid reaction to contemporary history, for it is a mechanism for producing and disseminating coherent world pictures with elements that are woven into the very fabric of modernity. For example, establishing a group identity, whether ethnic, national, or territorial, requires first the assertion that it exists, then the discursive elaboration of its shared language and its specific grammar, the subsidized search for its cultural heritage, usually in the form of literary artifacts, the writing of histories that show the gradual development of this collective tradition, its relationships to already established traditions, and the evolution of its concomitant consciousness. Although extremely complex and demanding extensive discursive resources, this process may take place in the briefest span of historical time. Such an elaboration would be impossible using the conceptual, historical, and institutional tools of medieval thought and discourse.

In historical terms, this scenario was often reenacted throughout the twentieth century, and the structure of this world picture, with its accompanying conceptual configuration, literally permeates all collective institutions, from the smallest principality to the United Nations. In fact, this age of the world picture or representation might best be designated the "age of modeling," of creating discursive models—models of concepts, figures, and their interactions—both to explain "reality" as it is perceived and to produce the means to render visible and comprehensible a reality that was at best inchoate. Although this modeling is specifically discursive in nature, it displays a marked resemblance to the hypothesis in the realm of scientific reasoning. A hypothesis, projecting an explanation involving disparate elements or events whose existence may be merely presupposed, conceptually shapes the future in the present.[9] In this sense, discourses, just like hypotheses, enable action and produce the context for interpretation and thus their own legitimation. Unlike with a hypothesis, however, one cannot test a discursive model and emerge with a definitive answer—one rallies to it or rejects it, but its empirical verification is rarely the deciding factor. As the twentieth century attests, contradictory discursive models often lead to physical conflict, but the attribution of values and modalities to the representation's figures does not come under scrutiny. These models, linguistic in nature and depending on technologies that guarantee their materialization— such as, for example, the stamping of ink on paper, the production of multiple copies, the binding of the sheets, and the distribution of the resulting physical product—rely heavily on continuous circulation and recycling, from past to present (to rejuvenate the physical material bearing its inscription) and from place to place (to expand the public domain). New forms of technological inscription—from photo and film to video games—have simultaneously contributed to a proliferation of disparate representations and called into question the simplistic claims of their timeless veracity.

The nonessential nature of these models has long been recognized, particularly in the scientific domain, but they are not arbitrary, an aspect that is perhaps more apparent in reference to discourses and economies of discourse, because they most explicitly belong to the larger historical and sociopolitical configuration of institutions. Nowhere is this clearer than in contemporary speculation about artificial intelligence, which has problematized the most fundamental aspect of modernity and its human-centered discursive universe—the human itself. For example, Marvin Minsky's remarks about the epistemological schemas of thought give an inkling of the extraordinary complexity of discourse and its motivating figures:

> Minds also make up pleasant worlds of practical affairs—which work because we make them work, by putting things in order there. In the physical realm, we keep our books and clothes in self-made shelves

and cabinets—thus building artificial boundaries to keep our things from interacting very much. Similarly, in mental realms, we make up countless artificial schemes to force things to seem orderly, by specifying legal codes, grammar rules and traffic laws. When growing up in such a world, it all seems right and natural—and only scholars and historians recall the mass of precedents and failed experiments it took to make it work so well. These "natural" worlds are actually more complex than the technical worlds of philosophy. They're far too vast to comprehend—except where we impose on them the rules we make.[10]

Minsky's brief characterization of the "artificial schemes" of knowing, whatever its own historical assumptions, touches on the way in which what is deemed "natural" becomes established. In the sense I indicated above, this mechanism for producing the natural is nonessential, which means simply that what is natural changes and has no possible definitive state and that no understanding of the natural is ruled by historical necessity.

The natural is not arbitrary, however, because it coexists with the sociohistorical, epistemological, and even political constraints at every given historical moment, which range from the structure of society, the available technology for preserving knowledge, and the financial resources dedicated to thought and research, to the means for obtaining executive and symbolic power. While the epistemological import of Minsky's observation is self-evident, introducing linguistic and, by extension, discursive elements into the equation complicates matters considerably. Concepts themselves, linguistic signifiers that necessarily involve immaterial human thought, and their naturalness are no less a product of historical, social, and epistemological forces than the artificial schemes of perception. Concepts or notions—inevitably embedded in discourses that explain, reinterpret, justify, or deny them—are even more tenuous than the codification of artificial schemes; discourses introduce an element of ambiguity, a slippage that always calls forth other discourses—to clarify, sustain, or rebut. The world of modernity is built on an infinite crisscrossing of interwoven discourses. These notions, ideas, concepts, or what have you, all of which share an immaterial aspect by definition, are the stuff of discourse and perhaps of thought itself. One can touch a table, a given individual, but can one touch a "self"? A people? In fact, these are figures: ideas whose existence is linguistic and discursive and that produce real material effects. Figures have juridical, institutional, conceptual, and historical existence; yet their existence cannot be thought separate from the discourses that express them.

The historical aspect proves the most thorny issue in attempts to discern the material forces of figuration and to avoid falling prey to their inherently powerful idealism. The principal difficulty in constituting history and figuration as an object resides in their inseparability from thought and discourse. In one of his countless prison letters to Tania Schucht, Antonio Gramsci hints at some of the aspects involved in considering material history on the basis of individual experience and critique, although, as is often the case even with Gramsci's most personal reflections, his remarks emerge in the context of broader historical concerns. In the midst of his critical comments on Tania Schucht's previous letter, Gramsci asks three rhetorical questions: "How many societies does each individual belong to? And does not each one of us make constant efforts to unify our own worldview [*concezione del mondo*], in which heterogeneous fragments of fossilized cultural worlds continue to subsist? And doesn't there exist a general historical process tending constantly toward a unification of the entire human species?"[11] These remarks resonate with Gramsci's incisive analyses of the historical efficacity of figures, of Machiavelli's concept of the prince in particular, and of how they might be tapped to describe and motivate contemporary historical transformation.[12] Much more schematic than Gramsci's notebook writings, this brief passage from his 1931 letter names three overlapping layers of historical experience that have decisive roles in providing parameters for individual consciousness. In the context of contemporaneity, which structuralism designated as synchronic, the individual belongs to multiple "societies" or groups that, on the one hand, furnish means for specific worldviews and that, on the other, are inevitably in conflict with one another. As Gramsci inquires in this same letter, "Doesn't every group, party, sect or religion tend to create its own 'conformism' (not understood in the gregarious and passive sense)?" In the twentieth century, worldviews cannot be boiled down to expressions of a single group, if indeed it was ever possible. In fact, the notion of multiple societies has today become commonplace; in anthropology, for example, one of the leading French anthropologists, Marc Augé, refers to individuals as belonging to multiple "worlds" and has made that multiplicity the object of much of his anthropological reflection.[13] Given the multiplicity of worlds to which each individual belongs, approaches to the question of hegemony and unitary consciousness are far from obvious; instead, one is constantly shuffling about, navigating through figures and discourses that, while perhaps tending toward conformism, are contradictory and incomplete.

This observation, fundamental for Gramsci's reflections, sets his version of historical understanding off from the hermeneutic conception of history that has been so influential in literary studies and the humanities generally. Contrary to hermeneutics, for Gramsci and for the notion of history he endorses, it is not possible to presuppose a homogeneous nucleus—of values, aesthetic objects, communal belongingness—that serves to guarantee a respective tradition's self-identity through time. Nowhere is this more evident than in the individual's efforts to fashion a historical worldview that privileges the present. In Gramsci's description, the historical past is not overcome; the present is an accretion of residues and sediments that not only cannot be sloughed off but also intrude into the worldview, striving to be integrally homogeneous. History is neither a sequence of ruptures, breaks, and the resulting self-contained epochs, nor a smooth unfolding of an overarching vision, whether emanating from the eyes of God or "man." It is a mass of fragments, ideologies, and beliefs that subsist to become more and more petrified, without disappearing, or to be reactivated in ever changing configurations in response to transformed conditions.

The third layer of historical experience described in the letter points to a historical current beyond the reach of individual experience. In traditional historical understanding, this general historical process emanates from the divine or, in more secular versions, from a transcendent agent who personifies a totalizing overview. For discursive and conceptual purposes, this historical trajectory marks the historical forces, consequences, and motivations that exceed human mastery. This notion, implicitly or explicitly part of every historical conception (Machiavelli, for instance, called it *"il cielo,"* the sky and, at times, *"la fortuna,"* chance), represents the limit of historical figuration, what at any given historical moment cannot be figurally expressed, much in the way that the limit-concept of infinity operates in differential calculus. The limit to historical thought is the necessary illusion of totality momentarily rendered or intimated in fragmentary figures. Even Gramsci's exemplary efforts to describe a unifying historical process ran up against the fragmentation of which he was one of the most important observers.

Like consciousness itself, a worldview, simultaneously individual and transindividual, is under continuous elaboration and reelaboration. It does not exist in isolation from the discourses that articulate it and the presuppositions that make its conception possible. In that sense, the notion of the world picture, intimating the static frame of a snapshot, is at best emblematic. Despite its infinite complexity, a worldview—whose possibility is coextensive with that of modernity (which here is shorthand for the largely unbounded "epoch" of secularization)—entails a number of identifiable elements that include an understanding of history, how it plays itself out and how the present relates to past and future, assumptions about how historical change takes place and about the role of human action in transforming the world, and a grasp of which figures can be discursively endowed with a power to act historically and how multiple figures can be related to one another. Figures, and the configurations that result from their combination, constitute the signposts of these worldviews; despite their similarity with concepts or ideas, they have an irreducible materiality because of their linguistic component.[14]

The linguistic substratum of the worldview—any worldview—explains in part why analyses of relationships between figuration and history have played a more significant role in literary studies than in other domains of reflection. Nevertheless, figures are not a phenomenon bound to conceptions of literature, all of which inevitably bear the disciplinary traits of literature's institutionalization. The linguistic aspect of figuration requires more precise elaboration to trace the figure's pertinence for a truly secular history and material critique. In the twentieth century, Walter Benjamin's reflections on the links between figuration, history, and the sociopolitical are a fundamental resource. Although much discussion of Benjamin's work has dealt with writings and projects from his final decade (most recently with the *Passagen-Werk,* but even before publication of those notes, with other works of the same period, including "The Work of Art in the Age of Mechanical Reproducibility" and "On the Concept of History," classics of twentieth-century thought), the same concerns are present in his earliest works, albeit in various guises.[15] Some of these earlier writings, such as his essay on translation, have been widely discussed, though rarely in the context of historical concerns that became more and more explicit in his later writings, while other texts dealing with the same issues, such as his "epistemo-critical" preface to the book on the German Trauerspiel, have been relatively ignored.

The translation essay, "The Task of the Translator," exceedingly difficult and dense (though without the plethora of textual variants complicating the interpretation of his later works) occupies a distinguished place in critical interpretations of Benjamin's work. In retrospect, if one wanted to adopt a classical narrative of Benjamin's intellectual trajectory, the essay seems to foreshadow the later historical concerns, even as it foregrounds the linguistic reflection that later becomes gradually less explicit. This juxtaposition of linguistic and historical concerns in conjunction with the figuration inherent in the act of translation makes the essay especially pertinent for understanding the epistemological and material dynamics of the worldview.

From the outset the essay seems anomalous: a highly theoretical text introducing a slim translation of Baudelaire's "Tableaux parisiens," a short section of *Les fleurs du mal*.[16] Nevertheless, Benjamin himself considered his essay on translation to be about "a subject that is so central for me that I still don't know whether I can develop it with sufficient freedom at my current stage of thinking."[17] Baudelaire's title for the section "Tableaux parisiens," fashioned for the 1861 edition of *Les fleurs du mal*, groups together eighteen poems that draw their themes from the Parisian "landscape," some of which were published elsewhere in the first edition of *Les fleurs*.[18] *Tableau* is the word for "picture," and both terms—along with "figure" and "image"—render the German *Bild* that was so important in Heidegger's and Auerbach's discussion of the worldview. In effect, Baudelaire's "Tableaux parisiens" endeavors to render the overlapping images of Paris as they are allegorically expressed in language, the elements that constitute the "picture" of Paris, a city that Benjamin will also consider to be representative of the experience of modernity.[19]

Despite the essay's apparent level of abstraction, it is extraordinarily forthright about its goals and precise in its descriptions. From its opening paragraph, which addresses the import of cultural production in general—music, painting, and literature are evoked—the essay bluntly states that referring to the public or some fictitious "recipient" is of no use precisely because they are linguistic idealizations. Such an approach merely affirms "the existence and essence of humankind as such."[20] In other words, in the terms I have used thus far, positing the ideal reader or public creates a figure, asserts the existence of a discursive entity that performs certain actions—reading, listening, watching. This figure, an object of discursive ventriloquism, fluctuates somewhere in the difference between a mere rhetorical figure—if in fact it could be *merely* rhetorical—and a living being. The goal of Benjamin's essay is ultimately to understand the process whereby these figures are produced and the materiality such a production implies.

Just as figures are the matter of thought, language is the touchstone of figuration. Benjamin therefore names this figurative process translation, and the translator, by derivation, becomes the one who undergoes or participates in that process. Embodying this process in the translator figure simultaneously demonstrates the difficulty in describing linguistic process using language itself and marks the limit of such reflection. The focus on process underlies the essay's trenchant critique of customary understandings of translation and, most particularly, its critique of the model of communication. Understood mechanically, communication means to treat the distinction between original and translation as a vacuum that should be semantically traversed; in the communication model, the translator simply transfers one semantic content to another representation. As Benjamin emphasizes throughout the essay, this way of approaching translation does not allow one to address the linguistic movement—which I am calling figuration—that exceeds the economy of representation. In his notion of the figurative process, he draws an analogy with theories of knowing (a line of thought he will continue more directly in his "epistemo-critical" introduction to the baroque Trauerspiel):

> To grasp the genuine relationship between an original and a translation requires an investigation analogous to the train of thought by which a critical epistemology has to prove the impossibility of a theory of imitation [*Abbildtheorie*]. There it is a matter of showing that in knowing there could be no objectivity, not even a claim to it, if it dealt with imitations of reality; here it can be demonstrated that no translation would be possible if in its ultimate essence it strove for likeness to the original. (*GS*, 12; "Task," 73)

Leaving aside the question as to whether there could ever be a pristine, unmediated experience of reality—the basis of a truly objective epistemology—the peculiar linguistic mediation of translation (and of thought) makes every *Abbild,* every representation or simulacrum into a *Bild,* a figure. It is for this reason that the example of nature, of the knowledge of nature, which has served in the West as the model for all forms of objective knowledge, is inappropriate for characterizing the linguistic mediation of the figure. Only history, not nature, exemplifies the concept of translation and the repetition it implies (that is, the original's "life" and "afterlife" [*GS*, 11; "Task," 71]).

History, for Benjamin, is a fragmentary stream of figural transformation whose meaning cannot be reduced to the purview of any given human present. Unambiguous in this regard, Benjamin's formulations echo in some aspects Auerbach's description of medieval figuration:

> Certain interrelated concepts retain their meaning, perhaps even their foremost meaning, if they are not referred exclusively to humankind. One might, for example, speak of an unforgettable life or moment even if all human beings had forgotten it. If the essence of such a life or moment required that it be unforgotten, that predicate would not imply a falsehood but merely a claim not fulfilled by human beings, and probably also a reference to a realm in which it *is* fulfilled: God's remembrance. Analogously, the translatability of linguistic configurations [*sprachlicher Gebilde*] ought to be considered even if for humankind they were untranslatable. (*GS*, 10; "Task," 70)

The linguistic precision of this passage bears commenting on. Just because one speaks of something that is not—in this instance, of an unforgettable moment that has been forgotten—the statement is not untrue. "The predicate is not false." (This portrayal of the way that language operates is not simply theoretical, even if this fact is rarely mentioned explicitly; for example, Benjamin's comments apply just as well to the presuppositions underlying the numerous signs at U.S. airport security checkpoints indicating that it was a serious offense to say that one was not carrying a bomb. After a brief time, the signs disappeared, presumably because language itself made the law unenforceable: was it also criminal to say that one is not going to say that one is not carrying a bomb?) In linguistic terms, that sort of negative statement, which seemingly contradicts the reality it would describe, makes reference (*Verweis*) to a figure—in Benjamin's text, God—whose figural existence makes it a true statement. In a very real sense, this is a model of meaning production, not a theology, that describes the linguistic mechanism whereby figures are conceived and, through extensive discursive elaboration, given substance.

From a theological perspective, all language is fallen language, and Benjamin's theory of meaning, which necessarily entails a theory of history, shows that there is no way to know if the figure—of the divine, for instance—is indeed subsequent to what it represents. There seems to be no totality of which figures or the translation that rewrites them are a fragment.[21] Benjamin's view projects no illusions of historical mastery, because language cannot be dispensed with in conceptualizing that history: "[A]ll translation is only a somewhat provisional way of coming to terms with the foreignness of languages. An instantaneous and final rather than a temporary and provisional solution of this foreignness remains out of reach of humankind; at any rate, it eludes any direct attempt" (*GS*, 14; "Task," 75). As is evident in this passage, translation—the name given to this essay's theme—brings together a vision of history and a theory of action, both of which rest on recognition of the linguistic foundation of human thought. No utopia or ultimate moment of collective wholeness guides human history; such a finality—even if it were potentially real—remains irrelevant because its revelation to humankind is impossible. This is why Benjamin's theory of history is ultimately neither a theology nor a teleology. At the same time, however, this foreignness constitutes an epistemological disruption that cannot be reduced to the models of history and understanding at hand. It is not a question of "foreign languages" but of the foreignness of language, the detritus of figuration. But this disruption that Benjamin later tries to articulate by referring to a flash of lightning both signaling and producing danger, does not depend on or emanate from an identifiable agent. Consequently, the foreignness it enacts can no more be relegated to a deterministic order than to one based on utopia.

This foreignness, which one would hesitate to call "otherness," does not belong to the modern paradigm that views foreignness as fodder either for assimilation or for elimination. Instead, it is linguistic—that is, a meld of material and conceptual elements—and marks a historical disparity. Benjamin's text becomes much more explicit in this regard: "While in languages that ultimate essence, pure language itself, is linked only to linguistic elements and their transformations, in linguistic configurations, it is weighted with a heavy, foreign meaning" (*GS*, 19; "Task," 79–80). Translations deal with "linguistic configurations," "*sprachlicher Gebilden,*" ensembles of language that are marked by history, the secular forces that power it and the figuration mobilized to present it. "Pure language," which in the context of this essay refuses to be read merely as a transcendental reference, is language unmarked by history, language against which foreignness becomes visible: "To turn the symbolizing into the symbolized, to regain pure languages figured [*gestaltet*] into the linguistic flux, is the powerful and only capacity of translation" (*GS*, 19; "Task," 80). From a historical or what Benjamin liked to call an epistemo-critical perspective, foreignness is the "natural," the objective that becomes manifest only as figurative, as having been constructed on the basis of idealized, historical, and epistemological needs that have no single identifiable agent or cause.

Linguistic purity, to the extent that it can be said to exist, is the presupposition of unfigured language that constitutes the backdrop of figuration. Without the assumption of unfigured language, however unrealizable in history, figures have no grounds of expression, no possibility to emerge. The essay's enigmatic concluding sentence, which affirms "the interlinear version of the sacred text" to be the original figure (*Urbild*) or "ideal of all translation" (*GS*, 21; "Task," 82), should be understood in this context. Measuring disparities between figures with no possibility of definitively recovering some pure language, whether it is more than a figure or not, one scribbles and glosses interpretations that become realizable in conjunction with the effects of historical forces. From the moment it achieves materialization in history, pure language—whatever it might be—cannot, even as a holy text, escape its own impurity. And that is the irrevocable condition of secular thought.

Unlike the medieval history portrayed by Auerbach, which relied on a divine vision anchored in worldly intentions, or the modern global picture of interacting subjects that Heidegger sets against his tidy narrative of the decline of being, Benjamin's theory of translation proposes a secular understanding of history that dispenses with the transcendent and facile attributions of subjective agency, simultaneously pushing into the foreground material linguistic concerns. Though wholly secular in its concern with unknowable transcendence, this historical conception shares its concrete, real aspect with Auerbach's medieval model. Nonetheless, in discarding the transcendental agent as a historical force, it necessarily entails questions of institutions, economies, secular power, and the material and conceptual forces that build ideas. In sum, it opens up a critical dimension to historical reflection, enabling a less idealizing understanding of meaning production and recognizing the presuppositions of thinking, as well as the consequences they produce. In examining the inextricable relationship between idealizing figures and theories of history, the following chapter interrogates the significance of this immanent space of historical understanding.

3

Illusions of Unfolding Time

Every cultural and political economy requires a coherent and compatible sense of the past, present, and future. A necessity more intensely felt since the advent of the modern state, this sometimes implicit historical understanding, with its attendant categories of knowledge and value, endows any present with stability by mediating between the need for continuity with the past and the inevitability of disruptive change. A quandary in historical understanding occurs when disruptive change outdistances the capacity to integrate it; at its most extreme, this quandary touches on the very concept of historical protagonist, a central element or figure of all historical thought. In modernity, however, when a transcendent deity gradually ceased being viewed as the primary agent of human events, the notion of historical protagonist has achieved unparalleled prominence. As shorthand for a social and ideological process, "modernity" is synonymous with the search for a secular agent to propel the movement of history and with the secular epistemology that derives from it. Endowed with recognizable characteristics, the historical agency of modernity has most insistently been attributed to collectivities, whether they take the form of the state, the nation, the class, or the people, and to the knowing subject, whether considered as the monadic individual or the personified *Geist* of idealism. Instability in the modern economy of agency places into question not only the tenuous historical continuity it produces but also the multivalent organization of knowledge that ranges from empirical institutions such as the university to presuppositions about how an object of knowledge is constituted.

In this context, the unfathomable acceleration of contemporary historical change, which affects realms of existence from the technological to the political, from the economic to the ecological, increasingly shows the impotence, if not the irrelevance, of traditional categories of knowledge. The incipient unraveling of traditional historical understanding can be readily pinpointed. In the words of a contemporary sociologist who has spent his entire professional career seeking to identify the shifting protagonists of history, "The Subject [in the sense of 'subjectivity'] is no longer the presence in us of the universal, whether one calls it the laws of nature, the meaning of history, or divine creation."[1] This statement about our historical condition, so to speak, like so many others that express a similar view, can be interpreted in various ways. Most interpreters oscillate between condemnation of our inability to posit universals and see them embodied in single instances, and celebration of the fact that today we live in a world of relative values. But the fundamental historical question is whether the currently misplaced universal results from a loss or from recognition that it existed only by virtue of massive social and political support.

While the perceived gravity and diffusion of the so-called historical problem is unprecedented, the issues involved in the collapse of otherworldly historical understanding have been openly debated since the emergence of industrialized states and the accompanying political economy. This has been particularly true in the United States, where industrialization went hand in hand with its emergence as a global power. In fact, without the slightest hint of irony, one could affirm that the most coldly analytical response to today's historical disjuncture was written by the American philosopher Charles Sanders Peirce at the end of the nineteenth century. Peirce's aggressive essay on historical agency, published in 1893 under the title "Evolutionary Love,"[2] is the fifth and final installment in a series of essays in which he attempted to construct the backbone of his entire philosophy, including his theories of mind and habit alongside his more widely known semiotic notions of firstness, secondness, and thirdness. Yet the essay's greater significance lies in its thematic concern with history, especially historical understanding as it pertains to the nineteenth and, in the essay's own reference, the latter part of the twentieth century.

As might be guessed from Peirce's extensive debt to the idealist tradition, his essay is a scarcely veiled polemic against materialist views of history. A critique of materialism is, of course, common among philosophers of history, who must make recourse to nebulous concepts such as "peoples," "states," and "historical epochs" to narrate their histories of progress and decline. But the essay's uniqueness resides in its attention to the implications of opposing views of historical understanding. These implications have a striking relevance for historical understanding at the dawn of the twenty-first century.

Peirce's analysis concedes from the outset that the form of historical understanding he endorses runs counter to the historical forces of his own time. To abstract his views from the historical present, therefore, Peirce describes the contemporary present through the eyes of future historians:

> The nineteenth century is now fast sinking into the grave, and we all begin to review its doings and to think what character it is destined to bear as compared with other centuries in the minds of future historians. It will be called, I guess, the Economical Century; for political economy has more direct relations with all the branches of activity than has any other science. Well, political economy has its formula of redemption, too. It is this: Intelligence in the service of greed ensures the justest prices, the fairest contracts, the most enlightened conduct of all the dealings between men, and leads to the summum bonum, food in plenty and perfect comfort. Food for whom? Why, for the greedy master of intelligence. (192)

The polemical, even sarcastic tone of this passage is unmistakable, and what it calls "political economy" bears the brunt of the critique. Yet, in characteristic fashion, Peirce's critique refrains from taking a narrowly construed political position. His attack on the centrality of political economy applies to capitalism no less than to Marxist critiques of it; although Peirce is far from a straightforward proponent of idealism, he shares with idealist philosophers a distaste for materialist views of history. In effect, in this entire essay he does not question the validity of political and economic conceptions in themselves but seeks to deny political economy as a basis for historical understanding. Peirce acknowledges that what he calls political economy, like universalizing theories of history, has a form of redemption. But that is precisely the problem: its redemptive moment does not transcend its own historical moment. It is, in fact, contrary to the logic of transcendence, because it has to do only with individual self-interest. Tying historical agency to individual action trivializes any attempt to explain historical change by referring to non-perishable, or eternal, truths and ideas.

This elevation of individual self-interest constitutes, for Peirce, the primary danger in giving precedence to political economy. Of course, what I am calling self-interest appears consistently in the essay as "greed," a term chosen for its obvious rhetorical power. But Peirce is clear about the repercussions of overemphasizing greed in explaining the individual's role in history. In addition to transforming values presumed to underlie Euro-American civilization, moving greed or self-interest into the foreground requires a shift in historical understanding. In his own words, it has resulted in "a philosophy which comes unwittingly to this, that greed is the great agent in the elevation of the human race and in the evolution of the universe" (193). Greed, in this instance, is the contrary of a universal concept that then becomes manifest in the individual. If this greed is a concept at all, it nonetheless has no other-worldly attributes. Greed as self-interest mediates between individuals and historical evolution. In this struggle that powers history, the more intelligent, aggressive, or perhaps simply the more fortunate wins. Fundamentally, this view of political economy embodies a theory of history based on perpetual conflict without the harmonizing force of universal ideals that transcend the individual.

Writing at the end of the nineteenth century, Peirce observed the contemporary effects of industrialized society to extrapolate the historical consequences of political economic thought. To flesh out other characteristics of this troubling conception of history, Peirce drew on Darwin's theory of evolution; in the words of the essay, Darwin's *Origin of Species* "merely extends politico-economical views of progress to the entire realm of animal and vegetable life" (196). Since an overarching idea does not guide history toward ever higher stages, the notion of progress is a qualified one at best.

This concern with progress, with the directionality of history, becomes the focus of the essay's comments on Darwin's work as exemplifying political economy. Peirce summarizes his critical judgment in one brief sentence: "Natural selection, as conceived by Darwin, is a mode of evolution in which the only positive agent of change in the whole passage from moner to man is fortuitous variation" (197). Darwin's notion of "fortuitous variation," change without causality and on the basis of no master plan, stands in opposition to Peirce's strong sense of developmental history, of history that proceeds from worse to better by means of a universal, nonhistorical idea. This apprehension about Darwin's theories was shared by many of Peirce's (and Darwin's) contemporaries, who were specifically perturbed by a historical conception that removed deities from intervention in evolutionary matters; others, some of whom Darwin mentioned in his reedition of *Origin of Species,* contained this implicit theory of history by integrating evolution into theological notions of historical change.

Ultimately, however, Peirce's concern, which becomes even more apparent when he counterposes his own historical model, has less to do with Darwinian evolution than with a theory of history that unfolds oblivious to any logic of necessity. It posits historical change and powerfully explains the development from a mass of protoplasm to human beings. Nonetheless, it does not tie agency to any notion or individual action that is not subject to the historical process. Consequently, its interpretation of the historical passage from the past to the present is most troubling to Peirce because the present human dominance, the end point of history, endows history with only a simulation of purposiveness. As a theory of history, it projects an endemically uncertain future; it is historical process without a center, an eternal point of reference. Unlike in theories of the unfolding of human consciousness, progress is far from absolute. From the perspective of human dominance, for example, evolution has made continuous progress, but it is doubtful that dinosaurs or other extinct species would agree. Even more to the point regarding Peirce's astute critique, zoobiologists—such as Claude Allègre—have begun to analyze the historical limit of human dominance, just as astrophysicists calculate the collapse of the solar system.[3] We are far removed from bickerings about whether the heavens revolve around the earth or the sun.

Briefly, therefore, Peirce's formulation seeks to fill the conceptual gap left by political economy's refusal or inability to give agency an immutable face, to assign a purposiveness to historical change, and its assertion that individual self-interest is the motor of history. This portrait of political economy represents the framework of his historical questioning. In devising a coherent response, Peirce predictably draws on the Christian tradition and, in a gesture characteristic of modernity, the obscured precepts of Greek philosophy. As the essay opens, it immediately sets out the parameters of discussion, although their significance becomes manifest only later: "Philosophy," Peirce writes, "when just escaping from its golden pupa-skin, mythology, proclaimed the great evolutionary agency of the universe to be Love" (190). This early philosophical understanding of the domain of human consciousness runs through Christianity as well. And although Peirce's argument would seem to have little in common with Christianity, he demonstrates its pertinence by interpreting the Gospel John's statement "God is love" as the "formula of an evolutionary philosophy" (192), which stands in opposition to the materialist view attributed to Darwin and political economy.

Nevertheless, even as he uses these modes of thought and belief, Peirce is no more interested in defending religious ideals than he is in debunking the Darwinian theory of evolution or challenging what he refers to as the "scientific character" of political economy. In the context of the essay's aims, it is thus not surprising that Lamarck's theory of evolution serves as the point of departure. It lends itself well to representing the historical agency of love because, unlike Darwinism, it is fundamentally an interpretive theory that closely resembles narrative history. When translated into the terms of historical and ideological development, Lamarck's theory of evolution works by taking "force," the movement toward change, and integrating it into already established history, even if this history refers to some generalized notion of biological heredity. Peirce uses several words to describe the workings of this "force" or agency: "Habit is mere inertia, a resting on one's oars, not a propulsion. Now it is energetic projaculation . . . by which in the typical instances of Lamarckian evolution the new elements of form are first created. Habit, however, forces them to take practical shapes, compatible with the structures they affect, and, in the form of heredity and otherwise, gradually replaces the spontaneous energy that sustains them" (201). The narrative sequentiality of this passage is readily evident. Habit, a concept that stands at the center of Peircean pragmatism, functions as a setting against which an event takes place. Yet, unlike many narratives, and contrary to the theory of history underlying Darwinian evolution, the events' outcome is unidirectional and irreversible because it leads toward an always improving accommodation to the world. Although even the most cursory knowledge of today's biogenetics would place these premises into question, that is really irrelevant for the theory of history that Lamarckian evolution is asserted to exemplify. This essentially narrative structure of historical change, change that occurs as a result of individual agents challenging habit and heredity only to have heredity incorporate the challenge, seems to mimic the model of tradition often associated with modernity.

Ultimately, however, Peirce's own conception of history differs from this both in its complexity and its explanatory power. This difference becomes evident when the essay shifts to a more openly phenomenological description of the process: "Everybody knows that the long continuance of a routine of habit makes us lethargic, while a succession of surprises wonderfully brightens the ideas. Where there is motion, where history is a-making, there is the focus of mental activity" (202). Consonant with a view that seeks historical constants to drive historical change, history requires mental activity to happen or to be produced. The reference to mental activity, to mind, is significant not only because it abstracts historical agency from the muck of materialism. In fact, the essay goes on to affirm that "all matter is essentially mind" and that historical consciousness rests on "a continuity of mind" (201). The continuity of mind proves to be the key concept that posits transhistorical continuity while providing both the space and the meaning for individual action. This formulation unites the possibility for individual agency, which in political economy lacks historical purposiveness, and an inexorable grinding out of history that shares features of Hegel's philosophy of history, which Peirce finds, in his own words, "superb, almost sublime" but lacking "living freedom" (204).

The essay's countergospel of love, which stands over against the gospel of greed, concretely expresses this continuity of history and action. Peirce's well-known penchant for Greek-based neologisms refashions the theory in terms of agape: "The agapastic development of thought should, if it exists, be distinguished by its purposive character, this purpose being the development of an idea" (212). In a most general sense, this formulation exhibits a striking resemblance to Hegelian history, but the differences are more suggestive because they address the perceived deficiencies in Hegel's theory. While here history and thought unfold in accordance with the idea, it is not a nameless abstract idea but one Peirce designates as love. This so-called agapastic theory of history contains within it the relationship between self and other, but it has virtually nothing to do with the subject-object dialectic that underlies much of the politics of identity.

Just as in the assertion that love explains historical evolution more effectively than self-interest, historical agency is produced through harmony rather than conflict. Although this emphasis hints at the ideological basis of Peirce's analysis, it proves necessary for the historical conception he so rigorously describes. In the essay's own terms, the dynamics of this series of conceptual relationships can be stated succinctly: "The agapastic development of thought is the adoption of certain mental tendencies . . . by an immediate attraction for the idea itself, whose nature is divined before the mind possesses it, by the power of sympathy, that is, by virtue of the continuity of mind" (205). In typical Peircean fashion, this view of history based on the idea (specifically, the idea of love because of love's conceptual characteristics) derives from Peirce's celebrated notion of thirdness. It offers a third way of historical understanding that incorporates purpose, absent from Darwin's theory of evolution, and the space of individual freedom, constricted in Hegelian idealism. Understood in this way, the idea of love, therefore, expresses the "continuity of mind" in time and in the individuals' bond to a community that transcends them, a bond here referred to as "sympathy." On this basis, the passage then proceeds to the idea's historical role, affecting the collective as a whole, or the "collective personality," the individual as a collective member, and the individual as individual.

Other of Peirce's essays treat in greater detail various of these issues, most notably the continuity of mind. But this essay essentially dissects the analytic of historical understanding that has characterized the modern era. Peirce lived in a century of mass movements surpassed only by the century that follows. His description of an ahistorical or transhistorical idea of love represents an attempt to explain individuals' belonging to mass groups, their like thinking even when such thinking would seem beyond specific individuals (213). Ultimately, after this painstaking analysis, Peirce concludes with a test that, if realizable, would establish the historical truth he endorses: "If it could be shown directly that there is such an entity as the 'spirit of an age' or of a people, and that mere individual intelligence will not account for all the phenomena, this would be proof enough at once of agapasticism and of synechism [or the continuity of mind]. I must acknowledge that I am unable to produce a cogent demonstration of this" (212–213). The spirit of an age is significant not because it represents a collective dimension but because it assumes the role of historical agent, that is, it takes the form of what I have designated as a historical figure. Interestingly,

Peirce's linguistic knowledge and integrity prevent him from asserting outright the existence of historical spirits, from claiming that the figure can be objectively substantiated. Instead, the essay demonstrates how collectivities are constructed, filled with meaning, given a temporal existence, and assigned the discursive power of historical protagonist.

In 1893 the "Evolutionary Love" essay was framed as a response to a conflictual, fragmented society. The dominance of political economy and what Peirce calls "Wall Street sharps" robbed history of its agency and its purpose. The essay indulges only once in historicizing, projecting toward a future where the conflict will be harmonized and agency restored to its rightful place. The future it refers to is at this point already behind us: "The twentieth century, in its latter half, shall surely see the deluge-tempest burst upon the social order—to clear upon a world as deep in ruin as that greed-philosophy has long plunged it into guilt" (195). This apocalyptic vision appears quaint today; the world we live in has become Peirce's worst nightmare, where agency has become more dispersed than he could ever have imagined. In effect, contemporary understandings of agency are considerably more radical and have none of the utopian hubris. For example, Pierre Lévy, a researcher on questions of technology and society, writes: "A disparate crowd of social agents explores new possibilities for their own benefit (and to the detriment of other agents) until a new situation is provisionally stabilized, with its local values, morals, and cultures."[4] The humanistic disciplines, with their attendant concern with values and culture, no longer provide the means for stability. Agency itself has been historicized, just as the sites of knowledge production and reproduction have been transformed, and agency's idealized guarantors, including the state and nationhood, are becoming less and less viable as the principal point of reference for determining collective action. In this context, nostalgic calls for a return to earlier concepts of social stability appear as ahistorical as the historical protagonists they seek to recuperate.

Even if Peirce's essay does not succeed in establishing the historical power of love, it unambiguously shows that the contemporary historical problem derives from an incommensurability between notions of agency and historical understanding. Although today the notion of agency is most often discussed as an attribute of subjectivity, it is closely linked to the much more widespread discussions about the disappearance of the universal, supposedly a condition of postmodernity. Postmodernity, perhaps best understood as a historical moment of profound instability, is further aggravated by the massive social and technological changes in the twentieth century. In the epoch of decolonization, which roughly corresponds to a recognition of the misplaced universal, histories have proliferated, most often striving to compensate for history's inability to grasp its own movement and drawing on ideas that are affirmed to reside outside of mundane time. These ideas have a broad range, including recourse to particularist ideas such as ethnicity and cultural identity, inevitably linked to affirmations of the present's historical continuity with the past and future. At the same time, however, a universalist concern with history still has its adherents, leading Alain Finkielkraut, for example, to resuscitate the notion of love in a historical formula not unlike that of Peirce.[5] In fact, this mechanism of historical understanding defined the historical thought and practice of the twentieth century, from Peirce's drive to recenter historical agency down to the fin de siècle obsession with the historical agency of cultural difference. But these proliferating ideas, all of which contribute to, rather than resolve, the problem of fragmentation, do not attempt to account for the historical specificity of contemporary society but rather operate according to the logic of unity that has become historically impossible.

To state the issue bluntly, contemporary historical understanding faces an unavoidable disjuncture between the reigning historical conception in modernity and the explosion in materialist, secular knowledge. The concept of agency, of how to conceive a contemporary historical protagonist, is the pivotal question of that disjuncture. Viewed in this way, the question of agency casts a different light on the omnipresent historical concerns and debates of the twentieth century. In this conceptual landscape, Walter Benjamin's writings on history starkly highlight the conflicts and tensions inherent in joining transcendent forces to earthly theories of history. Benjamin was, from the beginning, literally obsessed with the relationship between historical understanding and historical intervention, although it came to dominate other concerns only in his later writings. Interestingly, Benjamin's later work—which remained in large part unpublished during his lifetime and includes numerous versions of key texts as well as notes that served as supporting material—has been problematic precisely because it does not seem to endorse any established theory of history. As a consequence, the multiple interests of his interpreters have determined the reception of his work. Benjamin's later theory of history is alternatively seen as a botched or successful attempt at either historical materialism or theological messianism, and sometimes as a productive, or debilitating, synthesis of the two.[6] This series of banal oppositions has, in fact, become the tradition of Benjaminian interpretation.[7]

Rather than determining Benjamin's filiation, the tradition that might have claims on him, it would seem more fruitful to understand the way in which Benjamin takes elements from mutually exclusive theories of history to advance a historical understanding he considers appropriate for the age of mechanical reproducibility. Anyone who reads Benjamin's theses "On the Concept of History" immediately identifies the conflicting historical views that Benjamin juxtaposes. In the context of a devastating critique of historicism, the theses describe a new theory of history that they designate as historical materialism, although its apparent messianic elements indicate that this materialist theory of history resists being reduced to the customary historical materialism of Marxism. With the availability of Benjamin's texts and notes for his massive project now known as the *Passagen-Werk,* the range of Benjamin's thinking about materialist history becomes more apparent, and the nature of its resistance, both to historical materialism and to its messianic counterimage, more precise.

As Peirce's analysis demonstrated, a theory of history always entails a theory of agency, a notion of the idealized protagonist or force that propels historical change. Benjamin's critique of historicism, which plots the concerns he will rearticulate in his view of history, focuses on the assumptions and concepts that generate historicist interpretations. First of all, "historicism posits an 'eternal' image [*Bild*] of the past."[8] The eternal, an immutable idea that resists the ravages of time, marks a theory of history that exempts the historian, the contemporary interpreter, from the historical interests of the present, past, or future. This figure, idea, or image of eternity—in the case of historicism, a secular eternity—serves to anchor the theory of objectivity that was so much a part of positivist history. But it has other consequences as well: "Historicism rightly culminates in universal history, [which] has no theoretical apparatus. Its procedure is additive; it musters a mass of facts to fill homogeneous, empty time" (702; 262). From the universal perspective, all strife producing history disappears, including the relationship between the present and a past that coexists in the present, that exists only because it is not wholly past. Not only the historian but also history itself is dehistoricized: it becomes homogeneous and empty to enable the historicist interpreter to empty her mind and voyage into the idealized past. Theorizing universal history, which is the ultimate effect of Benjamin's analysis, means reintroducing the historical nature of all historical thinking and upsetting the chain of events that constitute historicist accounts of history. Historicism's assumptions about historical continuity motivate its recourse to causality as a fundamental element of historical understanding: "Historicism contents itself with establishing a causal connection between various moments in history. But no fact that is a cause is for that very reason historical. It became historical posthumously, as it were, through events that may be separated from it by thousands of years" (704; 263). As part of its very conception, historicism must remain blind to the process of historical construction that underlies all history. Causality, and the historical narratives it structures, is no more historical than the homogeneous time that provides its context.

Homogeneous time, ready to be filled with a series of facts marshaled to express a causal development, is the companion to modernity's secular notion of historical agency. The idea of progress, of course, best summarizes modernity's mode of conceiving historical change, and both the *Passagen-Werk* and the theses "On the Concept of History" identify progress as the lowest common denominator in historicist thought: "The idea [*Vorstellung*] of the historical progress of humankind cannot be sundered from the idea of its progression through a homogeneous, empty time. A critique of the idea of such a progression must form the basis of any critique of the idea of progress itself" (701; 261). In the same passage, Benjamin lists the characteristics of historicist progress as manifest in social-democratic theory. Progress implies: the progress of humankind itself; an open-ended temporality, corresponding to humankind's infinite perfectability; and a certain directionality. Progress anchors historical agency, the understanding of how historical change is propelled; not God but the very idea of human progress pushes along historical development. In somewhat tautological fashion—a consequence of all transcendental notions of agency—development (or, in a divinity-based transcendentalism, change whose direction and purpose are beyond human grasp) is inevitable because that is the way history plays itself out. And while today this may seem a naive, even ahistorical notion of history, it offers a stable narrative structure for historical understanding: the present is firmly located between a past that has been superseded and a future that will supersede our present. In the context of this formulation, Peirce's critique of evolution stands in even sharper contrast: evolution has a theory of change, but not of the future and not of absolute progress. There are too many factors, including even the environment, moving at different rates but also shifting position with respect to one another, to predict, even hypothetically, a better future. This denial of absolute progress hints at the ultimate materialism (or, perhaps, anti-idealism) of the Darwinian theory of evolution. For historicism, localizing the idea of agency in progress means assigning an idealized humankind the role of historical agent, for progress is always progress for humankind.

Benjamin's theory of history is articulated against this idea of historical progression and against the idealism that it implies. How is agency articulated in his materialist theory of history? In what might be called classical historical materialism, the proletariat embodied in the Communist party begins to exercise its collective will the moment it achieves self-consciousness as a historical protagonist.[9] But Benjamin explicitly rejects that historical conception. In an openly political reference, Benjamin remarks that the failure of the political opponents of fascism results from their misconstrued understanding of history: "This consideration proceeds from the insight that the politicians' stubborn faith in progress, their confidence in their 'mass basis,' and, finally, their servile integration in an uncontrollable apparatus have been three aspects of the same thing" (698; 258). Here, Benjamin's French version expresses more precisely the nature of the critique, which enumerates the leftists' "blind faith in progress, in the force, justice, and promptness of reactions formed within the masses, and in the party" (1263–1264). The text calls for a break with this sort of historical thinking, which claims to draw its impetus from the ideal of progress, a collective identity, or a bureaucratic organization. Rather than breaking with the political realm, however, Benjamin proposes regrounding it with a different understanding of historical agency.

As is often the case with Benjamin's affirmations, his analysis of agency is at the same time subtle and uncompromising. The historical subject does not represent or embody agency; instead, it produces epistemological effects: "The subject of historical knowledge is the strug-

gling, oppressed class itself" (700; 260). Benjamin's French version clarifies the nature of this subject by calling it "the artisan of historical
knowledge" (1264). The link between historical action and historical
knowledge is unmistakable, but the modalities of this relationship are
not specified at this juncture. And once again, Benjamin seeks to demarcate his conception of history by referring to the historical theory elaborated by the social democrats. By adopting progress as the motor of historical change, the text notes, they misunderstand the forces of history
and reverse even the temporality that they would adopt. From this perspective, today's oppressed class struggles in the name of a future that
history relentlessly approaches. In this sense, the notion of progress do-
mesticates a potentially quite different theory of history and of historical
knowledge; action in the present is robbed of its own presumed agency
because its meaning is perpetually postponed. An early draft of Benjamin's theses underscores the domesticating power of progress in conjunction with its ideal future: "The classless society is not the ultimate
goal of historical progress but its so often failed, ultimately realized in-
terruption" (1231). This displays only the faintest resemblance to historical materialism as it is generally understood.

In Benjamin's conception, conflict traverses history, just as the present
wrests itself out of the past, the oppressed struggle against domination,
and historical action disrupts the apparent historical continuity. Even
historical consciousness itself is manifest only in the instant and cannot
be sustained: "The awareness [Bewußtsein] of exploding the continuum
of history is characteristic of the revolutionary classes at the instant of
their action" (701; 261). Just as the oppressed class produces historical
knowledge by virtue of its struggle, the revolutionary classes, multiples
of the same historical conflict, become aware of the effects of their action
as the action takes place. They are not, however, agents of historical
change, nor are they protagonists in a historical idea that exceeds their
own time. This irrepressible historical conflict inhabits both the material
of history and its mode of transmission: "There is no document of culture that is not simultaneously a document of barbarism. And just as
such a document is not free of barbarism, barbarism also taints the manner in which it was transmitted" (696; 256). In this instance, the conflict
between culture and barbarism encompasses the two primary poles of
European historical understanding. At the same time, however, the example indicates the spatial and temporal aspects of any notion of cul-

tural tradition, never entirely separable from the historical theory that founds its interpretation. In a fragment from the *Passagen-Werk*, Benjamin affirms the conflictual nature of even the concepts of interpretation: "Barbarism is bound up with the very concept of culture, just as a treasure chest full of valuables is considered separate from the production process in which it endures, but not separate from the production process that created it."[10] This enigmatic attempt to juxtapose synchrony and diachrony, the treasure that both exists in the present and bears the marks of its conflictual production, serves as the dividing line between the historicist and the materialist. The "historical materialist" (696; 256) or the "materialist historian" (1262) refuses to be swayed by the lures of the treasure and does not lose sight of the conflict that inhabits it; the historicist, on the other hand, endorses the spoils of the historical victor. Yet, the materialist historian cannot escape the historical discontinuity and the knowledge it produces, just as all products of human history, from the immaterial concept to the material object, cannot be separated from the conflict that created and transmitted them.

In effect, the materialist historian, or the historical materialist, is a key element in Benjamin's theory of history. As if to underscore this link, recent interpretations of Benjamin's theory of history tend to include lengthy reflections on the role of the historian and interpreter. For example, Stéphane Mosès's *L'ange de l'histoire*, undoubtedly the most complete reading of this historical aspect of Benjamin's work, places the historian at the center of Benjamin's political theory of history.[11] In interpreting Benjamin's historical theory, Mosès draws extensively on the notion of "actualization," a process whereby the past and present collide in producing new constellations of meaning. For Mosès, the historian's "actualization" becomes the concept that unifies Benjamin's political materialism and the seemingly theological concepts of redemption (*Erlösung*), remembrance (*Eingedenken*), and the much discussed now-time (*Jetztzeit*). And Mosès's identification of actualization's importance cannot be overestimated. In the *Passagen-Werk* (in a passage that will be fundamental for Mosès's interpretation), Benjamin in fact counterposes the notion of actualization to that of historicism's progress. One of the *Passagen-Werk*'s aims, he remarks, was "to demonstrate a historical materialism that has annihilated in itself the idea of progress. Precisely in this respect historical materialism has cause to set itself off sharply from customary bourgeois thought. Its fundamental concept is not progress but actualization" (574). On its own terms, actualization is a problematic concept that seems to run counter to the affirmations of a materialist history that has dispensed with the eternal. Steeped in idealism, it tends to name the process by means of which something hidden becomes visible or, to render a temporal version, the process by means of which something past becomes present. And this nexus of synchrony and diachrony has a performative role in Benjamin's understanding of the workings of history. In the context of Benjamin's materialism, actualization refers to that instant when historical effects are produced, that moment when aspects of the past, which already belongs to the present, become contemporary. This instant has obvious epistemological implications, as indicated in "On the Concept of History."

Although the term *actualization* itself is rare in Benjamin's work, it describes the articulation of agency in his theory of history. As such, it expresses a moment of great instability in any historical conception based on the idea of continuity; theories of history, of course, emerged precisely in response to instabilities in order to explain them, render them understandable. Thus, historical theories tend to be totalizing, positing an origin, an ending, and a transcendental notion to power the course separating them.[12] It is difficult to appreciate the radical nature of Benjamin's historical theory because language (along with the concepts that organize thought) operates by assigning agency to linguistic constructions; in this sense, personification may be the single most important trope of modernity. But that is precisely the problem that Benjamin is grappling with in his theory of history and in the concept of actualization. Mosès, in fact, in what appears to be a startling departure from his own reading, ultimately advances a personified version of the materialist historian to whom he imputes historical choice, for all practical purposes making the historian the agent of actualization: "If this *actualization* of the past and future is necessarily political, it is because, for Benjamin, it depends on a choice. The historian who saves this or that past moment from the conformism threatening to swallow it up, to endow it with a new meaning in light of his own present, acts because he feels *responsible* for the past."[13] In this view, the subjectivity of the historian, whose actions result from a personal decision with historical implications, stabilizes the historical discontinuities. It introduces predictability into the historical equation by making it a function of personal identity, with its attendant ethical and moral decisions (153–154). Despite the inherent attraction of interpreting a conscious form of engagement into Benjamin's theory of history, the magnetic pull toward personification in modernity keeps us from knowing if such an interpretation derives from the formulation of Benjamin's theory of history or simply from the interpreter's methodological and historical concerns.[14]

At the same time, Benjamin's writings are filled with notes on the stakes of his theory of history, inevitably attempting to articulate his notions in contrast to other historical views, much in the vein of his discussion of historicism and certain understandings of historical materialism. One particularly significant note from the *Passagen-Werk,* in which Benjamin succinctly summarizes his theory of history and plots the differences between it and the then prevailing notions of history, deserves citation in its entirety:

> What distinguishes figures [*Bilder*] from the "essences" [*"Wesenheiten"*] of phenomenology is their historical index. (Heidegger's abstract attempt to save history for phenomenology by means of "historicity" [*"Geschichtlichkeit"*] is in vain.) These figures are to be thoroughly distinguished from the "human sciences" categories, from so-called habitus, style, etc. The figures' historical index means not only that they belong to a specific time but above all that they become readable [*zur Lesbarkeit kommen*] only at a specific time. And in fact this "becoming readable" [*"zur Lesbarkeit" gelangen*] is a specific critical point of their inner movement. Each present is specified by the figures that are synchronic with it: Every Now is the Now of a specific knowability [*Erkennbarkeit*]. In the Now, truth is loaded with time until it bursts. (This bursting is nothing more than the death of *intentio,* which also coincides with the birth of real historical time, the time of truth.) Thus it is not that the past sheds its light on the present or the present sheds its light on the past, but rather in the figure what has been [*das Gewesene*] and the Now meet in a flash of lightning to make a configuration [*Konstellation*]. In other words: the figure is the dialectic at a standstill. Thus while the present's relation to the past is purely temporal, the relation between what has been and the Now is dialectical: of a figural rather than temporal nature. Only dialectical figures are really historical, that is, not archaic figures. The read figure, the figure in the Now of knowability, bears to the highest degree the stamp of the critical, dangerous moment that forms the basis of all reading. (577–578)

This passage straightforwardly describes the disjuncture separating Benjamin's theory of history and the historical concepts at our disposal. Figurality describes the historical mode of his materialism. These figures are distinct from essences that exist outside of time, cannot be equated with Heidegger's historical events, resist reduction to human science (*geisteswissenschaftlichen*) categories, signal the death of intention, and cannot be expressed in a simple narrative that divides the past from the present. The characteristic of these figures is their readability, and reading itself serves as the epistemological model for the generation of historical time.[15] Reading describes an engagement with something that has material existence, to produce something that has a nonmaterial, though nonetheless historical, existence. This should not be mistaken for a hermeneutic moment, however: there is no community of interpretants, no unfolding of meaning in time, no sense of a temporal tradition. In sum, it indicates what seems to be an irresolvable contradiction: the absolute singularity of what can only be described as a historical action. In other words, readability is no less historical than the reading itself.

But how does one talk about agency in this context? The entire process that Benjamin describes, the actualization of historical time, does not lend itself to personification. A specific readability does correspond to a specific moment of the figures' "inner movement," but this movement merely opposes stasis—it is motion without direction or control. These figures, however, are distinguished by their "historical index" (*historischer Index*). The index, of course, has been a productive notion in theories of meaning, especially in modern semiotics. But at the outset it was no more than a general rhetorical term; Quintilian, for example, sees the index as simply a variant of the sign: "The Latin equivalent of the Greek *semeion* is *signum*, a sign, though some have called it *indicium*, an indication, or *vestigium*, a trace. Such signs or indications enable us to infer that something else has happened; blood for instance may lead us to infer that a murder has taken place."[16] For Quintilian, the term belongs squarely in the juridical tradition that gave birth to rhetoric. In this context of speculation about a prior event, it merely offers an indication of what might have happened, as would any other sign. And although Quintilian's definition has no direct significance for Benjamin's use of the term, it serves as a backdrop for Peirce's theory of semiotics, which is built on a series of distinctions between the various categories of sign and signification. The index plays an important role in Peirce's semiotics by being a signifying function that produces actions without depending on "resemblance" or originating in "intellectual operations": "Anything which focusses the attention is an index. Anything which startles us is an index, in so far as it marks the junction between two portions of experience. Thus a tremendous thunderbolt indicates that *something* considerable happened, though we may not know precisely what the event was. But it may be expected to connect itself with some other experience."[17]

The index ruptures continuity, breaks experience in two. And while it may point to an event, it does not specify what that event might have been and does not require interpretation, even if it poses the problem that might give rise to one. The index, which operates, as Peirce says, "by blind compulsion," has epistemological impact without being grounded in the need for meaning. It occupies a peculiar status even in contemporary, formalized semiotics precisely because it exceeds the linguistic while remaining an essential element of linguistic understanding.[18] As is the case with epistemological operations that skirt the edge of conceptual categories, the index is most often personified to render it more stable. Thus, it is not surprising that Peirce implicitly personifies reactions to the index, although his descriptions of the index itself are more carefully nuanced. To cite one of his many examples, a "rap on the door" calls one to attention, but, according to his logic, the "rap" as index does not depend on assigning protagonists.

Moreover, Benjamin transposes the index into history. The index, as *historical* index, loses even its illusion of a controlling consciousness. In his theses "On the Concept of History," Benjamin articulates other aspects of the index: "The past carries along a secret index [*heimlichen Index*] by which it is referred to redemption [*auf die Erlösung verwiesen wird*]. For did not a breath of the air floating around us once surround those who preceded us? Are not our sounds, when we voice them, an echo of those long since silent? . . . If so, there is a secret rendezvous between past generations and ours . . . Like every generation that came before us, we have been endowed with a *weak* messianic power, a power to which the past has a claim."[19] Here redemption is resolutely historical and firmly anchored in the indexical structure of history. This secret rendezvous or meeting between past and present takes place, as Benjamin never tires of repeating, in a figure that is historical but not temporal. It takes place in a configuration that stops time to become historical in Benjamin's sense. If we still breathe the same air, if we still hear the past in our utterances, then we have a historical relationship to that past. In other words, the past continues to be present, however diminished and fragmentary it might be. And redemption is simply the present's opportunity to "indicate" the past in a way that places a claim on the future. That is the weak messianic power of the present, always ensconced in the historical conflicts that not even a full-fledged Messiah can escape: "The Messiah comes not only as the redeemer; he comes as the subduer of the Antichrist" (695; 255). The Messiah, despite, or regardless of, the religious connotations, is a figure of the indexical structure of history.

For Benjamin, history is not an event, not a subject unfolding itself in time, and it is not controlled or generated by agents, even omniscient ones. Rather, it is a process of figuration characterized by its historicity and readability. The figure's historical index depersonalizes historical agency while retaining the phenomenological moment; but this moment, this experience (*Erfahrung*) with a past, bears no relation to the eternal and to the temporal as produced in historical narratives (702; 262). As in Peirce's description of the index, this experience is produced with lightning quickness; it refers to "seizing hold of a memory [*Erinnerung*] as it flashes up at a moment of danger. For historical materialism the point is to grasp a figure [*Bild*] of the past whose appearance catches the historical subject unawares, at a moment of danger" (695; 255). The historical subject acts or, rather, reacts in the face of an unpredictable relationship between the present and past. As noted in Benjamin's extensive quote on the process of figuration, that experience has to do with the historical process of reading the figure or producing it "in the Now of knowability." But, in the same passage, he also notes that one cannot separate the read figure from "the critical, dangerous moment that forms the basis of all reading." That danger is not personal, something that threatens the reader, even if such a threat is often enacted by the institutions charged with perpetuating social memory. For Benjamin, it is historical and has to do with the process of figuration itself.

As Benjamin stressed, the figure's primary distinction is its historical indexicality. Thus, depicting the nature of this danger requires a more precise understanding of the index's mode of signification. Peirce's theory of signs analytically describes the index's specific properties: "Such, for instance, is a piece of mould with a bullet-hole in it as sign of a shot; for without the shot there would have been no hole; but there is a hole there, whether anybody has the sense to attribute it to a shot or not" (170). The relationship of the index to its referent has no bearing on the existence of the index. In this characterization, a hole in the molding of a door frame exists as a mark, an index, by virtue of an event that is not so much lost as irrelevant, at least to the status of the index. When the house is remodeled or torn down, that index will exist as long as the wood it marks continues to exist, until the wood is consumed. Historicizing this indexical signaling gives an approximation of Benjamin's theory of history. But as a figure, the historical index does not escape the limitations posed by its readability. Figures have a specific historical existence: "they belong to a specific time" and they "become readable at a specific time." Furthermore, while the historical movement of this figuration operates independently, the historian has a role to play in it. In effect, Benjamin's frequent statement that the historian must bring the figures to a halt, reconstitute them into a new configuration, all of which is, of course, contingent on their historical readability, refers to one aspect of the historian's role. In other words, in reading that figure at the moment of its disruptive appearance, the historian constitutes a new figure. The danger resides precisely at that instant: the historian might fail to "save," to "indicate," to reconstitute and thereby relay the historical index. This danger, Benjamin remarks, "threatens the tradition's content as well as its receivers. The same threat hangs over both: that of becoming a tool of the ruling classes" (695; 255). Or, as Benjamin says in his French version, it is "the danger of enlisting [tradition's content and receivers] in the service of oppression" (1262). This danger exceeds the concerns of representational history that seeks to offer counterhistories to the dominant versions. Rather than interpreting indices, giving them a representation, the emphasis is on actualizing them, without ever knowing about the time of their (present or future) readability.

In Benjamin, the birth of historical time corresponds to the death of intention. Intention anchors the customary historical premise that agency, with its attendant willfulness, can be located in a subject, even if that subject is eternal rather than flesh and blood. This historical time distinguishes itself from the temporality of representational history because it is discontinuous, leads to no sure future, and cannot be grasped in a developmental narrative. Therefore, while Benjamin's concept of history advances a claim to truth, it is not the truth of epistemological verification. Benjamin's truth remains rigorously historical and is subject to the same process his concept of history attempts to render. Immediately following his elaboration of the figure's historical index, a *Passagen-Werk* entry remarks that "a decisive turn away from the concept of 'timeless truth' is called for. Nevertheless, truth is not only—as Marxism claims—a temporal function of knowing but is bound up with a time kernel that simultaneously inhabits the knower and the known. That is so true that the eternal is more ruffles on a dress than an idea" (578). Separating truth from the readability that actualizes history separates agency as well; that is why any theory of history is simultaneously a theory of knowing. And locating truth outside of history—a timeless truth—or asserting it to be a temporal manifestation of knowing—such as in Benjamin's reference to Marxism—has the same structure with regard to formulating historical agency. They each make history, or historical "truth," secondary to something that resides outside of it, a conceptual maneuver that allows the illusion that history can be grasped by personifying representations. The eternal is resolutely historical, attached to the cloth of history but not constitutive of it. The French version of the theses echoes this critique: "The immobile truth just waiting for whoever seeks it corresponds in no way to the concept of truth in the matter of history" (1261).

And the matter of history has to do with the specific relationship between the past and the present, itself the mechanism to produce a future that has no ideal existence: "The true figure of the past *flits* by. The past can be seized only as a figure that flashes up at the instant when it can be known [*im Augenblick seiner Erkennbarkeit*], never to be seen again" (695; 255). The historian, the materialist, or the historical subject, the names Benjamin gives to the indispensable reader in his conception of history, reads the figure, indicates the figure by reading it. This is all the future that Benjamin's historical understanding provides: rescuing by indicating what appears as a figural index. That is the context of Benjamin's angel, a powerful figure that has been subject to countless attempts at representation. It has its back to the future, the eternal's hiding place in any structure of temporality. Contrary to what appears to be a linear extension of events, of presents turning into pasts, the angel stares at historical time in its singularity. It reminds us not to confuse the temporal and the historical. The temporal lends itself to narrative, the historical only to figuration.

In Western modernity, the temporal and the historical have been collapsed together to provide the basis of secular representation. The historical force that Benjamin continually evokes becomes dissipated by becoming simply another genre of written discourse; it represents what

Benjamin calls "homogeneous time," which is opposed to the concept of history he undertakes to articulate. In flattening out uncontrollable historical force, modern figuration becomes a matter of assigning referents, however idealized they may be, to figures whose actions can be seamlessly narrated. This domestication of eternity, which has relied as much on the practical apparatus of print culture as on the gradual elaboration of literary understanding, has been fundamental for the modern organization of knowledge and for the figures of thought that furnish its cardinal points. Within this overarching perspective, the book's following section on the literary pillars of modernity seeks to illustrate both the role played by secular figures in the process of literary history and the unique place of literary understanding in the modern worldview.

II

From Europe to the Globe

4

The Epic Figure of Literary History

Staring, with a gaze sphinx-like and fatal,
Is the West, future of the past.

The face with which it stares is Portugal.
Fernando Pessoa, Mensagem

Modernity does not arrive spontaneously, as if emerging from the fumes of some alchemist's workshop. As an ongoing process of historical self-consciousness that simultaneously rewrites earlier history and its ideals, modernity has no discernible origin, no localizable point of emergence in space and time. Nonetheless the concept of modernity, with its multiple figures of thought, both accompanies and compels a shift in how the world is idealized. While modernity emerged alongside the development of print, whose process of materialization permits—even requires—a new organization of knowledge, it cannot be reduced to some form of material transformation. Modernity is first and foremost embroiled in a regime of representation, of idealized referents that can anchor historical narratives, be endlessly elaborated, support other figures or referents, and be spun off for use in other discursive contexts. For example, the modern nation-state, which has become ineradicably ensconced in the institutions of global representation, underwent centuries of painstaking elaboration before becoming an unquestioned figure of thought. In this idealizing framework of modernity, literary history has furnished the paradigm for secular history as a whole, particularly in regard to the figuration that is its scaffolding.

The panorama of European literatures has its hills and vales, its prom-ontories and abysses. From the perspective of world literature, a mod-ernizing European invention following closely on the heels of the founding of literary history, this supranational topography achieves representation through specific literary figures and masterworks lodged in their respective discourses of national identity. Perhaps even more than the works, these figures are known to all, even if they do not fulfill the same national role or enjoy the same universal status, and include Dante, Camões, Montaigne, Shakespeare, Cervantes, and Goethe. Nonetheless, despite the claims of individual literary and linguistic traditions—claims enhanced by nineteenth-century historical elaborations of national genealogies—these works and figures partake of a discursive regime that exceeds them and that glues together fragments of the modern world picture. That discursive regime, its conceptual underpinnings and the representations it enables, rests squarely on understandings of literary—or, in an epoch of multimedia, cultural—history.

Although the name of Luís Vaz de Camões—author of the epic poem, *The Lusiads (Os Lusíadas)*—may not have universal global recognition in the contemporary cultural landscape, the figure it inscribes has an unparalleled importance in framing the modern worldview. In addition to Camões's stature as the most significant Portuguese writer both within and without the Portuguese tradition, the figure of Camões and his epic play a founding role in the discursive regime of literary history. Within the Portuguese tradition, Camões's presence is overpowering and offers a required standard of comparison for any subsequent literary figure. Since the first publication of *The Lusiads* in 1572, mention of Camões has been unfailingly accompanied by the epithet "Prince of the Poets," which has been translated into modern criticism in various ways. Jorge de Sena gives an elegant summary of this aspect: "Camões is a great figure of a poet [*uma grande figura de poeta*], distinguished by secular devotion and universal renown."[1] In accordance with the demands of figural discourse, the more abstract image of the Poet takes precedence over the individual, who then becomes a representative of the idea. This image of the Poet can be expressed in any number of ways, of course, such as "[i]n the two fields [of poetic discourse], the Hispanic and the Italianate, Camões was to become the supreme Portuguese figure,"[2] a phrase that is all the more significant because in introducing a critical edition of the Portuguese-language text of *The Lusiads,* it presents the most legitimate and least controversial literary knowledge. Such an elevated figure necessarily lends itself to inscription within a historical schema, as is evinced by the same introducer in another article on Camões's epic, in which he refers to "the fullness of the sixteenth and seventeenth century of which Camões is such a commanding figure."³ During that epoch, literature of the Iberian Peninsula has been conceived as experiencing its "golden age," a term that is now synonymous with the period—a period that assumes a key role in the formulation of European literary history. These affirmations and descriptions are part and parcel of the historical enterprise of literary understanding and as such have a counterpart in other traditions powered by other figures. Evoking "Camões" overshoots the individual Camões and his writings' imputed value: his name is a figure, a discursive object, that is rhetorically deployed and intersects with countless other discourses. The figure signals the Poet and poetic creation and synecdochically represents a golden age that is already the protagonist of an entire literary history. Yet these remarks merely allude to the more extensive field of representation that this figure addresses. Already in the seventeenth century, as Maria Lucília Gonçalves Pires writes in *A crítica camoniana no século XVII, The Lusiads* represented the face of Portugal's "poetic universe": "Camões' poetic grandeur is displayed as the standard of superiority exhibited to the eyes of the world."⁴ Camões, a figure for the epic poem in which the Portuguese state was the protagonist, simultaneously represents the nation and its poetic excellence; this discursive intersection of state and literary culture comes to flourish in the constitution of national history.

Since the early eighteenth century, the figure of Camões has been linked to the concept of nationality and to an implicit comparative temporality that emerged alongside the historical shift of discourse and collective representation. Voltaire, in his *Essay on Epic Poetry* (1733), portrays the configuration of ideas that evolve more fully under the auspices of literary history: "While in Italy Trissino weakly and timidly followed in the tracks of the ancients, in Portugal Camões was opening up an entirely new course."⁵ At the same time that these two figures personify their respective traditions and countries of origin, the comparison and its accompanying judgment project the temporal coordinates that will be necessary for establishing national histories of literature and literary history generally. Voltaire's assertion combines the operative notions of belatedness and progress, distinctions that underwrite the linear history of European cultural development that will in part justify colonization as a civilizing process. (Italy, of course, serves as the counterexample within Europe because of its inability to evolve into a unified state, impose a single national language, and write a proper history.) At the same time, Voltaire declares the originality of Camões's *Lusiads,* which vaguely foreshadows Camões's conceptual role in Romantic literary understanding: *"Camões ouvrait une carrière toute nouvelle,"* he both "opened up an entirely new course" and "broke entirely new ground"; in other words, this new path or ground (*carrière* is both "course" and "quarry") conjoins the vertical and horizontal axes, an essential component in historical discourse tracing the horizontal or temporal evolution of a (vertical) identity impervious to the transformations it undergoes. This is no less true of a literary tradition than of a state or nation. In this sense, Camões in fact opened up the mine of national history, one that would give forth many new figures to supply Portugal with a discursive face. Voltaire's text makes an explicit allusion to the historical significance of Camões's account: "The simplicity of the poem is enhanced by fictions as new as the subject" (334). The subject's novelty repeats the same twofold structure: as an identity that transcends history, Portugal is the protagonist, the subject that propels the text and prompts the actions, while the poem treats the historically unfolding sea voyage that cuts a path to India. With Friedrich Schlegel, literary history incorporates this duality as a discursive object in its own right.

The Lusiads is an epic poem, a poetic discourse traditionally associated with history and with creating a literary monument to collective endeavors. In the case of the figure Camões (1525?–1580), "the greatest of all, a poet of international renown, the author of the Portuguese epic poem *The Lusiads,*"[6] the epic is inseparable from its subject matter, the originality attributed to its author, the Portuguese state, the launch of global colonization, and the historical discourse mediating the interplay between these various elements: "*The Lusiads* is the epic of new times, contradictory times. Nourished on these contradictions, the poem acquires its modernity and affirms itself to be the sole epic that is representative of the European Renaissance."[7] Its "modernity" stems from its depiction of the Portuguese state but also from its historical thrust: it traces the course of Portugal's—and therefore Europe's—face-off with the Orient, most prominently through Vasco da Gama's successful voyage to India, even if incorporating previous and subsequent encounters (such as that of Bartholomeu Dias). In this quote, the contradictions of the Renaissance refer to the relationship between humanism and feudalism as ideologies melded together in Camões's poem (17). This contradiction opposes a fundamental understanding grounded in divine omnipotence and a "humanist" secularism that places the human being in the role of historical protagonist. Extending beyond the localized formal limits of a given literary artifact, this contradiction inhabits the emerging discourse of modernity. *The Lusiads'* particular inscription of this incommensurability has contributed to its peculiar status in the annals of literary history.

On yet another level, António José Saraiva has written effectively about *The Lusiads'* constellation of ideas that orient and inform the protagonists' actions and perceptions. In this interpretation, the unity of the epic itself comes from the very abstract notion that the poem inaugurated: "The idea of the fatherland [*a pátria*] thus results in an abstract notion, outside history, with a merely subjective existence: it is in the perception [*sentimento*] of the Poet and not in the facts that he narrates."[8] The identity of the state correlates with the subjectivity of the Poet, and the "Poet" is not Camões the poet—as indicated by the capitalization—but the abstract subject as a producer of discourse. While this subject figure has become widely diffused in the literary traditions of modernity (for example, the notion of the *auteur*) and has an extensive presence in the tradition of Camonian criticism,[9] the more radical implications of Saraiva's comments concern the explicit connection between subjectivity, the state, and the discourse that will inscribe them both in the narrative of history.

The Camonian figure and its discursive circulation have been elaborated within an evolving tradition, which in modernity is characterized by a progressive self-consciousness of nationhood. Through the writings of the German Romantics, particularly those of Friedrich Schlegel, the figure of Camões (and, for different reasons, that of Shakespeare) occupied a crucial place in anchoring that modern paradigm of literary self-consciousness. Before turning to Schlegel's careful construction of the armature of literary history, it is important to detail the specificity of Camões's *Lusiads* in the Portuguese tradition, which in terms of what I have called the regime of discourse largely mirrors other national literary traditions. Perhaps because Camões and *The Lusiads* have been such a pillar of the Portuguese literary tradition, the work's historical trajectory, its reception and history of publication, incited much critical commentary in the late twentieth century. Although this trend makes itself felt today in virtually all critical writing on *The Lusiads*, the work's gradual historical construction has become the object of specialized studies, including Maria Lucília Gonçalves Pires's *A crítica camoniana no século XVII*.[10] Gonçalves Pires sets out to describe the "horizon of expectations" serving as the background against which Camões's work was received and evaluated. In the seventeenth century, the Camões figure was hotly contested, and the actual debates of that time are not always accessible. As she explains, the reigning consensus guaranteeing the supremacy of the contemporary Camões figure wrote the history and constituted the tradition, leaving a necessarily incomplete picture of seventeenth-century heretical arguments: "In this epoch the voice of those who dared to censure Camões was silenced: texts [were left] unpublished, manuscripts [were lost], and even the names of critics [were] consciously concealed" (26; see also 22 and 35). The process of institutionalization she alludes to exhibits a symbolic—and sometimes physical—violence that characterizes all traditions to a certain extent. In this instance, however, the seventeenth-century antagonisms revolved around aspects of figuration and, particularly, personification, issues that relate directly to nineteenth-century modes of figurative understanding mobilized around Camões's name.

While in Europe as a whole the seventeenth century was pivotal in elaborating the institutions, both real and ideal, that have come to be identified with modernity, in Portugal it ushered in a traumatic period of self-reflection. From 1580 to 1640 Portugal experienced what became known as the "Babylonian captivity," when Portugal lost its independence and became a part of Spain, albeit retaining a degree of autonomy. This is one of the greatest ironies: *The Lusiads*, glorifier of the Portuguese people, was published in 1572, a mere eight years before the loss of independence that would last sixty years.[11] As Gonçalves Pires suggests, during these sixty years Portugal as a nation was becoming a discursive object; in other words, it was achieving unity as an idea in the past through the poem that details its vanguard moment in the conquest of non-European peoples: "Thus a humiliated people would seek compensation for their present situation through recourse to the memory of past glories that Camões represented in such an exalting form" (65). But how was this idea constituted, and what were the issues involved in its figuration?

In an appendix to her study, Gonçalves Pires has published an abridged version of a seventeenth-century text by Manuel Pires de Almeida, one of Camões's critics, whose major works have remained only in manuscript, never having been printed. This highly analytical text constitutes a response to Manuel Faria e Sousa's commentaries on the 1639 Spanish critical edition of *The Lusiads*. Pires de Almeida's text is entitled "Response to the Judgment of the Poem of the *Lusiads* by Luis de Camões in which it is shown not to have the perfections attributed to it and to have others according to its invention and subject matter" (the "Judgment of the Poem" refers to a commentary written by Faria e Sousa).[12] At first glance, Pires de Almeida seems to address a purely literary issue, the definition of the Camonian epic and the disjuncture that separates it from classical epics: "[I]t has as its subject the perfections with which many mistakenly ennoble *The Lusiads* of Luís de Camões, a poem that is never sufficiently praised, for with these perfections they want it to be a heroic poem that follows the rules of Aristotle as well as the discourse of Homer's *Odyssey* and *Iliad* and Virgil's *Aeneid*" (80).

Although the text proceeds very methodically, listing seven perfections of the classical epic poem and demonstrating how *The Lusiads* fails on each count, all of its failings can be derived from its peculiar treatment of action. For example, the act of discovery is not a subject for a heroic poem: it does not "befit an action whose end is to form an idea and example of the prince and captain . . . and that should consist of not one simple action, which is a sea voyage, but of a number of noble actions" (81). The most striking aspect of this analysis relates to its introduction of the notion of idealization: *The Lusiads'* depiction of the act of discovery does not lend itself to forming an idea of the hero, which is a prerequisite for the heroic epic.

Put differently, the poem cannot be conceptualized according to a character who is represented in the text and who coalesces into an idea by means of actions attributed to him. Contrary to the *Odyssey* and the *Aeneid,* in which the voyage is secondary and subordinate to the hero, *The Lusiads* have failed to embody the actions in a hero. Thus the opposition is not between one action and many actions, a convenient reading that could perhaps be substantiated on the basis of just this passage, but between a series of actions that can be predicated of an actor and an action—the "sea voyage"—that has no idealized figure to perform it. This becomes increasingly clear as the text progresses and is formulated in surprisingly modern terms: "The unity of action [*acção*] and unity of

agent [*agente*] in Homer's *Iliad* and *Odyssey* are composed by their purpose [*proposição*] and their narration [*narração*] . . . That the hero is
constituted into a new state is very evident in Homer and in Virgil" (82).
In other words, the idea of the hero, the "identity," anchors the temporality of the epic project, permitting the constitution of a before and an
after, with the narrative movement from one moment to the other being
reflected in a change in the hero: he reaches a "new state."

The narrative in *The Lusiads* propels itself in a completely different
fashion, which prompts Pires de Almeida's critique, if not his perplexity:
"Our Poet lacks the idea of a hero, for he does not constitute in Vasco da
Gama actions that would form him as such [*pois não constitui em Vasco
da Gama acções que tal o formem*] . . . As Camões encompassed all the
most famous actions of the Portuguese, it was not befitting for him to
formulate the hero in Vasco da Gama, for the glory and Portuguese triumph was achieved by many and not by one alone" (83). With our discursive understanding that is conditioned by a plethora of idealized objects constituted in historical discourse, it is obviously impossible for us
to duplicate the bewilderment of the seventeenth-century reader. In fact,
Pires de Almeida's entire essay derives from the quandary posed by the
absence of the narrative's protagonist and attempts to explain what holds
the narrative together and propels it forward:

> It was necessary for Camões to follow the multiplicity of actions, held
> together by one action [*A Camões foi forçoso seguir a multiplicidade de
> acções, arrimadas a uma*] because he sang the glory and triumph of the
> Portuguese and on them he based his heroic poem: heroic for the gran-
> deur of actions, heroic for the stanzas that constituted it, heroic for its
> majestic style, and not for the qualities or excellences that are attrib-
> uted to it, for with its many actions it becomes in part superior to those
> based on one action alone. (82–83)

It is not a question of understanding that the poem sings the "glory and
triumph of Portugal" (83), which is a foregone conclusion; the issue is
how the narrative operates in the absence of a represented and even rep-
resentable hero—Portugal. Pires de Almeida is a great admirer of *The
Lusiads,* which he is not at all criticizing; his criticism is directed toward
those who misrecognize the extreme distance separating *The Lusiads*
from its supposed models and how this becomes evident in the mode of
narration.[13] Calling attention to such disjunctures between emergent
ideas and the baggage of historical understanding stresses the historicity

of ideas themselves. As I have repeatedly remarked in a variety of contexts, a prime operator of this disjuncture is personification. Pires de Almeida's ultimate concern involves the literary means of representing collective subjects, of the possibilities of grasping collective action in a solitary protagonist.

In attempting to debunk misconceptions about *The Lusiads'* hero, Pires de Almeida launched his polemic at the seventeenth-century tradition of Camões supporters by addressing Faria e Sousa, one of its most eloquent and authoritative adherents. Today's reaction to this seventeenth-century personification question, to the textual process of producing immaterial ideas, offers a very precise characteristic of what is at issue and how it concerns figuration. A present-day scholar of *The Lusiads*, Luiz Piva, provides a concrete example to demonstrate why he considers Pires de Almeida's criticism superior to that of Faria e Sousa.[14] In Piva's characterization, Faria e Sousa, a stalwart critic in the tradition, was "brilliant in the art of writing commentary" on *The Lusiads* but not always so brilliant in his understanding of the epic's ramifications (46); in commenting on the third stanza of the first canto, Faria e Sousa assigns a figural expression the wrong referent: he interprets the line in which the poet sings *"o peito ilustre lusitano"* ("The illustrious Luso heart") "not [as] an allusion to Portugal but to Vasco da Gama, [which demonstrates] that the celebrated Camões scholar did not understand *The Lusiads"* (47).

From today's perspective, after three centuries of institutional elaboration, it seems perfectly evident that Portugal is the subject, the "protagonist" of the poem, which leads to the assertion of Faria e Sousa's lack of understanding. But is it really so obvious? Within the language of the stanza itself, it would be more consistent if it referred to the "hero" da Gama:

> *Cessem do sábio grego e do troiano*
> *As navegações grandes que fizeram;*
> *Cale-se de Alexandre e de Trajano*
> *A fama das vitórias que tiveram;*
> *Que eu canto o peito ilustre lusitano*
> *A quem Neptuno e Marte obedeceram.*

> (Enough of the wise Greek and of the Trojan,
> Those great voyages they made;
> Silence about Alexander and Trajan,

> The famous victories they had;
> I'm going to sing the illustrious Luso heart
> That Mars and Neptune obeyed.)[15]

The figure in question derives from *peito,* literally "chest" and a host of other supposed figurative meanings, and in context should mean Vasco da Gama, for the references of comparison are all individual classical heroes, including Odysseus and Aeneas. Interestingly, even today there is no firm consensus about how one should say what it means, with Bacon's translation preferring "Lusian spirit," Piva, "Portugal," and Ramos, "Portuguese valor." Nevertheless, they all agree that it is not da Gama—that is, that the meaning of the figure does not appear as an acting character in its own representation. In its attempts to define and explain all the major rhetorical figures of the poem, Ramos's school edition of *The Lusiads* classifies the *peito* figure as a metonymy, which would in fact be an accurate description of the linguistic shift if the reference were to da Gama. Since, however, "Portugal" or some variant is held to be the referent, one cannot ignore that the trope could not be rhetorically summarized in the singular: it is both metonymy and prosopopeia.

At this juncture we can more accurately come to terms with the figure of the *peito:* whereas the poem states that the *"peito lusitano"* is the subject it will recount, as a prosopopeia of an abstraction that can exist only in discourse, the focus necessarily turns upon the production of that discursive object. The difference separating *The Lusiads* from the classical epic emerges in the economy of the prosopopeia, the inscription of a subject that does not lend itself to the reader or listener for identification, all of which implies a "new" economy of narrative propulsion. Prosopopeia, as a figure of thought and not merely as a figure of expression, underlies the volatile seventeenth-century debate about the meaning and value of *The Lusiads.* In this context, Pires de Almeida emphasizes the problem protagonist of the heroic actions in challenging Faria e Sousa's (and others') assertion of the epic nature of the poem. Moreover, the interpretation of *peito* as Portugal, as an idealized concept, cannot be considered as simply an alternative meaning to other possible meanings of the figure (including da Gama), which raises further questions for the interpretive tradition because it has inevitably presumed the referential existence of Portugal without acknowledging the economy of prosopopeia that produces it. Indeed, the structure of prosopopeia is such that misrecognition of its economy might be the determining factor of the tradition's constitution.

In Pires de Almeida's "Resposta ao Juízo do Poema," analysis of *The Lusiads'* narrative propulsion becomes more and more explicit:

> [Many episodes of the narration] neither assist nor impede the action of Vasco da Gama [*não ajudam nem impedem a ação de Vasca da Gama*], for they have no link whatsoever with it . . . And thus it becomes more than clear that the poem does not fit the Philosopher's precepts, nor the pattern of Homer and Virgil, and its episodes—which are actions—are with great awareness disunited and disjoined from the action of Vasco da Gama and addressed to the glory of the Portuguese name it celebrates. (85)

These passages seek to describe a narrative that seems to obey none of the paradigms handed down by tradition. The discourse proves unable to find the unifying core that accounts for the generation of the narrative and thus cannot even seem to secure a position from which to launch an interpretation. In effect, there is an outright denial of essentialism, even going so far as to assert the inefficacy of essentialist vocabulary: many of the actions are neither essential nor contingent. These actions appear as disjunctions and cannot be referred to a vertical unity, for they are not contingent, nor to a horizontal one, for they do not serve the forward propulsion of the narrative either as obstacles to be overcome or as positive contributions to the overriding diegesis of the story. Moreover, the poem is addressed to the Portuguese name, which is, however, not a literal but only a figural agent of the narration.

Contrary to what one might expect, the consequences deriving from Pires de Almeida's painstaking analysis do not entail a devalorization of *The Lusiads* but merely a recognition of its difference from the classical epics—a difference that the contemporary discursive experience was unable to rationalize: "And thus we conclude that the Homeric and Virgilian perfection is missing and there are many perfections that Greece and Italy, because they followed Aristotle's precepts, did not know but that are found in the novelty of *The Lusiads*" (85). *The Lusiads* cannot be understood in the same way as preceding epics, for it operates according to a different economy. If it is neither a heroic nor an epic poem, how does one describe it? Pires de Almeida gives an indication, but its peculiar status does not allow for rigid categorization: "[B]ecause of these considerations some minds [*engenhos*] have avoided calling *The Lusiads* a heroic poem, being satisfied with calling it a work [*dando-se por satisfeitos de lhe chamarem obra*], which is an equivocal term that embraces the romance [*romanço*] and the heroic poem, among which *The Lusiads* attain a position of sovereignty" (84). It is a work because of the way in which its figures operate and the discursive economy that works according to a different mode of idealization. But for the category of literary work to prevail as a concept for *The Lusiads,* the legitimizing discourse of literary history is needed, which may account for the privileged position accorded to it in the constitution of literary history as a discursive force in the early nineteenth century.

From the very first publication of Camões's *Lusiads* (1572), readers have experienced a great deal of trouble in constituting the work as a unified whole. Those commentators subsequently given legitimacy by literary history have resolved the issue of unity, or at least have rendered the question banal, by making the poem an expression of the Portuguese state, whereas Pires de Almeida's analysis points out the text's "workings," the operativity of a discourse that itself constitutes as a discursive object the very abstraction it was to glorify or monumentalize. Contrary to institutional accounts of *The Lusiads,* which down to the present day repeat the commonplaces of poetic "creation" and national expression, a careful reading of Pires de Almeida reveals that the "novelty" of *The Lusiads* is not due to its newness and originality: the attribution of novelty marks the appearance of what cannot be readily absorbed by current categories of the understanding. Traditionally, this series of concerns—regarding the work's unity, meaning, and historical or artistic significance—have revolved around the unstable figural relationship between Christianity and paganism. To say it differently, the poem serves as a point of transition between figures of thought based on a theological order and those that usher in a secular worldview. And, as Frank Pierce informs us in his opening sentence to an essay on the theme, the indecision about their interaction to a certain extent persists: "It is a surprising fact that a poem of the stature of Camões' epic . . . should still present a major problem of interpretation."[16] But this figural conflict is substantially more than a tame discussion about the work's overlapping mythologies.

António José Saraiva recapitulates the problem in somewhat different terms: "From the priest who censored and mutilated the Poem, up to the most modern commentators, all have noted the disparity [*o disparate*], for some substantial, for others formal, that consists in having the pagan gods intervene in a historical action whose objective was the expansion of the Christian faith."[17] The reference to "disparity" seemingly only reiterates the work's inability to achieve unity on the basis of its narration. Nevertheless, whereas Pires de Almeida envisioned a more radical disunity that could not by any stretch of the imagination be summarized as the conflict between two opposed autonomous levels, for he analyzed the disjunction within the historical narration as well, Saraiva conceives of the disparity in bipolar terms. To a certain extent, this bipolarity derives from the figural confrontation itself. As Saraiva's description intimates, the work's figural problem is simultaneously political and ideological. There is a complex disparity between the epic's subject—the Western Christians' encounter with the pagan Orient—and the predominantly pagan figuration representing that religious and "civilizing" mission.

On the basis of this affirmed disparity, Saraiva's interpretive solution restates the problem according to the traditional formula of substance and accident or, as he calls it, substance and form. He concludes that "[i]n *The Lusiads* the gods are not simply rhetorical but the same figures with which the very story of the poem is articulated and disarticulated [*mas as figuras com que se ata e desata a própria fábula do poema*]" (190). Fully in the modern, secular tradition of Camonian criticism, this approach argues for the absolute essentiality of the pagan gods, even as it implies a theory of figuration irreducible to that essentialism. In other words, if the gods are not merely figures whose proper meaning can be reached in order then to discard them, they do not simply represent underlying meaning but are simulacra whose presence in the work is indispensable and ineffaceable. Yet this solution does not entirely resolve the figural question: it asserts a necessary relationship between the figures and the work, whereas it was the disparity of the work that led to the question in the first place. In its own terms, then, this interpretation claims the pagan figures' primacy in propelling the story, which would make the so-called historical action subordinate, although textually it is difficult to confirm such a primacy, for the times of figural intervention are determined by rigorously historical events that *The Lusiads* endeavored to render. Displacement of the question of figural intervention in the working of the narrative permits Saraiva to contend that resolution of the disparity has indeed occurred: "And, in this way, the incongruity or disparity [*disparate*] indicated by Camões' critics does not exist from an aesthetic point of view" (181). Assertions of aesthetic unity, a version of the organicity fostered by Romanticism's literary history, consolidates the work itself into a figure whose only requirement is institutional consensus.

This figural disparity recurs incessantly among those reacting to Camões's *Lusiads,* even when the stakes are neither religious nor aesthetic. In his comments on the epic, for example, Voltaire proclaims that the conflict between the pagan and Christian elements of *The Lusiads* "disfigures the entire work in the eyes of sensible readers [*des lecteurs sensés*]" and that "Camões almost always falls into such absurdities [*dans de telles disparates*]."[18] This critique has often been discussed by Camões's champions, with Voltaire becoming emblematic of the unsympathetic reader bereft of literary sensibility. However, the continuation of Voltaire's critique displays a less arbitrary and subjective aspect: "But the greatest of all the defects of this poem is the scarce connection that governs [*le peu de liaison qui règne*] in all its parts; it resembles the voyage that is its subject" (336). In this sense, representation does not operate as it should in *The Lusiads,* for the poem's inability to effect its own governing unity prevents the representation from being separated from that which is represented. Contrary to attempts to unify the poem through aesthetic sensibility, Voltaire presumes that the text cannot attain unity even as an example of artistic form.

The stormy history of Camonian criticism thus derives from the unstable figurality of the poem: the peculiar status of the figures and their effects and actions in propelling a largely historical narrative. Bertholameu Ferreira, the initial censor of the poem, was also the first to offer a judgment on its figurality:

> I have reviewed, by order of the holy and general Inquisition, these ten cantos of the *Lusiads* of Luís de Camões, about the valorous deeds in arms which the Portuguese performed in Asia and Europe, and I did not find in them a single thing that was scandalous or contrary to the faith and good social behavior; but it seemed to me necessary to warn the readers that the author, in order to exalt the difficulty of the voyage and entrance of the Portuguese into India [*pera encarecer a difficuldade da nauegação & entrada dos Portugueses na India*], makes use of a fic-

tion of heathen gods . . . Nevertheless, as this is poetry and pretending, and the author as poet intends nothing more than making the poetic style ornate, we did not hold it to be unsuitable for this story of the gods to be included in the work [*na obra*], recognizing it for what it is, and considering that the truth of our holy faith, that all heathen gods are demons, remains secure.[19]

The low-key tone of the Inquisition evaluation belies any controversy regarding the text—a slight misgiving, perhaps, but not controversy. Yet the qualified acceptance of the figures, in the form of a warning to the readers, has implications that go far beyond the statement about this poem. In fact, as in the subsequent course of Camonian criticism, Ferreira presents as solved what he in retrospect first introduced as a problem: the unity of the work and the place of the figures within it. At the time when the permission was written, there was no national literature cognizant of itself as such, and the distinctions between history as the language of truth and fiction as the language of the imagination, of poetry versus prose and their respective cognitive values, were not firmly drawn.

But Ferreira (and the Inquisition he represents) takes a position with regard to these distinctions, one that will be compatible with future organizations of knowledge. The figures exist to enhance historical truth, to underscore the real-life difficulties of the voyage; this relationship between the ideal and the real, the figures and the history they supposedly incarnate, emerges over and over with regard to *The Lusiads* and will be decisive for Schlegel's formulation of literary history. The distinctions implied in Ferreira's permission have certainly been in force and enforced during the epoch of literary history, and twentieth-century readers are more than familiar with them, but this brief text reveals other facets of interpretation worthy of remark. The notion of figurality, or, rather, the notion of language itself, sees the rhetoric of its deployment in terms of essence and accident, meaning and expression, which just so happens in this interpretation to correspond to an encounter between Christians and pagans, a more than appropriate distinction in view of the poem's confrontation between agents of a Christian Portugal and a series of "heathen" others. These interpretive assumptions hold a great deal in common with the allegorical methods of biblical interpretation, a method designed to eliminate or domesticate scriptural contradictions.

For *The Lusiads,* a text on the way to becoming sacred in a secular tradition, this method of biblical interpretation becomes a recommendation about how a text should be read. Ferreira's text advances a theory of rhetoric, fiction, and reading, in addition to situating the poetic text in a communicative framework that joins author and readers. Although the tradition of Camonian criticism has opposed this conception of the figures as mere "window dressing," Ferreira single-handedly drew the line of debate that would thenceforth occupy the tradition of Camonian criticism; Saraiva, who attempts to reverse the devalorization of the "pagan" figures, serves as one example among many who reject the formulation only to endorse its distinction. It would, however, be anachronistic to align Ferreira's reference to the "work" with the aesthetic impulse of modernity. The notion of the work did not yet exist as a reified concept displaying and effecting unity; here *obra* simply suggests the operation of the text and not the "work" as an idea.

Undoubtedly Ferreira himself came to realize that such powerful discursive concepts cannot be established by fiat, for he was still censor in 1584, when the so-called *piscos* edition of *The Lusiads* was published, also with approval by the Inquisition. This permission to print is much briefer:

> I have reviewed, by the order of the very illustrious and most reverend Archbishop of Lisbon, General Inquisitor of these Realms, the *Lusiads* of Luís de Camões, with some glosses; this book, emended in the way that it has been, contains nothing against the faith and good social behavior and can be printed. And in it the author has shown much wit and erudition.[20]

This 1584 edition excised reference to pagan figures, thus eliminating the mediation of figurality that the reader had to traverse before arriving at the historical sense and Christianity of the mission. The Inquisition deemed it no longer sufficient to warn the reader and frame the interpretation; editing greatly reduced the possibility of erroneous readings, partly because of the suppression of figures but also because of the added "annotations," which restricted possible readings even further. These two endorsements present opposing modes of containing potential resolutions of the work's disparities, constraining the work within the guidelines of faith and custom: it is not a question of eliminating reading per se but of two methods of controlling it. The first method posits the parameters within which the text can effectively be read—

thus the warning to the reader—and the second seeks to limit the contradictions present in the text by excising key passages, and to channel possible ambiguities by supplying interpretive glosses. With historical hindsight, the first method has proven more effective; it has successfully accompanied the growth of institutions that pronounce upon and manage the meaning of cultural and literary artifacts, for which *The Lusiads* is merely an example, and it is compatible with the discursive objects that owe their existence to literary history and historical narrative in general.

In 1639, on the eve of Portugal's release from its "Babylonian captivity" and its reacquisition of sovereignty, Faria e Sousa's Spanish edition of *The Lusiads* appeared. Although printed in Madrid with the necessary approvals and licenses, the work was banned in Portugal by a 1640 edict of the Inquisition that has now been published in facsimile.[21] In this instance, the Inquisition is more concerned about Faria e Sousa's commentary than about the poem itself:

> We, the Apostolic Inquisitors against heretic depravity and apostasy in this city of Coimbra and in its district and elsewhere, let it be known to all who see this letter or who have any notice of it by any other way, that they are informed about a book which has recently appeared entitled Lusiads by Luís de Camões, annotated by Manoel de Faria e Sousa, associate of the Order of Christ and of the Royal House, printed in Madrid by Juan Sanches in 1639. In it are contained many things that are obscene to the purity of our Catholic religion and scandalous and offensive to the ears of faithful Christians, for the author interprets many passages from the Holy Scripture, applies them with little piety to profane things, speaks immodestly about the holy trinity, the holy spirit, the sacraments of the holy mother of the Church, and the holy virgin our lady, and places it on a level with sordid and lascivious figures and profane stories.

As the text continues, it bans reading of *The Lusiads* under penalty of excommunication. Because the "author" that the edict condemns is unequivocally Faria e Sousa and not Camões, the question of figurality and reading come into another light altogether. The condemnation emerges out of a perceived leveling of distinctions between sacred figures and profane ones; according to the edict, the inalienable boundary between the two types of figurality has not been respected; the author uses interpretations of biblical figures to interpret the profane text and explains biblical figures by referring to profane figuration. To paraphrase the edict, the author puts the profane figures on a par with Holy Scripture, literally placing them in proximity *(lhe apropria figuras torpes)*: the kind of exchange that can take place indicates a laterality instead of a vertical relationship. In other words, instead of the pagan figures being rendered dispensable to a deeper, underlying meaning, Faria e Sousa shows their figurality to operate in the same rhetorical universe—and not simply in a like way, the parallelism of which would still allow for the integrality of biblical interpretation.

This assimilation, a sort of figural desacralization, attenuates the absolutism of official, hierarchizing rhetorical projects, which include that of Ferreira and the Inquisition. Yet the different modalities of interpretation that are being articulated here surpass encroachments of the secular on the theologically ordered universe. The problem is much more sweeping: if reading signifies the transmuting of figures into figures, a translation not based on hierarchy but on lateral reiteration, there is conceptual—and, perhaps, political—anarchy. In other words, the suppression of meaning that was guaranteed in the theological sphere can no longer be maintained if literacy seeps out of its institutional confines, and in the early seventeenth century it was not at all clear how a conceptual (and social) hegemony could be established to stave off such anarchy.

History requires its telling, even if the discourse recording it rarely does justice to its most extreme transformations. *The Lusiads* stands at a peculiar juncture in the cartography of modernity. As a literary account inscribing an unprecedented series of historical forays into the unknown, it personifies a national consciousness in its quest to embrace the globe and encounter "others." The conceptual and figural problems posed by that literary and historical representation were set aside only in subsequent centuries, aided by the hegemonic aesthetic dimension and authorial supremacy. The drive toward personification, which has resulted in an epoch dominated by ideas of the author, artist, star, and creator of culture, has folded these divergent elements of *The Lusiads* into the Camões figure itself.

The figure of Camões, as the product of a constellation of discourses, plays a curious role in the tradition of Western Europe: Camões inscribes historical representation itself, marking the actor who represented Portuguese and European self-consciousness and representing the nation in its literary expression. The importance of the Camões figure's pan-European diffusion exceeds the local interests of a national tradition and directly concerns the regime of modern historical discourse. The figure coalesced in conjunction with nineteenth-century nationalism and literary history, two concepts whose coincidence is not at all innocent. As is the case with literary history generally, German Romanticism pioneered Camões's revalorization; a critical essay sketching some aspects of this valorization describes Camões in precise terms: "[T]he German cultural intelligentsia was the first to fully recognize Camões as a national and nationalistic poet, actually a *Kulturträger* of a very particular moment of Portuguese, and hence of European, historic evolution: the moment of consolidation and national expansion."[22] The article in which this passage appears participates in the wave of historical studies on the emergence of Camões and Camonian criticism, although it may very well be the first to consider Camões as exemplary of and in European self-consciousness. Moreover, the essay concludes by acknowledging that Camões's nineteenth-century revival also occurs at a moment of national consolidation, when culture is itself "nationalized" as the expression of a given people, language, and geographically bounded state (199–200). Thus Camões, as a figure, becomes at the same time the bearer of Portuguese culture and paradigmatic for the relationship between culture and state that literary and national history presuppose. But to understand the nineteenth-century multiplication of references to Camões as simply a belated European recognition of his greatness would be to fall prey to the historical conception of literature that his name was then invoked to establish.

As remarked by Melczer, Friedrich Schlegel was decisive in the revival of Camões (197), although it is equally well known that in his lectures under the title *History of Ancient and Modern Literature* (1812) Schlegel also provided the historical model linking culture and state.[23] Although Camões has an important place in the *History*, he also figures prominently in an earlier work (1803) that seeks to sketch briefly what would be entailed in a history of modern poetry.[24] In the section entitled "Portuguese Poetry [*Dichtkunst*]," Schlegel describes Camões much in the way we have traditionally come to expect: "The perfection [*Vollendung*] of Portuguese poetry is all the more apparent in the beautiful poems of the great Camões" (v3: 28). This, of course, refers to both the lyrical and the epic poetry, but it is *The Lusiads* that merits special attention, particularly because of its historical significance, including its importance for the nation: "That great national poem, the swan song of a fallen heroic people, can be considered as the highest moment of this short but masterful [*herrlichen*] epoch [of discovery]. Just a few years after the completion [*Vollendung*] of the poem, the nation itself collapses. The aged poet did not long survive the grief of a nation that to a certain extent continued to exist only through this work in which a richly endowed mind so masterfully adorned and immortalized its glory" (v3: 29). Historically, the passage refers to Portugal's loss of nationhood to Spain, which took place in the year of the poet's death (1580) and lasted until 1640. During that time, Camões was considered a Spanish poet, and the linguistic and literary links between Camões and Spain will be effectively exploited in Schlegel's full-blown narrative of national literary development. Here, however, there are already intimations of a theory of history that situates Portugal's (and Camões's) idiosyncratic centrality: *The Lusiads* is simultaneously the most masterful expression of the greatest, most masterful moment of Portugal's nationhood and its summation. It is the *Vollendung* of the nation in all senses, signaling the nation's end and its perfection. In other words, this monumentalization of Camões and his poem's relationship to the idea of Portugal has an important discursive role to play in Schlegel's own formulation of literary expression; within the project of literary history, it freezes a synchronic moment that represents the highest degree of nationhood, but its synchronicity is of historical import, for it represents the outcome—if also the loss—of a development of national self-consciousness. In addition, if nationhood formally ceases, its greatest monument becomes even more monumental, for the nation lives on only in its monument and not as a nation at all. The implications for the discourse of history will be developed only in Schlegel's later text on literary history.

Nevertheless, one should not assume that the general project of literary history does not already, in this earlier text, come to bear on the figure of Camões. As I discussed earlier in this chapter, it has been traditional for every critical reader of *The Lusiads* to come to terms with the disparity among its figures, if only in passing. Not surprisingly, Schlegel considers the contradiction between underlying Christianity and the pagan figures of representation to be easily resolvable and among the work's many positive aspects. His description of this resolution must rely on an important trope, perhaps the one most often identified with Schlegel: "Camões uses [pagan fables] as beautiful figural language for meaningful allegory [*als eine schöne Bildersprache für sinnreiche Allegorie*], as they are considered and used, often with a great deal of inventive innovation, by other poets and painters of the romantic period" (v3: 31). As with Saraiva and others discussed above, Schlegel's assertion of the meaningfulness of the pagan figures is predicated on a certain conception of the literary work as having an objective existence, as "reified." But Schlegel's notion of what he distinguishes as "romantic" allegory expresses a temporal aspect and linguistically produces the effect of duration, that is, it generates a narrative (discussed by Paul de Man in a completely different context[25]). Through the discursive operation of literary history—itself a projection in time—allegory is woven into a configuration of concepts that exist only in the history that proclaims them.

For example, in the *History of Ancient and Modern Literature* Schlegel refines the concept of allegory that belongs to the modern state. This discussion takes place in Schlegel's twelfth lecture, one of the book's most widely known because it addresses Shakespeare, Spanish drama, and the novel. The following comments appear in a paragraph discussing Calderón, one of Schlegel's principal authors, and the Spanish nation, which for Schlegel occupies a prominent position in grounding literary history: "Under allegory in the true sense of the word one should here understand the aggregate of Christian figuration and its meaning [*der ganze Inbegriff der gesamten christlichen Bildlichkeit und Sinnbildlichkeit*] as expression, covering, and mirror of the invisible world, in accord with Christian knowledge itself. This is the spirit or the soul of Christian poetry, and the body and external matter is the romantic legend or even national life" (v6: 286). The concept of the nation owes its very formulation to Christianity. Discursively speaking, the nation-state shares many characteristics with a divine agent, perhaps the most fundamental being that it cannot literally be present except through its manifestations. Thus Schlegel, in order to affirm the existence of a national spirit, a literature expressing it, and a history able to describe it, draws on Christianity and the traditional notions of figuration and meaning. Nonetheless, these notions enter into a configuration in which the nation concept mediates the underlying unity of Christianity even as it displays an analogy with it. In other words, Schlegel's text on the *History of*

Ancient and Modern Literature carefully and systematically constructs and conjoins a series of idealized discursive references that plot a new understanding of history and of (literary) culture.

The mutual relationships between nation, masterpiece, and literary figure or author coalesce into a constellation of ideas that cuts across the multiple discourses making up the Western tradition. At the same time, they overlap with other fields of knowledge (philosophy, for example) sharing the same economy of discourse. These notions form the assumptions of Schlegel's *History*. "Poets and philosophers" therefore become "manifestations" (*Erscheinungen*), show themselves as a "proof and general measure of the spiritual power and culture [*Bildung*] of their respective nations" (v6: 17). In this theory of cultural history, thinkers and their writings—if they leave behind written traces—exemplify synecdochically their nation; in this sense, they become its figures. Schlegel's historical text portrays a discursive economy whose elements render the state allegorically. On the basis of this figural expression, representative figures manifest their national origin to a greater or lesser extent, and the historical narrative they enable places them in a temporal continuum.

The judgment on Camões and *The Lusiads*, briefly recorded in Schlegel's 1803 text on modern poetry, reappears in the *History of Ancient and Modern Literature*. Although the general thrust of the passage is maintained, in the *History* it belongs to the powerful machine of historical discourse and is embroiled in many more conceptual relationships. Although only one reference among many, this most extensive treatment of Camões (approximately three pages) was well known among Portugal's nineteenth-century literary historians, who cited portions of it as evidence of Camões's recognized greatness.[26] The passage restating the opinion of the earlier passage falls within those three pages: "This poem encompasses the entire poetry of his people; among all the heroic poems of ancient or modern times, not one is national to the same degree, and not since Homer has a poet been loved and revered by his nation to the same extent as Camões. Thus all the patriotic sentiment [*Gefühl des Vaterlandes*] that remained in the nation, which after him fell from its masterfulness [*von ihrer Herrlichkeit*], is linked to this one poet, who can rightly take the place of other poets and of an entire literature" (v6: 266).

The synchronic aspect once again introduces the passage, but now the representation has become dual: the poem is the summation of national literature and the nation. In other words, this passage holds a much more developed notion of literature that must be understood in its entirety as expressive of the nation. More importantly, however, what he elsewhere calls the state becomes diversified into multiple references, each somewhat different and including the "fatherland" and the "people" *(Volk)*. The people proves to be an essential concept of Schlegel's history, for he uses it to explain the historical existence of the nation and national culture: the people will ultimately be the repository of national culture, an aspect of the nation concept that remains a mere suggestion in this passage. The schema of interrelationships renders not only synchronic comparisons but also temporal ones: comparisons between the poem and other poems, between the poet and other poets, between *The Lusiads'* relationship to its nation and that of other poems to their respective nations. Although this passage only intimates the larger discursive process it supplements, it hints at the complexity such a discursive regime entails. It is impossible to designate any single concept of the configuration, whether it be nation, people, literary work, or authorial figure, as the origin and power behind their interrelationship.

For Schlegel, this discursive web is called history: "[I]f a people is to have value, it must also come to a clear consciousness of its own acts and destinies. History is this self-consciousness of a nation that expresses itself in reflective and representational works" (v6: 16). It is very common, particularly since Hegel, to link history to self-consciousness. For Schlegel, however, history means becoming aware of oneself as a protagonist both in history and in representing that history; this formulation therefore calls for another category, that of the work. The people, or the nation that signifies its idealized unity, cannot act; there is simply no way for it to exist in flesh and blood and acquire a singularity of mind. This notion of history comes close to being tautological. History is the nation's self-consciousness, but that self-consciousness, and therefore that history, can come to be only through the mediation of works that represent the nation self-reflexively, that is, with an awareness that they are presenting the nation. Historical works, in other words, leave a material residue to represent moments of national self-consciousness. The category of the work, fundamental for literary history, emerges from this distinction between history as the self-consciousness of an ideal, nonmaterial mind and history as self-consciousness that merges the idea with empirical matter.

In introducing the necessary category of the work, Schlegel must address an issue that is implicated in every theory of history: writing. A conception of truth and meaning as present only in the mind must treat writing as external and superfluous to meaning, a corruption to the sense. Schlegel, however, cannot dismiss writing so easily, because while history depends on the subsistence of artifacts, it also relies on the transformation and increasing consciousness of the national spirit. Without transformation of the spirit, there could be no history. But as an essentialist enterprise that claims historical validity, Schlegel's *History* maintains the inseparable unity of "Spirit and Language" *(Geist und Sprache),* "Thought and Expression" *(Gedanke und Wort)* (v6: 14). How then does Schlegel's *History* conceptualize writing? For the ephemeral products of human activity to become historical objects, they must "form enduring works through writing and representation" (v6: 14). Language is the most adequate expression of the spirit itself, but this language encompasses another familiar distinction: voice and writing. Voice is given by nature *("Die Natur konnte den Menschen keine schönere Gabe verleihen als die Stimme"),* but writing is something else altogether: "Above everything that the human Spirit has invented, writing is the most wondrous and important and brooks no comparison" (v6: 14). The difference between writing and voice is a very significant one, for unlike simplistic conceptions in which writing represents the original voice, here writing—as opposed to voice—represents the greatest achievement of the human spirit. In other words, writing represents the spirit's recognition of itself; the history of the spirit, its materialization, does not simply supplement the voice. As a divine gift, the faculty of voice does not originate through intervention of the spirit.

In beginning his history of the human spirit by reflecting on the epistemological status of writing, Schlegel followed a time-honored tradition of historical writing. Because early historians were concerned about bequeathing their material legacy to subsequent generations, they often felt compelled to reflect on the precise nature of their written legacy. To understand the ramifications of Schlegel's view, it can be contrasted with that of another "historian" writing in Portugal when, in Schlegel's own terms, the nation first achieved its modern form. In fact, the historian João de Barros told the story of the Portuguese "discovery and conquest of the Orient," and his text served Camões as a guide in writing *The Lusiads.* In his prologue, Barros gives a justification for his writing (which I cite only in part):

The invention of the artifice [of writing] is owed to several authors, although it appears to be inspired by God rather than invented by any human understanding. And just as he established that by means of the palate, tongue, teeth, and lips, a breath of air propelled by the lungs and caused by a power that the Latins call "affatus" join to form meaningful utterances, so that the hearing, their natural object, represent to the understanding diverse meanings and concepts according to their arrangement, so he intended that by means of the characters of the letters that we use, which are arranged in the meaningful order of value that each nation has given to its alphabet, the sight, receptive object of these characters, forms the essence of things and rational concepts, in the way that speech in its function utters them. And, furthermore, he intended that, for the benefit of perpetuity, this artificial mode of elocution through the letter take precedence over the natural elocution of speech. Because speech, when animated, does not have life for longer than the instant of its pronunciation and loses its similarity to the time that is past, and the letters, being dead characters without animation, contain in themselves the spirit of life, for they give life to all things around us.[27]

The differences in orientation between this text and Schlegel's are striking. Writing, first of all, is described as a divine invention, for it supersedes human understanding. Just as absolute knowledge prevailed only in the mind of the divinity—a formulation that not even Kant (nor Schlegel; see v6: 225) challenges—the guarantee of the written word's meaning suffered no consequences from the invention of a time-resistant medium. Speech determines writing, and the only distinction between them is that writing, as materiality, opens up a future dimension, even if that dimension is merely the continued realization of past speech. But this introduces the unbridgeable difference between any historian of the sixteenth century and the premises of modern history. The nation in Barros's praise of Portuguese exploits is not equivalent to the state, for it has no existence as a discursive object: it is a synchronic community, bound by a common language, that does not change in time. Thus the future dimension could only mistakenly be conceived as a temporal future in which the community would need a mediator to explain its own past deeds to it. In effect, even though this history is written, it is fundamentally a product of an oral culture: written language reproduces the referentiality that only a spoken, gesturing speech can have. The "spirit of life" does not, as in Schlegel, have anything to do with consciousness but has to do with the here and now; Schlegel's history demands as its prerequisite that the here and now be lost and irrecuperable without mediation.

In the *History of Ancient and Modern Literature*, literature is the means by which the spirit signals its stage of consciousness, but literature is neither belles lettres nor simply that which is written in a manuscript: it is any activity that comes about through the intervention of the human spirit. Literature refers to "all those arts and sciences, representations and creations [*jene Künste und Wissenschaften, jene Darstellungen und Hervorbringungen*], which have life and human beings themselves as an object and operate only in thinking and language, without broaching external action and material effect, and without representing, in expression and writing, any extraneous physical matter to the spirit" (v6: 13). The only criterion for admitting materiality—"materialists" are throughout the text an object of scorn—derives from its ability to produce a discursive object. Nevertheless, this production of ideal objects—that is, humanity as the ideal object, thus legitimating the object as exemplary of the human spirit—cannot be equated with a simple idealism, for it must retain the materiality even as that materiality contradicts its project. No discursive object can escape its tenuousness, which irremediably depends on the material inscribing it and on the idealizations arising from it. As a general term, *literature*—which in today's usage would be called culture—entails nothing less than a boundless summation of all human creations. In this perspective, the concept of the state and its concomitant linguistic identity emerge to give direction to the discourse of history.

In setting the parameters of this history, Schlegel declares his intentions to be "to make visible [*vor Augen stellen*] the spirit of literature in every epoch, the whole of literature, and the course of its development among the most important nations" (v6: 6). Yet this vision of national history and the human continuum requires examples, even if it can be sustained in a narrative that has the spirit as its primary protagonist. Because the state and its literary culture depend so heavily on language, Spain and, to a lesser extent, Portugal—European states achieving an early cultural and linguistic unity—serve as models for Schlegel's theory of history. How does Schlegel bring all these elements together under the auspices of the nation? The qualities that must coalesce to define a state capable of bearing and producing a history preclude an easy separation between Spain and Portugal: for example, in the face of the Castilians, whose victory over the rest of "Spain" assured that "all the beauty of poetry was also brought together in Castilian poetry, . . . [o]nly the Portuguese, since they formed their own people and realm, retained their own language and poetry" (v6: 261). The year the Spanish realm is consolidated corresponds to the beginning of an imposition of Castilian as the national language at the expense of others (and Schlegel touches on the literature of Catalonia and Aragon only to offset the grandeur of Castilian poetry). Nevertheless, it is essential to the establishment of the concept of a national literary history that Portugal and Spain be in some way linked, if only because of Camões's national epic: "The poetry of each nation is so closely related that it is not easy to separate them" (v6: 261). Historically, of course, Camões was often referred to as a Spanish poet, particularly by Severim de Faria and Manuel de Faria e Sousa, both of whom wrote during the years when Portugal was a part of Spain.

Despite the asserted connection between Spain and Portugal, in the text it is Spain as a state formation that embodies the relationship between cultural production, nation, and language. The text reverberates with reference after reference to Spain and the perfection of its national model; because the argument is not built on demonstration, for the discourse of history proceeds by narrative rather than by syllogism and depends on interwoven concepts offering mutual support, the underlying assumptions about the Spanish ideal have to be ferreted out. The process of idealization, however, is depicted with great precision: "No other poetry stemmed from such a manifold of elements as the Spanish. But these elements were neither dissimilar nor incompatible; they were individual notes of fantasy and sentiment that first conjoined into a full accord, and Spanish poetry properly bestows the highest magic of the romantic. Not only is this poetry rich, but it is thoroughly one in spirit and orientation, and one with the character and sentiment of the nation" (v6: 263). The process, therefore, is clear: on the basis of particulars that evince a similarity, the concept of Spanishness emerges to be the general category of which the particulars are manifestations.

Although the perspectives are different, this appears to be a more sophisticated variant of what Barros collectively called the nation. But "this poetry is not merely rich," it also forms a spiritual unity and expresses the nation. At first glance, the phrase seems only to restate what had preceded, but a conceptual shift takes place that is fruitful for

Schlegel's *History*. Building on the metaphor of discordant harmony, the concept of the nation emerges full-blown: the concept of Spain becomes a particular that manifests a more abstract generality, the nation. Spain can be an example—the example—of nationality only if it is one nation among others. In the same way, establishing the nationhood of Spain and its relationship to the culture expressing it immediately consolidates the concept of nation, along with the countless nations against which it defines its own identity. These distinctions are not insignificant details, for they must be operative for history to produce the validity it claims, and without the attendant concepts of literary history, the historical enterprise fails. As the passage quoted above continues, this mutual reliance becomes clearer: "Since that glorious time under Ferdinand the Catholic and Charles V, there has in general been no literature as wholly national as that of the Spanish [*ist überhaupt keine Literatur so ganz national gewesen, als die der Spanier*]" (v6: 263). The only good idealization is a past idealization, one that can serve as a historical model for history.

But what are the peculiar characteristics of Spain that make it appropriate for founding literary history? Because literary history depends just as much on the facility of representation, which means the possibility of integrating the narrative that tells the story of respective literatures into already established ideas, more is involved than simply nationality or "statehood": "Everything [in Spanish literature] is permeated with the noblest national sentiment; strong, moral, and deeply religious, even where morality or religion is not immediately under discussion. There was nothing that could undermine the mode of thinking, confuse the sentiment, or invert the meaning. Throughout, one and the same spirit" (v6: 264). Thus literary history is located at the intersection of the philosophical and the political, which places the production of national culture in a completely terrestrial context. As in the notion of historical manifestation borrowed from Christianity, the monotheistic divinity reveals itself through the mediation of the national concept. In fact, Schlegel makes it explicit that Christianity is the philosophy of the modern period, for all of modernity owes its existence to the victory of Christianity over pagan philosophy. Moreover, "for cultural history and for the development of the formation of the spirit," the spiritual struggle between these two tendencies (which for Schlegel was won by Christianity) "also marks the universal focal point around which everything turns and out of which all is elucidated" (v6: 90). Christianity or, rather, the idea of Christianity is both a temporal and a spatial anchor; without it neither cultural nor literary history would be possible. It is the close collaboration between the government and religion that makes Spain a very apt model, above and beyond the status of its poetry and the spirit manifest there. In Schlegel's own conception, the national import of the literature under Ferdinand the Catholic (who with Isabella fashioned the Spanish state out of victory in an essentially religious war) and Charles V (the Holy Roman Emperor) became paradigmatic for literary and historical understanding.

Furthermore, on the long list of Spain's virtues as a model for literary history, as a national idea, was its early political commitment to molding a national language. And in the analysis and correlation of literary history, this shows another facet of Schlegel's affirmed relationship between spirit and language, for an autonomous and solitary national spirit expresses itself most clearly in a single language. In effect, Schlegel even implies that nation and language go together and provide stability along the lines of the traditional family: "The more one's memories and sentiment of the fatherland are stimulated, the greater is one's love for the mother-tongue" (v6: 10). In this regard, Spain again offered historical insight: the Castilian language was the first vernacular to have full-scale grammar.[28] Because Schlegel's ultimate goal is to provide the philosophical basis and political-literary conception for establishing a truly German literature, the material basis of a historical German spirit, his comments on language often take the form of admonishment: "In any case, use of indispensable foreign languages in daily life should be restricted to the barest minimum" (v6: 238). Language and its univocity is a concern that informs all relations between self and other, between empire and colony, between progress and belatedness, and between canonized works and those that are considered unworthy. Literary history, as the articulation of this discursive economy by means of which effects of univocity are produced, has been the ground upon which the discursive conflicts regarding institutionalized meaning have taken place, but, as a reading of Schlegel's *History* suggests, literary history is itself a product of that same discursive economy that it institutes.

Above and beyond specifically literary and linguistic factors, however, Spain is for Schlegel an idea with massive conceptual and, more important, historical baggage. This historical aspect, which refers more to a secular understanding of historical reality than to the narratives recounting it, involves precisely the figure of Camões. For reasons that only superficially have to do with the Portuguese loss of sovereignty, Schlegel invariably discusses Spanish and Portuguese literature together and consistently mentions Camões in tandem with Cervantes and Calderón.[29] In the epoch of discovery, at the outset of "modernity" (what Schlegel calls the "new"), Spain and Portugal evolved in historical synchrony; their literatures achieved self-consciousness, and the resulting literary artifacts represented material manifestations of their national spirit for posterity.

Camões's special place in this constellation derives in part from the epic genre that gave ideal form to the national spirit's material legacy. Schlegel's 1804 lectures are unambiguous in this regard: "A historical poem, however, which should comprehensively treat a nation's heroic traditions, must necessarily be *one* work, an integral unity at the center of which everything could be concentrated, and can therefore be accomplished only in the epic form."[30] This form ideally lends itself to an integral and totalizing representation of national history and tradition. The kernel of this idea has marked subsequent reflection on the representational power of the literary artifact (Lukács's *Theory of the Novel* is an obvious example). But in Schlegel's historical conception, this view of the epic's power of representation gives Camões and *The Lusiads* their historical distinction. "The ancients did not have a national poem of this sort" (v11: 158), principally because they had no nation in the modern sense. In contrast, *The Lusiads* offers a comprehensive manifestation of Camões's nation's history and "is the most perfect epic poem" (v11: 158). This particular confluence of factors makes Camões's epic exemplary: "His work achieved what many nations and eminent poets have vainly strived for"; in a broad historical perspective, "Camões's work corresponds perfectly to a concept for which one has often sought an example in vain" (v3: 30–31). It is an instance in which the example creates the concept.

But what is the nature of Camões's exemplarity? Schlegel's writings are peppered throughout with references to Camões, but there is no major study of the author or his work. Although he is repeatedly linked to the Spanish tradition, which also has a prototypical role to play in Schlegel's conception of modernity, Camões's exemplarity is not wholly commensurate with that of Spain. Nonetheless, they share a common historical ground. In his fragmentary notebook written from 1817 to 1820, "On Poetry and Literature," Schlegel continued his reflections on Camões and Spain: "The poetic presence of romantic life in reality predominates among the Spanish, and in this respect *Camões* also belongs entirely to Spanish poetry."[31] Camões belongs to the Spanish tradition because he shares a literary model of representing life in the world, of producing works that integrate literary expression, "life," and "reality." This vague and elliptical note becomes more comprehensible in a later entry that pinpoints Camões's difference from comparable authors in the Spanish tradition: "In *Camões, real external life* [*das wirkliche äußre Leben*] is conceived and expressed with the inner life's inspiration [*Begeisterung*]; in *Cervantes,* the inner life beautifully shines through the annihilation of external life; in *Calderón,* external life is transformed by inner life" (v17: 428). In this context, Camões's singularity becomes more readily apparent: inner life, and the spirit that powers it, seizes living external reality and expresses it, renders it in a work. Although the works of Calderón and Cervantes equally reside along the axis of inner life and reality, they collapse the two poles into a single topographic plane.

In preserving the real world in an act of representation, the figure of Camões crystallizes a model of historical agency. The elements of this model are made explicit by yet another of Schlegel's entries, this one in the form of diagrams. The entry's two diagrams that concern Camões are displayed following their original layout (v17: 451). The first diagram lists four faculties of the mind as well as the literary figures embodying them:

	Cervantes	
	Understanding	
Calderón		*Shakespeare*
Fantasy		Reason
	Camões	
	Will Inspiration	
	[*Wille Begeisterung*]	

Given his honored place in the conceptual firmament of German Romanticism, Shakespeare occupies the fourth coordinate. Apart from Camões, each of the figures has one description; the two terms characterizing the Camões figure refer to opposing modalities of (mental) action. Inspiration comes from elsewhere, as if on its own, whereas will emanates from an intending subject.

The second diagram registers what Schlegel calls the "four basic powers":

                              Intell[ect]
                              Shakespeare
        Calderón   *Camões*
        F[antasy]   Id[ealism]
                                                          Emp[iricism]
                              Cervantes
                              Id[ealism]

Once again, the figure of Camões receives two terms, but in this instance they signal two intellectual orientations that traverse all the philosophical, scientific, and historical thought of modernity. In Camões, idealism and empiricism come together to provide a model for historical (and literary) representation. In the same way that the inner life conceives and expresses external reality, Camões's literary inventory of Portuguese material actions and manifestations produced the very idea of Portugal. His exemplarity, and that of his work, actuates the concept whose examples can be infinitely repeated. The figural problems of *The Lusiads* introduced from the very first moment the merger—or, at the time, the clash—between the ideal and the real, representational figures and the history they describe.

Nevertheless, Schlegel's image of Camões has an additional dimension. More than simply an empty idealized figure to fill with arbitrary dreams, the Camões name belonged to an empirical individual, and *The Lusiads* inscribes Camões's concrete existence. That existence was specifically historical, conjunctural, and not merely individual lived experience: "Camões was a soldier and a knight. He himself lived a part of his life in India. Everything in his poem breathes the genuine courage of heroes and heroic meaning, is created out of the fullness of his own perceptions, his own experience" (v11: 159). In a sense, Camões becomes Schlegel's evidence of historical agency, proof that literature—writing in the form of a work—can grasp history and represent the national spirit. Camões, then, becomes the figure of literary history, the figure of modern figuration. As Schlegel writes in his early poem addressed to Camões: "*Sei, Camoëns, denn mein Vorbild!*" ("Thus, Camões, be my model!").[32] He literally invokes Camões as a prefiguration, as *Vorbild*, to prepare his way. One image begets another, and literary history laces them together.

5

Cosmopolitical Grounding of Literature

The ethos of modernity was born of a clash with the other, and the resulting global projection incorporated otherness as a counterbalance to social, political, and cultural self-identity. Thinking about relations between self and other, between representatives of highly divergent societies, surfaced in tandem with the encounters that occasioned it. In the history of this phenomenon, Montaigne's reflections on "cannibals" occupies a privileged place and in the past two hundred years has become an inescapable point of reference, frequently in combination with discussions of Shakespeare's *Tempest*.[1] Montaigne's essay is notable for various reasons: it was written early in the history of colonization, it is critical of European haughtiness, and it succinctly presents general lines of thought that have become paradigmatic for anyone broaching the issue. Moreover, it has direct and incontrovertible implications for formulating the figural basis of otherness.

The essay "Cannibals" (an ironic title in light of its subsequent critique) begins with concerns of an entirely different order. It opens with consideration about how *idées reçues* frequently run counter to experience, particularly when experience involves unfamiliar others or, as the Greeks called them, barbarians. After offering a number of historical examples to illustrate its point, the first paragraph closes with the remark that "we should hold off from espousing prevailing opinions and judge them by way of reason, not by common word."[2] This reason is individual reason, which often diverges from collective preconceptions, as Montaigne never ceases reiterating throughout all three books of the *Essays*. Montaigne's recommendations call for a twofold effort: remain aloof

135

from received ideas and, in that state of relative detachment, give empirical reason its full reign. However, the close, symbiotic relationship between individual reason and preconceived notions cannot simply be sundered, any more than an individual can hastily slough off one ideology and slip on another. In fact, the strain between perception and preconception constitutes this essay's basic theme.

Yet Montaigne's discussion stresses specific aspects of this issue that in the following century (with Spinoza and, later, with Locke) become buried under the modern discourse on tolerance. In referring to Brazil (or, as the sixteenth-century French called it, "Antarctic France"), Montaigne observes "that there is nothing barbarous or savage about that nation, from what I've been told, except that everyone calls barbarism what follows other customs; indeed, it seems that we have no other standard of truth and reason than the example and idea of the opinions and customs in the country where we are. *There* is always the perfect religion, the perfect government, the perfect and accomplished customs in all things" (203; 152). Confrontation with the other, with what is unfamiliar or unknown, provokes judgment. Rather than critiquing a bland and unassuming ethnocentrism, this passage evinces a concern with how that predictable knowledge and judgment of the other come about. It's a question of measure, of the standard against which the other is measured and found wanting. This target (*mire* is the actual word Montaigne uses) stands off in the distance, the object of the mind's eye, which measures the shortcomings accordingly. This standard is furnished by the example or idea we have projected of our own country's opinions and customs, not the opinions and customs themselves. Thus the idea or idealized example becomes the measure against which all others are perceived by default.

Shifting the question of otherness to the plane of mental image or figure has profound consequences for considering European encounters with unknown others and for tracing their assimilation into the discourses of Western knowledge. This shift was also necessary for confirming the essay's own discursive authority and explaining how it avoids falling prey to imposing inapplicable ideal images. Much of Montaigne's information was based on the eyewitness account of a man in his employ:

> The man I had was simple and unrefined, a condition proper to bearing true witness; for clever people observe more things and more curi-

ously, but they offer glosses on them; and to make their interpretation more effective and persuasive, they cannot help altering history a little. They never represent things as they are [*choses pures*], but bend and mask them according to the facet [*visage*] they glimpsed; and to give credence to their judgment and attract you to it, they are prone to add something to the matter, to stretch it out and amplify it. (202; 151–152)

No historical account, no matter how accurate, is insulated from the ideas and figures of understanding. But Montaigne's information was reliable because his conduit, whether by nature or because of lack of education, had no inclination or means to embellish his story and therefore remove the account even further from the experience it tells. Thus from the perspective of historical veracity, that is, of experience less subjected to discursive artifice, Montaigne's essay seemingly rests on firm ground.

But in the essay the question of otherness, of how the other merges with multiple discourses, becomes enmeshed in modes of understanding, arises rather in the more elaborate reports of the "clever people." These persons, *"fines gens"* in Montaigne's French, are more refined, discursively aware, and integrate their experiences more readily into prevailing knowledge, if only because they must convince their knowing public. The description of these finer observers' methods enumerates all the elements in the modern economy of discourse. It presupposes a historical basis, experience marked to a lesser degree by preconceived ideas, that then receives discursive elaboration according to the general precepts of rhetoric. In this process of rhetorical appropriation and diffusion, both branches of classical rhetoric, persuasion and figuration, have intertwined roles to play. These imaginative persons in Montaigne's presentation gloss, interpret, and transform history to meet the demands of persuasion; they represent by means of figures, masking things to reproduce the visage that appeared to them, modifying the matter in all its dimensions.

All discourse proceeds by figuration, even those discourses that consider the figurative process, as Montaigne's figure of "clever people" shows. The *Essays* in their entirety repeatedly examine this question and define this irrepressible tendency to realign experience with discourse as consciousness itself. In the essay on experience, for example: "There is more to do in interpreting interpretations than in interpreting things, and there are more books about books than about any other subject: we do nothing but write glosses among ourselves."[3] Immaterial because they derive less from things than from idealized discourses, the glosses that this statement describes result from modern discursive understanding generally. Yet in the context of the "cannibals" or, more precisely, the radical others of sixteenth-century Europe, this immaterial figuration finds a test case: encountering the unknown cracks open the material constraints of the historical experience and of the figuration process that assimilates it. Although his concerns led him elsewhere, Montaigne's portrayal of the discursive economy of otherness summarized the terms of the debate in the sixteenth century and has been decisive for subsequent reflection on the historical grounds of representing otherness.

In the wake of the so-called epoch of discovery, the relationship between the historical and its figuration, which in the perpetual circulation of figures becomes an avalanche of idealized images, most generally of literary origin, was from the outset and has remained a key problem in modern historical understanding. As the preceding chapter indicated, Friedrich Schlegel's conception of literary history drew heavily on the fact that Camões's epic *The Lusiads* had a historical basis and that Camões was better able to depict the events because of his own personal and historical experience in the East. In effect, Camões's epic plays an exemplary role in representing European self-consciousness and the Portuguese spirit as metonymically representative of it. In tracing Vasco da Gama's successful foray to the East, thus paving the way for European colonization, *The Lusiads* enshrines the physical and ideological engagement with the other. The poem, conceived and written more than fifty years after the events it reenacts and published eight years before the first edition of Montaigne's *Essays,* was built on all available information of the time it relates, including eyewitness accounts and historical elaborations. Its goal was to idealize, to render an idealized literary version, of these historical events. In the words of a twentieth-century scholar, *The Lusiads* "is a remarkable poetic record of the rise of Portugal and its emergence as a power of European importance and the creator of the first modern overseas empire."[4] It has itself become a part of the historical record.

From the very beginning, the relationship between idealization and the history it embodies has been an issue for *The Lusiads*. One of the poem's most celebrated and, at the same time, contested passages concerns the appearance of the figure Adamastor. The figure rises up at a crucial moment in the voyage, at what is today called the Cape of Good

Hope; in the flow of the poem, it stands near the midpoint. In the economy of the historical narrative, Adamastor appears at the moment when Vasco da Gama rounds the cape and reaches beyond his predecessor for the first time. Passing through the figure, which in the poem's account takes some doing, breaks the barrier of the unknown. Ultimately, the disjuncture between the historical and the figural, between experience and its idealization, come to a head in the looming figure of Adamastor.

The first critical work to tackle the Adamastor passage head-on, in its historical and figural implications, is José Agostinho de Macedo's *Critical Reflections on the Adamastor Episode,* which was published in 1811, one year before Schlegel's *History.*[5] Because of Macedo's thrashing and at times outrageous critique of Camões, the work has been largely ignored by the imposing institution of Camonian studies. In Teófilo Braga's panorama of Portugal's literary production, which created the twentieth-century paradigm for Portuguese literary history, Macedo's text is mentioned as the low point in Portugal's cultural life: "Imitating the rhetorical criticism of the French pseudo-classicists, the priest José Agostinho de Macedo decided to crudely analyze the Adamastor episode in 1811, when Portuguese nationhood was at the point of extreme degradation."[6] Here Braga is implicitly referring to the Napoleonic invasion and the transfer of the Portuguese court to Brazil, which turned Portugal into a colony of the Brazilian empire. Nor was its idealized identity secure: Portugal had no literary history in 1811; following Schlegel's model, it came into existence with the revival of Camões and the nation in the 1820s. In Braga's own construction of Portuguese literary identity, this moment serves as the negative backdrop against which Portuguese literary consciousness emerges. In the words of Braga's history, Macedo's interrogation of the Adamastor figure belonged to that decadent period: "In the *Gazeta de Lisboa* of 26 December 1811, one could read in the announcement of *As Reflexões sobre o Episodio de Adamastor* that it manifestly demonstrated the greatest incoherence of Luiz de Camões. Such was the state in which Portuguese literary culture was found at that time" (658n). In subsequent histories, Macedo's criticism of Camões has been excluded from the critical tradition just as effectively as Braga suppressed the "critical" in Macedo's title.

Critical Reflections constitutes a peculiar document in tone, in theme, and in its forthright awareness of its own heretical position vis-à-vis

Camões and *The Lusiads*. Its preface, defensively entitled "To Whoever May Want to Read," remarks on its own hereticism:

> When his students noticed some absurdity that escaped the most distinguished writers of antiquity, Quintilian asked them always to proceed very modestly and circumspectly, keeping in mind that the writers were great men [*Varões*]. I would be for this canon of rhetoric if it could prove to me that the ancients had the authority to write with impunity whatever nonsense [*disparates*] they wanted; and if the modern masters want this rule to be observed, let them show me the reason why a Giant is to have the freedom to produce absurdities, and why a Pygmy is not to have the freedom to say: "This, Mr. Giant, is absurd." (iii)

In the theatrical scene portrayed here, with Macedo representing himself as a pygmy confronting a personified literary giant, the pygmy claims that his modernity gives him the right to denounce absurdities. The mention of *"Varão"* extends the rhetoric of personification to the first line of *The Lusiads*, *"As armas e os barões assinalados"* (Arms and those distinguished heroes), which collectively incarnates the Portuguese ideal at the same time that it reveals a link to the Virgilian model (*"arma virumque cano"*). In this instance, though, the "nonsense," the disparity (*disparate*) that Macedo is going to point out, is the Adamastor figure.

According to Macedo, the figural disparities in *The Lusiads* are irremediable, and while the Adamastor passage proves to be their summation, they implicate other levels of discourse residing along the axis extending from history to figuration. In attempting to articulate these disparities, Macedo sets out to prove that Camões did not write poetry but prose: "In the long poem of *The Lusiads* almost everything is mere prose [*mera prosa*], with the difference that the more poetry was expected, the more intolerable it becomes" (5). Such an accusation is obviously meant to be provocative, combining with negative pronouncements regarding the poem's "frigid and prosaic style" (6), which is his way of saying that *The Lusiads* is unsuccessful in idealizing the historical events it recounts: in other words, that its figuration fails and its literary status is unfounded. Beyond a simple provocation, however, Macedo's *Critical Reflections* seeks to demonstrate textually why, from its narrow perspective, *The Lusiads* is bereft of poetry and full of prose: "Numerous passages of pure, rigorous history that you find in *The Lusiads* have been translated by

Camões from Barros without doing anything more than rhyme and re-cast the chaste prose of this illustrious writer" (7). From within the con-fines of Macedo's neoclassical mindset, history is the language of repre-sentation, which could be the basis for poetry, but Camões falls short of producing idealized discourse and succeeds only in rhyming the prose. "To recast" *(rebater)* is the prosaic word par excellence; in Littré's defini-tion of the French equivalent, *rebattre* is akin to the production of clichés; his example of its usage is, *"Ce ne sont que des lieux communs, des thèmes usés et rebattus"* (They are nothing but commonplaces, worn-out and recast subjects).[7] Macedo's allusion to Camões's literary failure be-comes one of *Critical Reflections'* litanies: Camões "never stopped trans-lating Barros, and without altering the meaning or phrases, without re-membering even to give it a poetic hue, he is content to rhyme those very plebeian expressions" (9). For Macedo, because Barros was a histo-rian, prose was his proper mode of expression and utilizing common-place language was to his advantage and credit. Camões, however, pro-duced some sort of a hybrid, an anomalous writing that did not clearly represent the events of history, for its language, though "merely prose," could not be entirely reduced to description; it did not achieve the status of poetry or literature because it was unable to rise above historical rep-resentation. *Critical Reflections'* description of this in-between writing, which belongs neither to the rational discourse of history nor the figural invention of the poet, identifies the problem as one of translation, of transfer from one domain to another.

Ultimately Macedo's efforts to specify the figural abnormality of Adamastor, its rhetorical abomination, lead him to reiterate the parade of oppositions used in determining the status of the literary artifact, in-cluding originality and imitation, poetry and prose, and history and imagination. *The Lusiads* jumbles the contraries, short-circuiting the clear and distinct schemas. Even the customary pair of form and content prove problematic: "There is nothing in Camões that we can properly call his own, for if the content is his, the form is foreign; and if the versification is his (which rarely happens), the subject matter is from elsewhere, and borrowed" (11). From a rhetorical standpoint, this sen-tence enacts a classical, logical chiasmus that, nevertheless, displays none of the chiasmus's typical rhetorical power. Instead of locking form and content into a symmetrical vise, this chiasmus subjects both form and content to the process of translation, to an insistent foreignness.

There is no moment of resolution: the disjuncture between form and content is complete and asynchronous; no discursive imagery congeals to heal the disparity. Situated along the same fault as Montaigne's preoccupation with the passage from history into discourse and the tension between preconceived ideas and experience, *The Lusiads'* failings derive from Camões's supposed inability to create a coherent idealization that sublimates its sources.

In *Critical Reflections,* the passage of *The Lusiads* in which the figure of Adamastor appears becomes the primary focus of the critique. As a figure, Adamastor brings together the negative prosaic elements in the poem (as Macedo defines them), for, as his reading carefully illustrates, it is borrowed in substance and form and is unreasonable. Only indirectly connected with Macedo's critique, however, the Adamastor figure stands at a crossroads in the poem. It is a turning point in the narrative: the figure textually marks the moment when Vasco da Gama's fleet supersedes the farthest point reached by the voyage of Bartolomeu Dias; the story finds its reason for being in successfully traversing the cape, at which point a distinct da Gama begins to exist. Historically, on a parallel with the epic's storyline, the cape remained a barrier to Portuguese colonization. Finally, the figure of Adamastor has an epistemological charge that exceeds both the narrative and its historical inspiration: it works as a hinge between the known and the unknown.

In asserting the exemplary status of Adamastor, *Critical Reflections* defines it succinctly: "Abstractly, what is Adamastor? It is a figure, a phantasm, that erupts out of dark cloud [*carregada nuvem*] to appear in the air and at night to Vasco da Gama in the moment when he was passing the Cape of Good Hope" (15–16). This passage presents in microcosm what Macedo's thin pamphlet wrestles with throughout its entire length. The description it presents closely follows the language of the poem itself; at the cape "a figure reveals itself in the air" (V.39.i–ii), seemingly emanating "at night" from a "dark cloud" (V.37.v–38.i). Contrary to Macedo's claims of abstraction, his characterization of the figure literally restates that of *The Lusiads.* There is, though, one evident addition: the reference to the figure as "phantasm." Instead of a stable figure that functions like terrestrial representations of an original and always recoverable Platonic idea, this phantasm seems to represent nothing, to resist idealization. This phantasmic quality, which makes Adamastor an inappropriate figure, a figure *manquée,* is what troubles neoclassical Macedo. In fact, *Critical Reflections'* stated goal is to "throw this phantasm to the ground once and for all" (13).

Methodologically, analysis of the Adamastor episode pursues the same line of argument as in the earlier analysis of the poem's prosaicness. Yet the Adamastor figure was borrowed in both meaning and form: while the "matrix idea" (15) comes from Lucan, numerous other aspects are derived from Virgil, Benivieni, Sannazaro, Ariosto, and Ovid.[8] Neverthe-less, it is in Macedo's understanding of the passage as nonsensical or dis-parate that the question of prosaic otherness—that is, of the phantasm or, in contemporary idiom, the simulacrum—comes to bear most force-fully.[9] In denouncing Adamastor's disparateness, *Critical Reflections* re-peats itself to the saturation point: "Among the disparities [*os disparates*] of Luiz de Camões, the Adamastor episode is the greatest" (13); "this was the greatest among the disparities of *The Lusiads*" (28); "I judge that with this critical analysis, you will be convinced that among the dispari-ties of *The Lusiads,* this episode is the greatest disparity" (28). While the disparate nature of the passage refers to the episode as a whole, the epi-sode is defined by and is coextensive with presence of the figure, which does not appear again.

But what is disparate about the episode? Given Macedo's preoccupa-tions with verisimilitude, *Critical Reflections* raises questions about the logic of its appearance, about how it diverges from what would be its reasonable presence in the narrative. For example, why, in *The Lusiads,* does it make itself known to da Gama instead of to Dias? After all, Dias did squeeze past the cape, if only to turn back before beginning up the eastern coast of Africa. Yet the notion of disparateness necessarily links the Adamastor figure to an abuse of language, the denouement toward which Macedo's critical narrative builds from the outset: "the last of my reasons for calling it the mother of disparities [*altissimo disparate*] is what follows" (28). What follows is a discussion of the figure and its ca-pacity to use language. Whereas the episode treats the passage around the cape, the figure Adamastor recounts his own narrative to explain his generation from a living being into a geographical location. (Specifically, in the poem, Adamastor is a godlike figure who in the wake of a series of events becomes the cape's terra firma.) Thus Adamastor undergoes a transition in terms of being, which Macedo calls a "transubstantiation" (29), a movement from one substance to another. Accordingly, metamorphosis "is a passage from human nature to another nature, whether that nature is vegetable, endowed with sensibility though brutish, or possessing sensibility and organization" (28–29). Macedo judges non-sense or disparities in light of an ontology of nature and the qualities that should accompany respective states of being. Under the gaze of logic, then, whoever becomes transformed into a mountain or stone cannot by nature speak, for as Macedo remarks, they must lose their "sensible and rational nature" (29). This is the crux of Adamastor's disparateness: if Adamastor was not the cape, then he lied when making such an assertion to da Gama, but if he had really been transformed into the cape, then he could not have spoken (29–30). As Macedo concludes, "the magnitude of the disparity" derives from this "contradiction, an ab-surdity, that reveals a manifest lack of judgment" (30). The Adamastor figure not only personifies an inanimate object, a geographical place, but also takes on human trappings as part of his essence: he feels, speaks, and loves.

But, more problematic, the figure of Adamastor introduces an unre-solvable temporal disjuncture. The human figure recounts how he be-came the cape, that is, he tells his story after he is no longer a human figure. The figure's disparateness brings about an unresolvable contra-diction that defies logic, negates it. The operation of the disparate figure boils down to what seems to be a simple formula: "if it speaks it lies." Yet the critique does not address prosopopeia as such (the cape's speaking) but the fact that Adamastor's prosopoetic narrative contradicts his trans-formation; in Macedo's conception of evolutionary change that is being told, the loss of language would be a prerequisite for the transition. In other words, when the Portuguese arrive at the cape, they meet the Adamastor figure, its personification. In rhetorical terms, this is a classi-cal prosopopeia, giving voice to a nonhuman protagonist so that it can play an active role in the representation. However, in this case, the hu-man figure of Adamastor creates a temporal anomaly (which Macedo designates as a *disparate*): He tells the story of his transformation from a human figure into the cape's hard earth. Therefore, either the Portuguese arrived before the figure became the cape, and what the figure recounts as past is the future; or the figure is caught in a structure of repetition, much like a time warp in the worlds of science fiction, which perpetu-ally upsets the economy of figural representation in which the proper meaning knows its place.

Despite the bizarre nature of Macedo's text, the disparity the author unearths in the Adamastor figure constitutes a productive insight into the vagaries of figuration. Francisco Rodrigues Lôbo's *Corte na aldeia* (1619), which contains the sole Portuguese reference to *disparate* as a rhetorical term, underscores other aspects of the notion that have proved decisive in interpretations of Adamastor, as well as of the figure of Camões: "disparate writings seem in their words to diverge from their purpose [and] lead one to understand, as if in an enigma, the thought of whoever writes them."[10] Here the rhetorical figure applied to Adamastor is revealed as a figure of thought. In the Camonian tradition, however, the mandate to solve this enigmatic figure, to find the thought of which it is the figure, has amalgamated Adamastor's stature with that of Camões and of *The Lusiads* in its entirety. In other words, the question of Adamastor, of its figural disparity, inevitably comes back to Portuguese history, on the one hand, and Camões's lived experience, on the other. In addition to its problematic otherness, the cape, given voice by Adamastor, is the node where these issues come together.

Apart from Macedo's transgressive comments, the tradition of Camonian interpretation universally views this narrative moment (that is, rounding the cape and Adamastor's appearance) as the "episode of singular importance in the economy of *The Lusiads*."[11] Beginning at least with Francisco Leitão Ferreira's *Nova arte de conceitos* (1718–1721), the passage is singled out as exemplary of Camões's great art.[12] In later texts, such as that of Teófilo Braga, Adamastor becomes an aesthetic topos; in combating Macedo's attacks on this figure, Braga claims instead that the episode represents proof of successful idealization and that Macedo confused the "truth of history" and the "truth of art": "The old myths were used as symbols, along with a synthesizing intuition. It was this state of consciousness that saved Camões from banality; the representation of the giant Adamastor is the complete success of his aesthetic process in which the truth reflects his personal impressions in passing the Cape of Storms."[13] Endorsing the same theory of knowledge advanced by *Critical Reflections*, Braga presents the counterimage of its interpretation, asserting an accomplished (aesthetic) synthesis where Macedo saw only a hodgepodge of alien sources. Thus Braga will go on to say, in reference to the Adamastor figure, that "Camões's idealization was based on the knowledge [or experience, as in Schlegel: *conhecimento*] of tremendous shipwrecks" (650). Adamastor's disparity finds resolution in Camões's consciousness, which brings together personal impressions, historical experience, and figural expression to produce an idealized representation. And as Braga himself mentions (648), it is well known that giants, monsters, and other nonhuman forms of otherness are textually significant and bear on epistemological concerns.

The figure of Adamastor has assumed such proportions that it has come to overshadow and even engulf the figure of Camões. In *A literatura portuguesa e a expansão ultramarina,* Hernâni Cidade, perhaps the most influential twentieth-century reader of *The Lusiads,* who has literally defined the parameters of its study, describes Adamastor as "the most impressive creation of Camões's epic genius. The giant emerges [*ergue-se*] at the Cape of Storms, later called the Cape of Good Hope, because it was the passage from the gloomy mysteries of the Atlantic to the magnificent certainties of the East Indies and the Orient. And it emerged as if it brought together all the tragic gloom, all the terrifying legends that our audacity had been dissipating beyond the Atlantic, and there, so to speak, they made their final stand against us."[14] This anachronistic historical narrative, endowing past actors with consciousness of future events, illustrates the cape's historical importance to Portuguese and, by extension, European self-consciousness. As a temporal projection, it repeats the very disparity that underlay the cape's figuration. The travelogues and narratives of the time, even the "official" ones, are more apprehensive than certain about the Orient; as Cidade points out, even the European name of Africa's cape underwent a subsequent name change to redirect its historical meaning. The cape was a barrier that, once breached, became a turning point, and Adamastor is its figure.

A great deal hinges on this figure, for it articulates the known and the unknown, but discursively, as Camões's figure in all its ambiguity, its national prominence is linked with that of Camões no less than with the voyage of discovery. The figure "emerges," but more literally it "raises up" (*ergue-se*), poetically comes into view against the backdrop of dissipating fog—or, as Cidade would have it, in dispersing the tales that stand in lieu of knowledge. This discursive "arising" suggests a phenomenal emergence out of a continuum. Passed around from critic to critic, this description of Adamastor had by the eighteenth century already wended its way into French; as Voltaire writes: "It is a phantom that emerges [*s'élève*] from the bottom of the sea."[15] In Cidade's text, the figurality of Camões is expressed in precisely the same terms as the

Adamastor figure: "Luís de Camões emerges [*ergue-se*] at the historical moment that is singularly adequate to making his genius and his work the synthesis of the Fatherland" (259). The literary idealization of Portugal, itself crucial to the deployment of European literary history and the respective national self-identities it fosters, rests squarely on Adamastor, figure of radical otherness.

In building the discursive web of historical reference, Cidade's formulation repeatedly surfaces in the work of other commentators. In C. M. Bowra's *Heroic Poetry,* for example, which analytically restates the topos, the figure displays a dual function: "Adamastor symbolizes a natural obstacle, the passage around the Cape of Storms, the point where East meets West and disasters are common . . . The grisly and revolting phantom is an apt symbol of the horrors which may well appall those who break into the waters where no man has sailed before."[16] This last phrase takes up Camões's refrain recurring throughout the poem (*"mares nunca dantes navegados"*), a commonplace that draws a line at the cape. The figure analytically breaks down into two categories (for which Bowra uses the word *symbol*): on the one hand, it inscribes a finite obstacle; on the other, it marks the limit whose far side is accessible only by figuration because it resides beyond the known. A very different reader of *The Lusiads,* Reis do Brasil, gives a more historical slant to his commentary. First, as an expression of "phenomenal" experiences: "[T]he giant is the symbol of all the maritime difficulties of our voyages of discovery, difficulties that culminated in the passage of the Cape of Good Hope"; then, what I have called its epistemological charge: "Since this Cape represents a decisive moment in the evolution of discovery, Camões has to let it echo this occult feeling."[17] Although these general interpretations are omnipresent, Reis do Brasil broadens the spectrum somewhat by inscribing it into a temporal trajectory—the evolution of discovery—that has been necessary not only for conceptualizing history but also for establishing that Europe is the bearer of that history.

Furthermore, this figure, the historical cape and its idealized expression, belong to the modern regime of secular discourse and etch the infinite unknown in an understanding of historical finitude. In Saraiva's reinscription of these terms, "the gods of the sea and the giant Adamastor attempt to place limits before the audacity of men, which is a conquest of divinity."[18] In other words, transgressing these limits buttresses human agency and forces a reconceptualization of the relationship between human and divine. For Saraiva, this figure provides a linchpin for a general theory of personification in modernity: "Through mythology, Camões expresses some profound tendencies of the Renaissance: the victory of men over gods, who personify the limits that tradition opposed to human initiative, the confidence in the human capacity to dominate nature" (195). The personified limits are figural, just as their supersession is discursive. Caught up in this secular constellation, the Adamastor figure plays a profound historical role. But its relationship to history, its finite inscription of infinitude, cannot be subsumed under the concept of representation. That is the nature of its disparity.

In retracing the voyage of Vasco da Gama and the history of Portugal, Camões had at his disposal and made use of a number of texts related to Portuguese expansion. *The Lusiads* departed from this record of finite experience, won out of a discursive struggle with infinity, to produce an idealized understanding that would bring the infinitude of the unknown down to human scale. The events of fifteenth- and sixteenth-century voyages spawned a rash of narratives, which in Portugal constituted a historical record preserved as part of the national patrimony. As was customary in the incipient historical discourse of modernity, the accounts focused on events, and abstraction from and about those events was rare. Two of the most important texts that treat Vasco da Gama's voyage and in which the passing of the cape figures prominently are João de Barros's *Asia; dos feitos que os portugueses fizeram no descobrimento e conquista dos mares e terras do oriente* and Lopes de Castanheda's *História do descobrimento & conquista da India pelos portugueses*.[19] Scholars of *The Lusiads*—and in this respect, Macedo was no exception—consider these historical syntheses as the real history that Camões inscribes in his idealized rendering. In *The Lusiads,* the cape's figuration marks the intersection of Dias's and da Gama's voyages at the southern tip of Africa.

These respective narratives of the Portuguese discovery and conquest take a different point of departure: Castanheda's account begins after completion of the preparations for da Gama's voyage and therefore does not include Dias's expedition, which was merely a precursor for da Gama's (more) successful voyage; Barros, attracted more by the process of discovery, also recounts the earlier events leading up to da Gama's voyage to India. Although each narrative treats differently the two expeditions' point of intersection in southern Africa, their presupposed context is the same. After arriving at the cape, Dias's ships turned back before they could head north and thus free themselves of the obstacle that was the African continent. For da Gama's subsequent expedition, therefore, the cape represented a crucial moment in the voyage that was as much epistemological as physical. For the technology of the time, negotiating the cape constituted a formidable challenge: the Agulhas Current flowing from the Indian Ocean, combined with the effects of the Benguela Current coming from the South Atlantic, created an imposing hurdle. This physical, finite challenge was simultaneously a site of uncertainty, an engagement with the unknown that only the imagination could represent.

In this age of "discovery," representation was a practical issue related to geographical surveying and territorial claims. Portuguese explorers at least since Diogo Cão (1481) carried with them stone markers *(padrões)* to represent Portuguese claims, although symbolically, as a representational extension of Portugal, they function not unlike flags on the moon. During the voyage, Dias placed one of these stone pillars at each point he deemed significant, a practice that would be followed by da Gama and others. The word *padrão* figurally reenacts the function it fulfills. *Padrão* derives from *pedra* (stone), demonstrating an intermediary form of *pedrão*, clearly an augmentative of *pedra*. Yet *padrão* appears in other contexts, with other meanings, and with another derivation: *padrão* as "model, pattern" is said to derive from the Latin *patronu* (ultimately, *pater,* father) and is linked to numerous other words in Portuguese such as *padre* (father), *patrão* (boss or, more generally, "the one who gives orders"), and *pátria* (fatherland).[20] The circulation of *padrão* attests to the figurality of the role that it will play in representing Portugal and in plotting the coordinates of the Portuguese empire. This mixture of lines of derivation leads to historical judgments on *The Lusiads* that underscore the stone marker's larger figural context: *"Camões construiu n'Os Lusíadas um padrão eterno à soberania da pátria"* (In *The Lusiads* Camões erected an eternal pillar to the sovereignty of the fatherland).[21]

In Barros's account, Dias's encounter with the cape results in the placing of a stone pillar. In fact, the Dias fleet, which underwent such difficulty in passing the cape as to name it the Cape of Storms, did not know when they passed it. Dias could have sailed to India instead of da Gama, but his sailors reached a point beyond which they would go no farther, claiming that they had done enough exploring; they said "that it was enough of any voyage to have discovered so much coast and they had already gotten the most information [*nouidáde*] they could out of that discovery: they found that the land ran almost universally to the east, from which it seemed to them that back a ways was some great cape, and it would be wiser to turn around and discover it."²² This confusion regarding the unknown, the very end of the known, is repeated with the placing of Dias's final pillar; having convinced his men to go a few more days, immediately before turning back to "discover" and name the cape, he set down his most distant pillar from Portugal, representing the endpoint of his voyage (although he did travel a few leagues beyond it). The exact location of this pillar has thereafter been controversial, despite Barros's unequivocal statement that it was placed on what is today called St. Croix Island: "Having arrived at St. Croix Island, it was with a great deal of sadness and feeling that Dias departed from the pillar that he placed there, as if he left behind a son who would be exiled forever" (87). Each description of the discovery seems to favor its own personification, for just as Adamastor recounts his turning into a clump of rocks, so the stone representative of Portugal becomes a son who can only represent the land (being *desterrado*) but can never be a part of it. This dramatic description follows from Barros's correlation between the placement of pillars and the act of discovery itself (88).

Thenceforth, the voyage's uncertainty is associated not with the cape specifically but with the area surrounding this last Dias pillar. In Barros's narrative, for example, da Gama passed the cape with no trouble at all, "without as much storm and danger as the sailors expected, owing to the current of opinion among them, which gave rise to the name of Cape of Storms" (129). Nevertheless, this passage from Barros does indicate very briefly the way in which circulating stories (*"a opiniã que entrelles andáua"*) mediated the understanding of the course of their voyage. And although Barros does not elaborate on the difficulty in passing Dias's final pillar, at that moment of the voyage, the text overtly refers to the link between the first experience of storms and unknown seas: "And as this was the first storm that the sailors had experienced in unknown seas and climates [*em q os mareãtes se tinhã visto, em mares e climas nã sabidos*], they were so beside themselves [*andavã tã fóra de sy*] that the only thing they could agree on was to call out for God, being more concerned about penitence for their sins than in managing the sails, for everything had a shadow of death" (130–131).

In the fifteenth century, the ocean was infinitude itself, a fact difficult to grasp in an epoch when the earth can be seen in its orbit. The unknown calls forth speculation, and the sailors had soaked up layers of stories and had very specific expectations regarding the experiences that awaited them. The shadow of death, the personification of an event beyond which one knows nothing, restates the intermingling of known and unknown, discursive understanding and experience, and designating the primacy of one over the other is no simple matter.

In Castanheda's version the passing of the pillar took the form of a repetition: the ships passed it, only to find that they were again alongside it:

> And on this same day [when they realized they had gone backward] the fleet again passed along the same course [*passar a mesma carreira*] that it had passed, taking advantage of a strong stern wind that lasted three or four days and with which it broke through the currents [*rõpeo as corretes*] that they feared they would be unable to pass through. And thus they all proceeded, very pleased to have passed beyond where Bertolomeu Dias had reached, and Vasco da Gama pressed them on, saying that therefore God wanted them to find India.[23]

Discovery and the subsequent colonization entailed acts of violence, which have been endlessly catalogued even by their perpetrators, but Castanheda's text indicates that the violence is no less epistemological: a rupture, a breaking of the currents that also constituted a barrier in their understanding of the voyage. This act of force, overcoming the physical as well as conceptual obstacle, paved the way for the journey's successful conclusion. And because history, which depends on pathbreaking events to deploy its narration, is written to record and produce understanding, these events' discursive inscription takes on greater importance than the underlying natural obstacles that occasioned it. Thus, not unlike da Gama's fleet, Camões "broke new ground," as Voltaire remarked: the very narration of history hinges on this rupture.

In writing his history, Castanheda had access to what is now called the *Roteiro da primeira viagem de Vasco da Gama* (*The Logbook of Vasco da Gama's First Voyage*), the only text of the discovery written during the voyage by an actual participant (although there are still debates as to which of the crew actually kept the journal). Not only does Castanheda's detailed account indicate his knowledge of the text, but he frequently borrows entire phrases, a procedure highlighted when comparing his account of passing the Dias marker with the equivalent passage in the *Roteiro*. Since the nineteenth-century constitution of Portuguese history, the logbook has enjoyed a privileged status in the pantheon of national relics.[24] As Barros and Castanheda indicated, the passage around the cape posed no difficulty whatsoever. According to the definitive version of the *Roteiro,* this easy passage stemmed from the sailors' foreknowledge of the currents: they took what is known as the "indirect route," which from that moment forward served as the guide for all fleets going to the East (106–107). But the passage around the other edge of southern Africa, that is, in the vicinity where Dias's pillar was located (the exact location of which is still not entirely agreed upon, given the texts' numerous discrepancies), proved more problematic, as Castanheda's description intimated. In the words of the *Roteiro:*

> On the following Saturday [December 16] we passed the last [Dias] pillar . . .
>
> The following night we lay to, for we had gone as far as the Rio do Infante [presumably today's Groot Vis River], which was the last land that Bartolomeu Dias discovered. And on the following day [December 17] we proceeded with a stern wind, running along the coast until the evening hours, when the eastern wind sprang upon us and we veered out to sea [*fizemos na volta do mar*]. And we continued veering toward the sea and alternately toward the land [*andamos com uma volta ao mar e outra à terra*] until Tuesday [December 19] around sunset, when the western wind returned. Therefore that night we lay to so that on the next day we could reconnoiter the land or passage where we were. And when morning [December 20] came, we went straight to land and at ten o'clock we found ourselves at [*achamonos com*] St. Croix Island, which was sixty leagues abaft what we had figured. And this was caused by the currents, which here are very strong.
>
> And on this same day we passed along the course that we had already passed, with a strong stern wind that lasted three or four days, where we broke through [*rompemos*] the currents, which we were afraid would not let us have what we desired [*a que nós haviamos grande mêdo de não nos deixar haver aquilo que desejávamos*]. And from that day on God in his mercy wanted us to go forward and not aft: may it please him that it be thus always.[25]

According to the journal entries, the part of the trip that was repeated corresponded to the coast between St. Croix Island—where both Barros and Castanheda asserted Dias's last pillar to be, although the modern view is that the pillar was five leagues to the east of today's Bird Island, which is approximately ten leagues from St. Croix Island—and the Groot Vis, or Great Fish, River, which was the farthest point that Dias reached. Da Gama's fleet traversed the distance between these two points three times, for when they reached the Great Fish River, they could not move beyond Dias's endpoint but rather unknowingly retraced their path, in zig-zag fashion, turning first toward the land and then toward the sea. The third time over the same stretch of coast was merely a repetition of the first, direct course to the Great Fish River, at which point they "broke through the currents" and assured—at least in retrospect—the success of the voyage.

Although Castanheda's text takes greater pains than that of Barros with the description of this moment of the voyage, it nonetheless focuses on the result, the concluding paragraph of the passage cited from the *Roteiro*, which Castanheda's account repeats almost word for word. Yet there is a major difference: the author of the *Roteiro*, writing at the same time as the events transpired, attempts to conceptualize and record the activity of the actors themselves, and writes in the first person. In Castanheda's account, the first person shifts to third person, the historical tense that in the Western tradition has come to indicate distance, disinterested description, and veracity. Thus "fleet" becomes the subject of the actions. The conceptual and narrative distinctions between these two representations are striking: the first-person agent has no knowledge of the future, and its narrative propels itself differently than that of Castanheda, whose title proclaims its subject to be about the discovery and conquest of India. In the *Roteiro*'s narrative, "what we desired" has a diegetic role to play, for it suggests an orientation, a direction, but not an end, which must remain unknown; "what *they* desired" is an unspecified projection that is founded not on knowledge but on a continuous transition between the known and unknown. In the "historical" text, endless desire must be suppressed because it runs counter to historical discourse, which operates on the basis of an entrenched telos. And in the same way that the specified "India" of Castanheda's history replaces the vague "forward" direction of the *Roteiro*, the nebulous pronouncements of God speaking for himself—textually, that is—are made finite by allowing da Gama to speak for him and act out the interpretation. Thus these shifts underwrite the process of personification that attributes religious and patriotic feeling to da Gama—and, by extension, to his men. While none of these texts inscribes the empirical event in its unmediated facticity, they form the historical backdrop that Camões's *Lusiads* subjects to more intense idealization.

In *The Lusiads,* Adamastor's appearance marks the episode of rounding the cape and moving beyond the limits associated with the Dias expedition. The very structure of the Adamastor episode is intricate, for it functions in the poem as an autonomous narrative that offers a terrain for other self-contained narratives. This narratological relationship becomes possible because of the passage's peculiar figuration, both in terms of historical representation and in the overall figural economy of the poem. As in the poem as a whole, this episode assimilates the historical discourse of Castanheda and Barros, including the impersonality characterizing the language of truth; concurrently, however, the first-person veracity of the witness, here in the "person" of the narrator, duplicates aspects of the discourse recorded in the *Roteiro.* Early in the Adamastor canto, narrator da Gama thematizes the relationship between history and thought, experience and knowledge, which was at the center of Montaigne's reflection and Camões's project of idealization:

> *Os casos vi, que os rudos marinheiros,*
> *Que têm por mestra a longa experiência,*
> *Contam por certos sempre e verdadeiros,*
> *Julgando as cousas só pola aparência,*
> *E que os que têm juízos mais inteiros,*
> *Que só por puro engenho e por ciência*
> *Vêm do mundo os segredos escondidos,*
> *Julgam por falsos ou mal entendidos.*[26]

> (The things I've seen, which rude sailors,
> Who take long experience as their guide,
> Hold always for certain and true,
> Judging things by appearances alone;
> And which those with fuller judgment,
> Who only by pure intelligence and knowledge
> See the world's hidden secrets,
> Judge to be false or poorly understood.)

On the one hand is lived experience that never penetrates beneath the surface; on the other, reflection on those things or events that contradict those appearances. These oppositions, which inhabit human discourse, traverse the entire Western tradition but take on special significance in the context of secularization. Adamastor encapsulates these disparities in a figure of thought that leaves its imprint on the discursive and territorial topography.

After intervening skirmishes on land, Vasco da Gama's crew begins to break into *"os mares nunca de outrem navigados"* ("seas never sailed by others") (V.37.3), which provides the prerequisite unknown and context for Adamastor's manifestation. Initially unfolding in a linear narrative, the episode opens with a placid setting, which is then disrupted by the emergence of the figure, accompanied by a detailed description, all mediated through the first-person narrator. In the episode's first stanza, the calmness is broken by

> *Ũa nuvem, que os ares escurece,*
> *Sobre nossas cabeças aparece.*
> *Tão temerosa vinha e carregada,*
> *Que pôs nos corações um grande medo.* (V.37.7–38.2)

> (A cloud, darkening the skies,
> Appears above our heads,
> So frightful and weighty with darkness
> That it fills our hearts with terror.)

The *"carregada nuvem,"* an inscription of the *disparate*, announces the figure, alluding as well to the uncontrollable weather and currents that have traditionally been ascribed to southern Africa. The lapse (of six lines) between the cloud's appearance and the figure's emergence allows the narrator to evoke a "power" (*"O Potestade"*) to ask what is in store, the first apostrophe in an episode built on apostrophes. And then the narrator says

> *Não acabava, quando ũa figura*
> *Se nos mostra no ar, robusta e válida,*
> *De disforme e grandíssima estatura,*
> *O rosto carregado, a barba esquálida,*
> *Os olhos encovados, e a postura*
> *Medonha e má e a cor terrena e pálida,*
> *Cheios de terra e crespos os cabelos,*
> *A boca negra, os dentes amarelos.*
> *. . . .*
> *Cum tom de voz nos fala horrendo e grosso,*
> *Que pareceu sair do mar profundo.*

Arrepiam-se as carnes e o cabelo
A mi e a todos, só de ouvi-lo e vê-lo. (V.39.1–40.8)

(I had not finished when a figure
Showed itself in the air, rugged and powerful,
Of deformed and enormous stature,
With a gloomy face, a squalid beard,
Cavernous eyes, its posture
Evil and fierce, of pale and earthen hue,
Its kinked hair full of earth,
Black mouth, yellow teeth.
. . . .
It blasts us with a horrible and brutish voice
That seemed to issue from the depths of the sea.
Our hair stands on end and our flesh creeps
Just to see and hear him.)

The appearing figure is disfigured, has a distorted and deformed stature; this portrayal suggests that the figure does not obey the logic of form at all, inscribing instead an otherness not easily grasped by discourse. This dilemma accounts for the narrative necessity of describing the figure in such detail. The figure is a concatenated mass of predicates that does not correspond to forms of experience; the passage's explicit phenomenality mimics the linguistic shift from the figure that disrupts form to the experience of that disruption—thus the horror, terror, and fear at the sight and hearing of the "figure." In other words, the figure's cognitive charge relates to the impenetrable bond between historical and discursive understanding. This incommensurability seems to erect a brick wall that condemns the Camonian tradition to constant reiteration of the problem. In this figure, once again, "Camões provides one of his truly impressive poetic versions of historical reality. Adamastor symbolizes both a natural phenomenon and the dangers of the voyage."[27]

Discursively, new possibilities emerge in the wake of the figure's network of descriptions. Once arisen, qualified, and established in terms of the reactions of those who perceived it, the figure can be attributed with a voice—the voice of Portuguese history. As a textual voice, the figure can recount the past (the time prior to da Gama's voyage) and the future (up until the writing of the poem). The inscribed figure therefore proceeds to apostrophize the Portuguese people (still in Barros's and not in Schlegel's sense): *"O gente ousada"* ("O daring people," V.41.1), you will advance

Por todo o largo mar e pola terra
Que inda hás-de sojugar com dura guerra. (V.42.7–8)

(Over the vast sea and on land
That you are yet to subjugate in difficult war.)

To project the identity of a subject discursively, one must inscribe, idealize an other. In this figure, however, the mechanism of historical representation is laid bare. The Adamastor figure utters in an apostrophe the personified collective self of Portugal, and the juxtaposition of self and other—that is, the Portuguese and the sea and land to be subjugated—is the condition for the appearance of the figure in the first place. Within this framework, the figure recounts various incidents involving the Portuguese and the cape, making up the "historical" narrative of the episode.

Although this brief historical narrative hints at the role that otherness plays in the discourse of colonization, the episode's remaining portions focus more directly on the question of figuration. In the midst of the figure's evocation of the Portuguese, the narrator interrupts with an openly ontological question that redirects the entire course of the narrative:

Mais ia por diante o monstro horrendo
Dizendo nossos fados, quando, alçado,
Lhe disse eu: "Quem és tu? que esse estupendo
Corpo, certo me tem maravilhado!" (V.49.1–4)

(The horrible monster kept on
Telling our fate, when, standing up,
I said to him: "Who are you, whose overwhelming
Body has so astounded me?")

The apostrophe is reversed, and the figure is addressed; the overwhelming body, which cannot be encased in a form and exceeds the referential, requires a name. In fact, the question addresses the figurality of the figure: how does one come to terms with "you," this figure? The figure immediately acknowledges that it is a prosopopeia and then doubly offers its name:

"Eu sou aquele oculto e grande Cabo
A quem chamais vós outros Tormentório,
Que nunca a Ptolomeu, Pompónio, Estrabo,
Plínio, e quantos passaram fui notório.
Aqui toda a africana costa acabo

Neste meu nunca visto promontório[.]

. . . .

Chamei-me Adamastor . . ." (V.50.1–6; 51.3)

("I am that huge and veiled cape
That you call the Cape of Storms,
Never known by Ptolemy and Strabo,
Pomponius and Pliny, among countless others.
Here I cap off all the African coast
In this never viewed promontory.

. . . .

I called myself Adamastor.")

The figure has, so to speak, a split identity, for it makes a distinction between what "you others" call it (*A quem chamais vós outros*) and what the
figure called itself (*Chamei-me Adamastor*). The cape was outside the experience of the ancients; it revealed itself, became known, only to the
Portuguese. Although after Dias's voyage its name was changed to the
Cape of Good Hope, that does not explicitly bear on the alternation
pointed out in *The Lusiads*. This bicephalous answer serves as the response to the narrator's question concerning the figure's identity. Contrary to the reiterated consensus about the Adamastor figure's meaning,
the philological derivation of its name has produced no agreement. For
example, Macedo toiled to show how the name was stolen from various
classical writers, whereas Braga praised it and spent time tracing out its
etymology (652–653).

   The most detailed—and perhaps definitive—discussion of the name,
in Américo da Costa Ramalho's *Estudos camonianos*,[28] is relevant for the
figural concerns inherent in the passage of the cape. The name, instead
of being a mistake owing to Camões's bad Greek or to some other lack
of understanding, seems to have been current during the Renaissance
and appears in a revised version of Nebrija's Latin dictionary (Antwerp,
1545): under the listing "Adamastor" can be found *"nomen gigantis
staturosi."* In confirming that "Adamastor" was in circulation in the sixteenth century, Ramalho wants to defend Camões against the charges of
ignorance that result from the figure being called "Adamastor" instead of
"Damastor." More precisely, however, he wants to free Camões from the
responsibility of contradiction: in returning to Greek to understand the
noun *adamastor,* "the initial 'a' [has] a negative value in contrast to the

agential suffix of 'tor,' which is connected to the verbal stem 'dama' (to dominate)" (33). In other words, in the economy of the poem, it should not be a masterful, dominating figure, for it submits to the Portuguese. Therefore, the distinction between "damastor" and "adamastor" is significant in the poem, for the name emerges as an issue in the context of self and other, in the context of domination. This disjuncture, between a proactive Cape of Storms that provokes disaster and a passive rock outside the economy of domination (a "nondominator"), constitutes the figure of otherness that assimilates the radical unknown to understanding.

Following a narrative pattern that regresses into the past—that is, a narrative constructed through use of the past tense—to explain the present, Adamastor narrates the events that led to his becoming the cape, a prosopopeia that Macedo contended was only a disparity. To establish his genealogy, he crafts his identity in facing a beloved other, in this case the nymph Thetis. In the same way that the idealized Portuguese identity was forged in an economy of otherness, confrontation, and subjugation, the figure Adamastor was waging war to acquire Thetis. (In the ongoing amalgamation of Camões and Adamastor, the editor of the Portuguese national edition of *The Lusiads* remarks that "Adamastor, in the passion he experiences for Thetis, shares some of Camões's nature"![29]) A truce was reached, although Adamastor did not know it was merely a subterfuge: he would stop fighting and she would definitively be his, thus cementing his victory. At this point in his genealogical narrative—when he finally moves toward the conquest of the other, the nymph he loves—the deception becomes unveiled:

> "Já néscio, já de guerra desistindo,
> Ũa noite, de Dóris prometida,
> Me aparece de longe o gesto lindo
> Da branca Tétis, única, despida.
> Como doudo corri, de longe abrindo
> Os braços pera aquela que era vida
> Deste corpo, e começo os olhos belos
> A lhe beijar, as faces e os cabelos.

> "Oh! que não sei de nojo como o conte!
> Que, crendo ter nos braços quem amava,
> Abraçado me achei cum duro monte

De áspero mato e de espessura brava.
Estando cum penedo fronte a fronte,
Que eu polo rosto angélico apertava,
Não fiquei homem, não, mas mudo e quedo
E junto dum penedo outro penedo!" (V.55.1–56.8)

("Like a fool I gave up the war.
One night, as Doris promised,
In the distance appeared to me the beautiful form
Of white Thetis, naked and alone.
I ran like a crazy man, extending out
My arms toward her, life
Of this my body, and I began to kiss
Her eyes, her cheeks, and hair.

"Oh, I am so choked up, I can hardly tell it!
Believing to hold in my arms my beloved
I found myself locked in embrace with a rugged mount
Full of rough woods and thickset wilderness.
Being head to head with a rock
That I held to be that angelic face,
I did not remain a man, no, but became dumb, immobile,
A rock joined to another rock.")

In these stanzas, the language attributed to Adamastor stresses the phenomenal aspect of otherness, of his relationship to Thetis: once he had fulfilled his part of the bargain, she appears to him in the distance. The language literally traces the process of conceptualization: the other gives this body life, although the body cannot achieve wholeness until the other has been conceptualized, which in this passage is literally a grasping. This seems to be a classic repetition of the way that identity is constituted, always through mediation of the other. The moment Adamastor grasped Thetis she disappeared—she turned into him, so to speak, and he realized that the other he reached for was in fact himself. Moreover, it would seem that the Hegelian dream of absoluteness has been realized, for the end product has become a reified clump of rocks; the process of self-consciousness has satisfactorily come to a complete halt: the other is definitively annihilated.[30] Nonetheless, questions remain.

Here resides the motive for Macedo's assertion of the episode's disparateness, which is emblematically expressed in the verb fiquei (in line V.56.7). As in contemporary Portuguese, the infinitive ficar simultaneously means "to remain" and "to become." However, to make sense of the last two lines of stanza 56, it must mean both, a confusion that is overcome only through the double negative: *"Não fiquei homem, não, mas mudo e quedo / E junto dum penedo outro penedo"* ("I did not *remain* a man, no, but *became* dumb, immobile, a rock joined to another rock"). The definitive completion of consciousness not only stops the process of history but also does away with language. The passage confirms that silence, for Adamastor loses his humanity and becomes "mute." Stanza 59 is even more explicit:

> *"Converte-se me a carne em terra dura,*
> *Em penedos os ossos se fizeram;*
> *Estes membros que vês e esta figura*
> *Por estas longas águas se estenderam[.]"* (V.59.1–4)

> ("My flesh gets converted into solid earth
> And my bones made into rocks:
> These limbs that you see and this figure
> Stretched out into these vast waters.")

Reaching out into the boundless waters, the figure, the figure of the cape, is there, solid as a rock; and it tells its own tale of woe, of how it became snared by the other it sought to grasp. Yet how does one come to terms with the voice, and the figure that gives it a mouth, that tells us about its own loss? Macedo's own condemnation merely rejects the episode as a betrayal of logic, which he conceives of solely in the sense of formalistic syllogisms, and places the episode—and the poem as a whole—outside the realm of acceptable discourse. But such policing cannot guarantee that discourse will be free of disparity, particularly when the linguistic mediation that produces the *disparate* must be disparate in order to produce it. In the passage itself, the figure not only debunks its own absolute consciousness in the telling that asserts it; it also reintroduces the other—again, in an apostrophe—that had to be annihilated for that consciousness to close upon itself. As a figure, therefore, Adamastor proves incapable of totalizing otherness but only renders it finite. It is its own negation, its own aberration, the agent that cannot act, the dominator that cannot dominate, the figure that cannot overcome its disparateness.

But Adamastor is more than an inscription of some vague radical otherness. As a prosopopeia indivisible into the contraries of proper and figural meaning, the Adamastor figure opens up a different dimension of sense. It is a secular figure of thought, earthly in its mélange of the literal and the figural, like Melville's reference to "Camoën's Spirit of the Cape, an eclipsing menace mysterious and prodigious,"[31] which prefigures and forebodes at the same time that it acts. The finite economy of meaning produces but does not rely on the primacy of self-consciousness, identity, and instrumental action. Is it merely happenstance that the collision of discoverers with the discovered created this discursive impasse? Conquest must be discursive and immaterial, perhaps to a greater extent than it is bodily oppressive and tangible. Foregrounded in the Portuguese history of nationhood, this encounter has provided the skeletal structure for European self-consciousness as well as coordinates for the multiple historical narratives recounting the course and unity of European culture. In other words, the conquistadors did not simply vanquish "discovered" lands and peoples, the "unknown"; the conquest's most enduring outcome has been the figuration of its accompanying social order and discursive hegemony.

The phantom of Adamastor has not yet been cast to the ground, and every repetition wrestles anew with the historical unknown and its figuration. Like the phantasm of Adamastor, the figure of otherness it inscribes is as old as modernity and has underwritten an adamantine economy of global knowledge. At the contemporary cape, following the collapse of legislated otherness, the Adamastor figure resurfaces to retell his story through five centuries of retrospection. Reappropriating the cape's provocative dimension, André Brink's narrative, *Cape of Storms: The First Life of Adamastor,* takes up the figure, reacting to the "eurocentric revulsion implicit in that image."[32] In the story, the figure becomes another and remains the same, victim of a more intricate and uncontrollable love, and casts a divergent gaze on the events of colonization. Brink's assumptions reveal the general limits within which the narrative unfolds: "Suppose there *were* an Adamastor, a model for the giant of Camões's fanciful history; and suppose that original creature, spirit, or whatever he may have been, has survived through the centuries in a series of disparate successive avatars in order to continue watching over the Cape of Storms: how would *he* look back, from the perspective of the late twentieth century, on that original experience?" (13). An idealized Adamastor anchors a figural projection in time; whereas in *The Lusiads,* the historical unfolding told by the figure applied to the Portuguese, here it applies to the figure itself. The disparity is successive, transposed into time; repetition, powered by the worn and imprecise memory of conscious Adamastor, punctuates the historical duress of colonization.

Nevertheless, the life of Adamastor's modern caprice revolves around yearning for an other, although in this instance the woman of his desire comes from the colonizers' ships. Just as Camões's Adamastor sought to grasp, to possess Thetis, Brink's figure seeks to possess his beloved other in heart, soul, and—especially—body; once the marriage is consummated (a feat whose final accomplishment is prepared throughout the entire book), his beloved is retaken, and Adamastor is successfully domesticated by the sailors, who follow the plot as it evolved in the Portuguese epic. Thus, the trap:

> "Come to the beach tonight and you will have her. There must be no one else with you. We shall bring you the woman. But you must wait patiently until the full moon has fully risen." (132)

And the trap sprung:

> I suddenly noticed the dark figure between me and the dazzling path of the Moon on the water. Motionless, tall, pale, with long hair: the woman . . .
> At full speed I ran into the heavy figurehead. For that was what it was. The figurehead from their main ship, which they had planted in the sand for me. Half dazed, I fell down in the shallow foam. (133)

This modern story endeavors to reenact an "unwritten Urtext" that could have served as Camões's "raw material" (13).

In other words, its project was to sketch Adamastor's prototype, turn history on its head by creating an antecedent to the Camonian figure that inspired it. Perhaps this orientation influenced the narration, giving the story a linear development, with identifiable agents, represented enemies. After clanging his head against the figurehead, the Adamastor figure is whisked off, bound to a boulder, beaten, and exposed to the elements. The figure's head meets the figurehead, but this modern Adamastor suspends that disparate figuration by rendering it successive, by the offspring of his union with the European woman: "[T]he child . . . would live on . . . And then I died, the first of my many deaths, as far as I can remember" (135).

In a sense, in endorsing the logic of the Urtext, Adamastor's modern story, with its full elaboration and narrative coherence, assumes a historical tone, of which Camões's poetic version would be the idealization. But, finally, the problem of the Camões figure has from the outset been linked to its inability to idealize history. As sublime as it might be, *The Lusiads*' Adamastor fails at idealization and calls out for interpretation (what it shares with Montaigne's *Essays*): the vast chasm of sense it opens cannot be bridged, even by a deluge of discourses. In sum, despite the attempts of this "first life of Adamastor" to ground an immemorial South African identity, the disparate Adamastor has no avatar, no idealized resolution; only in the domain of ideology, a domain in which radical challenge is rendered "natural" and therefore banal, does miscegenation (historically, official Portuguese policy in colonizing the other) enact a synthesis, merge the contraries in the service of an illusory historical resolution. At bottom, while figures of thought offer a way to seize and represent the unknowable, they do not wholly domesticate the unknown in itself. They present a mechanism for processing the unknown, for confronting epistemological and physical antagonism. A secular agent of otherness, Adamastor grounds the figuration of global modernity, and the figure of thought it incarnates has been essential for projecting the modern worldview.

III

Unplanned Obsolescence

6

The Use and Abuse of the Human

Contemporary concerns about the organization of knowledge (including the disciplines and their discourses), the social function of universities, and the role of intellectuals have emerged in the wake of destabilizing technological, cultural, and economic change in the last half of the twentieth century. This volatile configuration of change, often referred to as "globalization," has placed into question a number of the ideas we have concerning the world—ideas ranging from the nation, collectivity, and cultural production, to how to describe fields of knowledge and integrate those knowledges into a larger historical understanding. This instability of modern understanding and knowledge has affected both material and symbolic domains; the theme has become omnipresent in specialized journals as well as in the popular media.

An example is useful in making more concrete this seemingly abstract challenge to prevailing concepts of understanding, to the picture of the world that accompanies modern institutions. In the same way that *Time* or *Newsweek* views the world from a North American vantage point, *Le nouvel observateur* often contains lengthy considerations on the global force of French culture and regularly devotes a large percentage of its pages to evaluating the French national culture's vitality and viability outside its borders, in all fields of cultural production from cinema to architecture, including literature, philosophy, painting, and even rap music. In trying to represent the contemporary dynamism of French knowledge and ideas in the age of what it has called "computer intellectuals," the magazine (in Didier Eribon's "Quand la pensée française voyage sur Internet") opted for a statistical analysis of data reported in the

167

American *Citation Index,* which lists authors and texts cited in academic journals. Needless to say, the French were very well represented globally: in 1994, Foucault was cited 1,085 times, followed by Bourdieu (624 times), Derrida (293 times), Baudrillard (232 times), Levi-Strauss (186 times), Lyotard (183 times), Ricoeur (177 times), Barthes (154 times), Lacan (118 times), Sartre (90 times), Braudel (86 times), and so on. Furthermore, Foucault was quoted significantly more than *any* other writer: Habermas, for example, was cited only 918 times and John Rawls, 664 times.[1] As the author was quick to point out, French culture and knowledge are obviously holding their own in the global marketplace; they seemingly have no trouble transcending the confines of national debate and contributing to transnational debates of a more universal character.

But the author did glimpse some shadows in this otherwise bright picture of the planetary status of French intellectual production. To put it simply, the French works, authors, and ideas are read, cited, and known almost exclusively in English. The article's author comments that this "nuance" needs to be considered in determining the significance of the global circulation of French culture. This is ironic, to be sure, particularly with regard to the obsessive defensiveness of French cultural policy concerning the intrusiveness of English; but this account succinctly articulates a series of interrelationships and issues implicated in any contemporary discussion of the organization of knowledge, whether thought of according to disciplines, university departments, or area or thematic studies.

While French knowledge, if one could really conceive of such national knowledge today, shows its face to the world in English guise, the underlying translation process results from a strangely asymmetrical opposition. Contrary to customary French interpretations, it is neither a question of two or more nations in ideological or cultural conflict nor some sort of linguistic battle between two powers vying for world domination. In fact, rather than simply being the result of some national imperative, the massive diffusion of English expresses a new global condition that is at the same time a loss of cultural specificity or identity. In this sense, English is a linguistic vehicle of a globalization that problematizes claims for territorial, cultural, and epistemological distinction between the national and international spheres, even as it disrupts prevailing worldviews that project a static relationship between the universal and the particular, the global and the local.

As this example suggests, it is not easy to characterize the nature of this challenge to the ideas of modernity, for the configuration of modernity has from the very beginning been bound up with the idea of globalization. Even Marx and Engels saw global awareness as fundamental for modern historical interpretation: "The need of a constantly expanding market for its products chases the bourgeoisie over the whole surface of the globe. It must nestle everywhere, settle everywhere, establish connections everywhere. Through its exploitation of the world market, the bourgeoisie has given a cosmopolitan character to production and consumption in every country."[2] For Marx and Engels, globalism belonged to the economic and historical logic of capitalism, a fact that is more evident today than ever. The notion of "cosmopolitan" meant precisely "global" in the sense that whatever it referred to was not tied to a specific country, culture, or tradition. In this view, modernity, in both its historical and economic manifestations, is necessarily accompanied by global awareness. Interestingly, in the Marxist tradition, global ideas are linked to production and consumption, two notions that have once again come into the foreground in debates about contemporary global culture.

Nonetheless, this world idea as the conceptual framework of modernity does not in any way originate with Marx or even with Hegel. It in fact results from the wide-ranging secularization process of the eighteenth century, a process that attempts to place the human being at the center of historical understanding. Although discussions of the modern university and its concomitant organizations of knowledge rightly refer back to Humboldt, Humboldt's reflections on the university follow on his theories about the science of man, what he calls "anthropology" (not at all the same thing as today's discipline of anthropology).[3] Not surprisingly, however, the first systematic account of the science of man was *Anthropology from a Pragmatic Point of View*, which Kant completed and published in 1798, after having taught the basic doctrine for thirty years.[4] The notion of the human being articulated in *Anthropology* belongs to the Western project of secularized thought that was to be first ordered and expressed in Kantian philosophy.[5] The science of the human being that makes up Kant's object "contains the knowledge of man as a world citizen [*Weltbürger*]" (400). In other words, the modern science of man as an autonomous agent was from the outset part of a global projection and derived from the idea of an abstract human without local limitations.

Yet Kant was far from being simply an abstract theoretician detached from contemporary political and economic concerns. Developing human science as a mode of understanding requires extensive experience with and knowledge of individual human beings; this sort of experience can be obtained only under certain conditions. In this context, Kant notes the advantages of "a large city at the realm's center, which houses the country's governmental institutions, which has a university (for cultivating knowledge) as well as a disposition for maritime trade that, thanks to its river network, favors both a circulation coming from the interior and exchanges with distant or bordering countries, with different languages and customs . . . Such a city, like Königsberg on the Pregel, for example [!], can already be considered a site well adapted to increasing the knowledge of man as well as the knowledge of the world" (400n). There is obviously a synergy between a global—or cosmopolitan—point of view, which is achieved through the experience of diversity and subsequent abstraction from it, and the human idea, along with the characteristics of its manifestations, such as language, country, nation, traditions, and customs.

In the latter part of the twentieth century, this configuration of figures, ideas, concepts, and presuppositions began to change its shape dramatically; nowhere have the effects of this metamorphosis been more apparent than in the human sciences (or the "humanities"), whose disciplines seem gradually to be losing their objects. In a very real sense, technological transformation, and the resulting knowledge it permits, is on the verge of outstripping the human figure that has sustained modernity. This is true whether one notes that presumed French culture becomes global only in another language, that literary traditions are becoming increasingly irrelevant to cultural production and even to collective identities, or that a global identity seems to be in the making by virtue of mass media visualizations. In this regard, for example, confrontations between chess master Kasparov and the supercomputer Big Blue, which one commentator designated as "species defining," mark the outer limit of the human figure or idea as it has been historically defined.[6] In a parallel context, the discovery of planets that could support life contains the germ of a radical reconsideration of the human idea and its relationship to life in general. As Paul Davies remarks, "The discovery of life beyond earth would transform not only our science but also our religions, our belief systems and our entire worldview. For in a sense, the search for extraterrestrial life is really a search for ourselves—who we are and what our place is in the grand sweep of the cosmos."[7] Furthermore, this transformation would include universities and institutions of knowledge generally, which inculcate and disseminate these worldviews. While the chances of eventually finding life may be good, it is unlikely that such life will be in our own image. This does not bode well for a theory of history and knowledge that rests squarely on the science of the human figure.

Ultimately, the human figure of thought—the idea of the human as a point of departure for grasping historical change—is first and foremost an epistemological notion that emerged at a specific historical moment to lend a unifying perspective to the way history is conceived and told and to anchor the organization of knowledge reproducing those basic historical tenets. Radical challenges to this notion, produced by contemporary pressures of historical, technological, and epistemological change, have provoked numerous attempts to resuscitate and redefine the eighteenth-century idea of the human being and its accompanying historical vision of progress and reason.[8] In this chapter, the focus will be on analyzing the dynamics of modernity's human figure, particularly with regard to questions of language, history, and contemporaneity.

In his essay "The Age of the World Picture," Heidegger sketches the philosophical context for converting the idea of the human being into the touchstone of modernity. After asserting a fundamental difference between the natural sciences (*Naturwissenschaften*) and the human sciences (*Geisteswissenschaften*), the essay compares and contrasts their respective methodologies and approaches. In the exact or natural sciences, the methodology delimits its object-sphere as precisely as possible and proceeds to regulate the variables in a way that can be measured. The human sciences display another mode of operation:

> The humanistic sciences, in contrast, indeed all the sciences concerned with life, must necessarily be inexact just in order to remain rigorous. A living thing can indeed be grasped as a spatiotemporal magnitude of motion, but then it is no longer apprehended as living. The inexactitude of the historical humanistic sciences is not a deficiency, but is only the fulfillment of a demand essential to this type of research. It is true, also, that the projecting and securing of the object-sphere of the historical sciences is not only of another kind, but is much more difficult of execution than is the achieving of rigor in the exact sciences.[9]

In sum, the human sciences, which by definition are concerned with products of the mind or spirit that do not easily admit of quantification, *render* rather than measure their objects. The inexactness of the human sciences is in the rendering itself, for that rendering, presenting, explaining, and so forth, comes about through discourse. Perhaps for this reason the essay generally refers to the human sciences as *historical* human sciences to distinguish them from the natural sciences. In terms of being part of institutionalized knowledge, however, the humanities or human sciences have necessarily elaborated an economy of discourse that demarcates and guarantees the perimeters of their objects or fields of study.

Just as the concept of history combines the element of pastness with that of discourse, the human sciences' distinction vis-à-vis the natural sciences derives, on the one hand, from the humanities' reliance on language and discourse and, on the other, from the way the human sciences incorporate the past into that discourse. To elaborate on an example mentioned briefly in Heidegger's text, a physics experiment, even one seeking to break new ground and extend beyond the known, embodies all previous physics. Previous physics must be mobilized, activated to push beyond itself. The accumulation of past knowledge reenacted by humanist science belongs to a different order of complexity. In the words of Heidegger's essay: "Correspondingly, in historiographical [*historischen*] research, funds of source materials become usable for explanation only if those sources are themselves guaranteed on the basis of historiographical explanation" (124; 77). The discourse of humanist knowledge resembles nothing more than a web or network of interrelated ideas, concepts, and representations that are repeated and associated in what seems to be an eternal digression. Each textual object, whether a mere concept, a full-fledged text, or an entire tradition or corpus of work, must be sustained by numerous discourses. For Heidegger, that describes the nature of the "system" at work in the modern human sciences; it powers the legitimation process and permits the human sciences' integration into the institutions of knowledge.

Consequently, knowledge comes about and reproduces itself in bundles, in configurations. In this context, post-Renaissance modernity signals the gradual setting into place of a specific configuration in which the idea of the human—of the human subject, of what is universally human—constitutes one of the leading figures. This configuring, which intimately inhabits the workings of discourse itself, entails the positing of immaterial figures whose manifestations are then inventoried, catalogued, and registered in discourse; this discursive process characterizes language use and even thought itself. Even if figures of thought are not simply arbitrarily interchangeable, different figures, from within very dissimilar historical strictures, combine in a multiplicity of ways with different notions of temporality, permit diverse attributions of subjectivity, and so on. In this context, as I discussed above in chapter 2, Auerbach's painstaking analysis of *figura* details the nonlinear historical vision that dominated medieval Western knowledge,[10] just as Heidegger's "World Picture" essay depicts the philosophical import of valorizing the human idea. Though without material existence, figures enable discourses and sustain historical conceptions; modernity's perspective on and of the human has been exceptionally productive. The current organization of knowledge, elaborated and bequeathed to the present by successive generations of humanists, is inextricably linked to that human perspective or figure.

With regard to the idea of humanism, the interpretive or discursive process Heidegger alludes to is readily visible. While the nineteenth-century construction of Renaissance humanism has begun to solicit critical attention,[11] the discursive characteristics of the human sciences appear with exceptional clarity even in the works of Paul Oskar Kristeller, who remains an important figure in Renaissance scholarship despite the fact that many of his essays were written more than fifty years ago. Kristeller was one of the first to elucidate the nineteenth-century origin of the humanism concept; nonetheless, his work in its entirety aims to establish the centrality during the Renaissance of what he calls "the emphasis on man, on his dignity and privileged place in the universe."[12] The figure of the human comes to occupy a nexus that associates the numerous conceptual threads of modernity.

In "The Philosophy of Man in the Italian Renaissance," an essay in which Kristeller confronts the question directly, the discursive argumentation and strategies of humanist knowledge are placed in relief even as the essay's subject matter is the human itself. Near the conclusion of this text, Kristeller summarizes his goals in the essay: "It has been my intention to show that the three major intellectual currents of the early Renaissance were all concerned with the purpose of human life and with the place of man in the universe, and that this concern found its expression not only in definite standards for individual conduct, but also in a strong sense for human relationships and for the solidarity of mankind."[13] The three factors or historical currents—the tradition of medieval rhetoric, the study of classical Latin literature, and the later interest in classical Greek literature—intersect at the idea of humankind to express a historical epoch. Assertions, however, are inseparable from the discursive operations that contextualize them. From a rhetorical perspective, the essay advances an underlying unity to these three currents, characterizes that unity as the purpose and place of humankind in the universe, and proceeds to marshal citations and authorities in support of that figure or idea. The contemporary production of humanist knowledge stays within the same parameters, whether one refers to theses or dissertations or to the briefest of articles or reviews. To a large extent, this rhetorical movement describes the general discursive economy of knowledge that begins with an affirmation, usually in the form of an idea, whether articulated or implicit, establishes its authenticity or veracity by the liberal use of citations, and extrapolates accordingly. This mode of discourse, constituted by an interactive relationship between asserted ideas, by recourse to peripheral sources, and by explanatory digressions, belongs to legitimized knowledge in the same way that interactions between events, protagonists, and description belong to narrative discourse.

The concluding sentence of Kristeller's essay foregrounds the historical significance of both the human figure as matrix of Western knowledge and the humanist methodology of discourse that derives from it. As Kristeller remarks, the early humanists occupy a distinguished place in Western thought: "Many of their ideas are merely a matter of historical curiosity, but some of them contain a nucleus of permanent truth and might thus become a message and an inspiration to present-day Italy, and to the rest of mankind" (139). As has long been affirmed, humanism signals a shift toward secular historical understanding, away from a historical vision based on divine transcendence. Nonetheless, while the governing historical idea undergoes transformation, resulting in a massive change in the historical interpretations that the new model permits, the humanist discourse strangely manifests characteristics similar to the theological discourse it supplanted. Historical accidents are peeled away to reveal the "nucleus of permanent truth" that resists the ravages of history, of prosaic events and facts linked to specific temporal moments. In the same way that divine action could intervene at any historical moment precisely because the divinity resided outside of history, the human idea, the kernel of humanity exempt from the forces of history, can inspire historical action at any given present. Kristeller's essay, published in 1946, calls on the human idea to inspire post-war Italy and, by extension, humankind.

Even the least idealist of thinkers, such as Machiavelli, bound their rigorously materialist views of history to an underlying notion of human consistency. In fact, the human idea encourages a restrained materialism that stops short of historicizing the human itself. A more radical materialism would submit the emergence of the human idea to historical reflection and demonstrate that, instead of representing an unchanging set of characteristics that define the human essence, the human idea is no more resistant to the vagaries of historical understanding than events that supposedly issue from that idea. In contrast, Machiavelli's historical accounts, materialist in a powerful yet more restricted sense, rely on an unexamined notion of human nature; his depiction of the tension between the human idea and the history it permits represents the outer limits of the figure's materialism. In Book 3 of the *Discourses*, Machiavelli writes:

> Wise men say, and not by happenstance nor without reason, that whoever wants to see what will be must consider what has been; for all things of the world, at any given time, have their own resemblance [*il proprio riscontro*] with ancient times. This arises from the fact that they are produced by men who are and have always been animated by the same passions, and thus they must necessarily have the same results. It is true that their actions [*opere*] are more or less virtuous [*virtuose*] in one region or another, according to the nature of the education by which those people have formed their ways and habits of life.[14]

Virtù, the word and notion so important to Machiavelli's view of the individual, belongs to secular history and to the institutions of knowledge, customs, and habits of life. The underlying passions—that is, what motivates and moves one to act, the energy propelling human events—have no history and remain unchanged throughout time. Those passions' manifestations, however, the works and deeds that are historically produced, vary according to particular peoples and their institutions. This brief characterization hints at the explanatory power of the human figure. Presupposing a steady nucleus of humanity, Machiavelli's discourse is free to study the diverse manifestations that provide the grounds for secular inquiry. Distinctions between essence and accident, when infused into a secular historical conception, easily translate into the concepts we have come to recognize as modern: the diversity of peoples, their specificity vis-à-vis one another, their differences in culture and civil society, as well as worldviews and means of articulating them (language).

This humanizing view of the world and of history, which became part of institutionalized understanding in the nineteenth century, has underwritten a global projection of enormous discursive power whose consequences, modalities, and limitations became objects of reflection only in the twentieth century. Nonetheless, in the fifteenth century a personal letter from Ficino to Tommaso Minerbetti already expressed in a rudimentary way a notion that would undergo extensive elaboration in the following centuries. Ficino's letter, which discusses Nero's brutality, affirms that Nero's inhuman treatment of others proves his inhumanity. He wrote, "For as individual men are under one Idea and in one species, they are like one man."[15] Unlike Machiavelli's projection of the human idea into history, the definition in Ficino's letter emphasizes the logical, spatial aspect of the human idea, in keeping with Ficino's Platonism. But this kernel of an idea, and the series of conceptual relationships it encapsulates, serves to generate a truly "modern" theory of history that incorporates the question of technology by providing a means to explain the vast differences in knowledge separating past and present and to assert its continuity.

The transposition of this human idea into a temporal formula expressing the advance of scientific knowledge lays the foundation for the necessarily linear notion of progress. Since our discourses of knowledge, the conceptual tools at our disposal, tend to take this temporality for granted, I think it would be useful to examine the components of its construction. Undoubtedly Pascal's "Préface pour le traité du vide" contains the most analytical dissection of these elements and of how they combine into a new configuration of knowledge. Pascal's ongoing reflection on infinity, which appears in the diverse contexts of number theory, rhetoric, and personal salvation, is well known; in "Préface" the notion of infinity marks the human as distinct from the animal. Animals enjoy a state of "limited perfection," whereas man, that is, the human being, "is produced only for infinity."[16] This open-endedness proves necessary for mobilizing the notion of progress; progress requires the possibility, however unrealizable, of each moment's infinitely surpassing itself as it becomes a subsequent moment. The progress of knowledge is evident in the life of an individual human being, who is born defenseless and unaware. This observation, anchored in empirical experience, serves as the point of departure for assertions of a more abstract order.

Pascal thus drafts the corresponding theory of history, continuing: "That gives rise, by a specific prerogative, to the fact that not only does each man advance daily in the sciences, but all men together make constant progress as the universe grows older, for the same thing happens in the succession of men as in the different ages of an individual. So that the entire chain of men during the course of so many centuries must be considered as a single man always subsisting and constantly learning" (533–534). The epistemological framework often associated with modernity can find no more elegant and succinct expression. This vision of epistemology, presented as a sort of personification, evinces a structure irrefutable in its logic: just as an individual acquires knowledge from birth to death, constantly adding to his or her store, the student surpasses the teacher, and succeeding epochs surpass what precedes them. The progress is cumulative, and there is no end in sight. This wholly terrestrial understanding of science and knowledge poses no ambiguities in itself; Pascal's personal conundrum, which does not concern me directly here, is of an altogether different sort and involves the problem of integrating this terrestrial projection of knowledge and history with a divine history that unfolds according to opposing criteria and ends abruptly in a last judgment.[17]

Yet, within this secular schema of history, technology has a significant role to play, as Pascal's essay clearly indicates. Neither *technique* nor *technology* appear in Pascal's texts; the words had not yet made their way into French. In discussing what we would today call technology, Pascal, as one would expect, draws on contemporary examples. According to his interpretation of history, it is natural for the present—that is, his present—to have moved beyond the ancients in their understanding of the heavens, specifically of the Milky Way (or, as he calls it, the "Milk Way"). While such a historical vision seems unduly innocent today, it is perhaps not coincidental that Giordano Bruno was burned a few decades earlier precisely because of his cosmology, his notions of infinity and progress, and, most important, their historical implications. In this in-

stance, the difference between past and present knowledge has a verita-
ble reason: the ancients had only their eyes for observing, "not having
yet received help from inventions" (534), what Pascal's text literally calls
"le secours de l'artifice," an abstraction perhaps best translated as "artificial assistance." That is "technology" in Pascal's text—artificial assistance that extends the senses of the knowing subject to previously in-
discernible segments of nature. From the perspective of this model of
knowledge, technology is a tool for broadening the area subject to human observation, calculation, and thought. As such, technology becomes a necessary element in the model of historical progress, subsid-
iary and subservient to the human being.

On the basis of the human being and the configuration of concepts accompanying it, a highly productive and hegemonic theory of history
emerged whose only blind spot is its inability to account for its own
emergence. This historical interpretation, however, has been decisive for
modernity, which doubtless would have been impossible without it. The
logic of this history, delineated in some of its aspects by Machiavelli and
Pascal, though present to greater or lesser degrees in virtually every text
of historical reflection since the inception of the modern state, has had
enormous consequences for the organization of modern knowledge, itself closely linked to institutions of civil society. In the Heidegger text
I cited above, "The Age of the World Picture," some of these consequences are laconically mentioned. Heidegger's peculiar obsession with
subjectivity, and with how to insert it into a collectivity, will lead the argument elsewhere, but in passing he alludes to a number of the historical elements making up the configuration of modernity. After Descartes,
the text states, "Man has become *subiectum.* Therefore he can determine
and realize the essence of subjectivity, always in keeping with the way in
which he himself conceives and wills himself. Man as a rational being of
the age of Enlightenment is no less subject than is man who grasps himself as a nation, wills himself as a people, fosters himself as a race, and,
finally, empowers himself as lord of the earth."[18] In discursive terms, the
figure of man or the human being as a knowing subject and touchstone
of historical understanding underlies the history of the Enlightenment,
which is a secular history with very specific characteristics. Its accompanying notions that Heidegger partially enumerates are readily familiar
and include nation, race, culture, a people, and so forth, discursive categories that result from personification and thus accrue to themselves a

subjective status. Through the discourses that describe them, they co-here, think, act, even though they have no *real* material existence, de-spite the heavy discursive investment in their corresponding figures.

In effect, history—not the history that one recounts but the history that gives one the ideas, tools, and means of recounting—marks all concep-tual production. The notions constituting the configuration of moder-nity belong to no single discipline of knowledge but permeate them all. While recounting the history of this configuration's emergence may rel-ativize the configuration's power and question its universal application, it does not necessarily render an account of how it operates and of its historical efficacy or even necessity. For example, Machiavelli's rudimen-tary notions of underlying humanity that manifests itself in diverse his-torical and cultural ways share a fundamental perspective with Pascal's more abstract and theoretically informed version of the human and its history. Going from the concrete—the individual's seeming empirical existence that is blocked off and constituted by the events occurring in the interim between birth and death—to the abstract affirmation of hu-manity's parallel existence, Pascal makes a rhetorical argument based on analogy. Similarly, reference to the artificial invention or technology, which for Pascal extends humanity and promotes its progress without damaging or affecting the underlying human idea, reaffirms human con-sistency and continuity by claiming the artifice's inconsequentiality. In the same vein, Heidegger's comments on the way in which the figure of "man" personifies a host of other subjects—categories of sociopolitical, cultural, and philosophical understanding basic to modernity—signal the inescapable linguistic or rhetorical aspect to any historical or inter-pretive project.

As Lévinas intimates by referring to Pascal's view of "man surpassing man" in the context of an "anthropology of humanity,"[19] the emergence of anthropology was an integral part of Enlightenment elaborations of history. In this sense, of course, I should reiterate, anthropology does not refer to the contemporary discipline of organized knowledge but rather to the "study" or "science of man." Kant's *Anthropology*, which I mentioned earlier, is the first complete statement calling for a new focus on the human being. As usual, Kant's statement of purpose is exceed-ingly clear: "A systematically conceived knowledge of man (anthropol-ogy) can be expressed from either a physiological or a philosophical perspective. The physiological knowledge of man is concerned with inquiry into what nature makes of man, whereas the pragmatic knowledge of man is concerned with what man, as a free-acting entity [*freihandelndes Wesen*], makes, or can and should make, of himself" (399). Kant's anthropology adopts the pragmatic approach, which focuses on the intellect's modalities, products, and consequences. Ultimately, it deals with the investment of the world and historical attempts to render account of it, including the categories of race, culture, and so on. But above all it involves the question of action and its attribution to a subject called "man."

Even on its most basic level, anthropology has always been concerned with the attribution of action. Coining neither the word nor the concept, Kant radically alters anthropology's status by redefining and systematizing it, but also by secularizing its accompanying theory of action. In this regard, Diderot and d'Alembert's *Encyclopédie* summarizes the contemporary backdrop against which the precise nature of Kant's intervention becomes visible. The *Encyclopédie* has two entries for anthropology that roughly parallel Kant's two anthropological categories; the second concerns a descriptive anthropology, and the first involves a rendering of action. The second and less significant entry concerns anthropology "in the animal economy" and refers to what Kant calls "physiological" anthropology, or man as a product of nature. The *Encyclopédie* proceeds to define the term ("it is a treatise about man"), to give its etymology ("the word comes from the Greek *anthropos,* 'man,' and *logos,* 'treatise'"), and to offer various examples of such a treatise.

As in Kant's *Anthropology,* the anthropology dealing with action receives the greatest attention. In the *Encyclopédie,* this anthropology derives from the domain of theology; anthropology in this sense is the

> mode of expression by means of which the sacred writers attribute God with the members, actions, or feelings that apply only to man, in order to adapt to and enter into just relation with the weakness of our intelligence. Thus it is said in *Genesis* that God *called Adam,* that he *regretted having created man;* in *Psalms* the universe is called *the work of God's hands;* it is still said that *his eyes are open and watch over the destitute.*
>
> With all these expressions and others like them that are so frequently found in the Scriptures, the Holy Spirit only wanted us to understand the things or effects that God produces [*opère*] as if he had hands, eyes, etc., without compromising the singularity of his being [*la simplicité de son être*].[20]

From a literary or rhetorical perspective, the *Encyclopédie*'s anthropology is a figure—specifically, prosopopoeia—in which god's representation necessarily assumes human attributes. As other entries in the *Encyclopédie* indicate, anthropology is the general concept of this figurative process, which logically subsumes more specific genres of attribution, such as "anthropopathy," the process of endowing god's representation with human passions. Thus the *anthropopathie* entry, after a very brief definition, refers the reader to *anthropologie*, the general term englobing the mode of representation at issue. This anthropology, as personification or prosopopoeia, is not simply a figure of speech but is a figure of thought that must be used to represent god, to render god presentable and intelligible. Through anthropology, the idea of god comes into (linguistic) existence.

God's unique indivisibility, which is undamaged or unaffected by its own figuration, remains wholly on an otherworldly plane that offers no access on its own terms. The singularity—or, as the *Encyclopédie* states, the simplicity—of the divinity's nature refers to the various aspects of divine omniscience. Unlike human thought, to which god's representation has fallen prey, divine "allknowingness," in its very essence, permits no time to lapse between yesterday and today, no difference between knower and known, between subject and object. In other words, there is no mediation produced through discourse. The terrestrial necessity of discourse underscores why all history, even history of the divine, is unavoidably mundane history. From a linguistic point of view, assertions of god's existence presuppose by definition that he resides elsewhere, isolated from the discourse announcing his existence.

Against this backdrop, Kant's radical reorientation of anthropology achieves greater precision. Kant's anthropology takes over the notion and sifts away the theology and the rhetoric. Rather than the process of rendering god and his actions, anthropology becomes that knowledge concerned with rendering the human being's own actions, their products and consequences. Contrary to divine omniscience or to its idea, human knowing is inevitably mediated by language itself and is therefore grounded in temporal and spatial separation; as all human-oriented theories of history attest, human knowledge is a process of discernment and reflection, producing a necessary distinction, however tentative or nuanced, between subject and object, between the "now" that is past and the "now" yet to come. Modern anthropology, the application of human language to human endeavors, shunts aside the question of fig-

uration that thrusts itself into the equation only because of the presumed essential difference between human language and the divine. Human language is commensurable with human action, and, in a secular
perspective, the question of figuration loses all sense of urgency.

Nonetheless, the notion of figuration does not disappear; true to its
name, it reemerges in another form. In severing anthropology from the
divine and attaching it to the human, thus giving a conceptual basis for
objective description of human action and history, Kant's *Anthropology
from a Pragmatic Point of View* mobilizes yet another term that resides
along the same axis as anthropology. In *Anthropology,* this other term,
anthropomorphism, describes the necessary mental process by means of
which the imagination represents "reasonable beings."[21] This notion of
anthropomorphism, which Leibniz had taken from the theological regis-
ter in applying it to human knowledge generally,[22] already appeared in
greater detail in Kant's *Critique of Pure Reason.* Not unlike the *Encyclopédie's* definition of anthropology, the *Critique's* anthropomorphism
proves necessary in describing the ultimate unity of nature or the "cause
of the world"; without anthropomorphism, Kant remarks, "nothing
whatsoever could be thought" about the cause of the world.[23] This re-
articulation of anthropology, which wholly secularizes it and distinguishes it from its tropological aspects, signals one of the most important elements of Enlightenment thought and the modernity it will
underwrite: Knowledge (and the discourses that convey, describe, and
produce it) claims for itself an objectivity exempt from the vagaries of
figuration. Figuration becomes an issue only at the limits of knowledge
itself.

In sum, this anthropology, the science of man that anchors Kantian
and modern philosophy, ushers in a form of historical understanding
that bridges two seemingly contradictory notions. On the one hand, a
theory of knowledge and understanding based entirely on the anthropos, on generic man, is inescapably secular, bound to this world. On the
other hand, a unitary idea of the anthropos, whose historical manifestations allow for recognition of terrestrial difference (whether based on
race, culture, or knowledge, and whether spatial or temporal), conjures
up images of divine essence, residing beyond history though implicated
in it. In this sense, such an anthropological notion represents a partial
secularization that perhaps dispenses with the necessity of divine unity
but maintains its discursive framework by replacing it with a unifying—
ultimately nonhistorical—figure from the prosaic world.

Kant's careful transformation of anthropology, removing it from the realm of figuration to redefine it as an objective science of man, indicates the logic of this partial secularization. In strict terms, anthropomorphism, or personification, while necessary to human thought, can represent only that which is not human, whether otherworldly or simply mired in the terrestrial mud. For Kant, the discourse of pragmatic anthropology dispenses with personification because the (human) object can be experienced daily as a living referent; it becomes the figurative point of reference for understanding all that is not human, whether it is a matter of describing thoughts, god, or the forces of nature. Consequently, the figurative aspect of language drops out of anthropology when it is conceived as the science of man, which must deny the figurative aspect of language in order to claim the objectivity of its description. In this logic, one describes rather than personifies a human, even if that human is no more than an idea; this aspect of anthropomorphic discourse has important consequences for the human sciences constituted according to a separation between "anthropology" and its figural aspects, and expresses the limitations inherent in efforts to historicize the human idea in this framework.[24]

In the twentieth century, particularly in the latter half, social, political, cultural, and technological upheavals placed unforeseen pressures on the multivalent configuration of modernity. These upheavals or disruptive transformations, which have had repercussions for the universalizing tendencies of humanistic interpretation, its presuppositions, concepts, and categories, have most specifically challenged the nonhistorical idea of the human. In a very precise sense, knowledge itself has become openly enmeshed in the mechanism that previously applied only to its objects. Transcendent or ahistorical notions are scarcely posited before they are rendered immanent or somehow explicable by historical or epistemological circumstances and interests. This process of questioning or debunking transcendent claims runs the gamut of knowledge production, whether one refers to paradigm changes in scientific research or to contestation of literary, philosophical, or social canons of thought and culture. This process is strikingly visible in the fields of literary studies, in which the specificity of the object(s) of knowledge is becoming increasingly difficult to articulate and grasp.

But how does one go about describing this historical or conceptual situation with regard to the human idea itself, a touchstone of the configuration of modernity? Long before the author achieved status as a cult figure, Jean Baudrillard's *La société de consommation* (1970) analyzed the impact of twentieth-century cultural production on Western knowledge and thought. The book's formulation of the issues remains pertinent, even though its moral indignation seems quaint and anachronistic, while its tone alternates between celebrating as inevitable and condemning outright the demise of human transcendence. J. P. Mayer's preface succinctly lays out the book's fundamental premise: "Consumerism, as a new tribal myth, has become the morality of our contemporary world. It is destroying the foundations of the human being, that is, the balance that European thought from the Greeks on has maintained between mythological roots and the world of the logos."[25] Thus cultural production, which when the book was published in 1970 was in its global infancy, underlies the conceptual collapse of the human being, an idea viewed as continuous with that of the Greeks only in modernity. From the perspective of modernity, contemporary cultural production disrupts or accompanies a disruption of the reigning discursive regime, which for Mayer maintains a balance between myth and reason, between transcendence and immanence.

Tracing the implications of omnipresent consumerism, the context producing a new concept of the human, the book offers a vision of culture that finds echoes in today's cultural criticism. In summarizing the "organizing principle governing all of today's 'mass' culture," it draws on the notion of recycling:

> What all those who are culturally integrated have a right to (and, ultimately, not even those who are "cultivated" will escape it) is not culture but cultural recycling . . . It is being subject to this narrow-band constraint, in perpetual movement like fashion styles, that is the *absolute contrary* of culture conceived as:
> 1. A hereditary patrimony of works, thoughts, and traditions;
> 2. A continuous dimension of theoretical and critical reflection—critical transcendence and symbolic function. (151)

This passage attempts to portray the consumer logic of cultural production—or, to be precise, the production of immaterial goods such as ideas, traditions, and concepts. Rather than enjoying a status as treasure to be guarded and interpreted, culture becomes directly integrated into the financial and production economy; in other words, culture no longer enjoys privileged links with political economy—links with national identity, for example—even if those links have been diluted rather than severed. This new logic, which Baudrillard calls consumerism, runs counter to the construction of tradition and the ensuing cultural identity that is produced through shared beliefs, values, ideologies, and other immaterial references. Traditional forms of culture, constituted by an immaterial patrimony repeatedly bequeathed to successive generations, provided a temporary continuity and have underwritten the institutions and subjectivities of modernity. This same continuity, however, also characterized the means and mechanisms of critical thought, which in this model of historical understanding requires a transcendent dimension, the postulating of universal ideas to motivate human action. Ultimately, this lost transcendence, this lost possibility of transcendence, is the most significant by-product of a consumer economy that necessarily subjects immaterial production—that is, culture, ideas, and so on—to economic forces.

Needless to say, this insight into the economic dismantling of transcendence, which Baudrillard articulates with great clarity, can be traced back at least to the Frankfurt School's 1930s critique of the culture industry, which was itself a continuation of the debates in the 1920s on "Americanism." But the accelerated diffusion of this cultural economy, which became a global reality in the late twentieth century, merits dispassionate consideration before calling for a return to Enlightenment models of human reason and critique. With that proviso, it is useful to follow Baudrillard's analysis, which sketches out the fundamental transformations arising from the cultural economy of consumerism. Today's cultural production, which disperses and recycles the cultural patrimony, provokes a rupture in the continuity of tradition: "Culture is no longer produced to last. It is of course kept as a universal instance, as an ideal reference, all the more so when it loses the substance of its meaning (just as Nature is never as exalted as when it has been widely destroyed). In reality, however, by its very mode of production, culture responds to the same call of 'contemporaneity' [*actualité*] as material goods" (151–152). In Baudrillard's description, the model of culture that has been displaced represents culture as enduring, as something that transcends the moment of its creation to remain pertinent in subsequent historical moments. It is not by happenstance that challenges to this cultural model were occasioned by the dynamics of twentieth-century mass culture and its multiplicity of media.

In fact, this model is inextricably linked to written culture; in the age of print, it has reigned supreme. The continuity of meaning derives from successive generations who share cultural artifacts that can be interpreted in perpetuity. That is the patrimony to which the earlier passage from Baudrillard referred. The written text remains the paradigm for this model of culture, just as hermeneutics, the founding vision of historical critique, theorizes the present understanding as an ongoing renewal of meaning from within an established tradition. In the case of a text, its fundamental materiality may remain unchanged in time (same words, same chapters printed on separate pages and bound together, and so on), but within the limits of its materiality, its meaning shifts and is inexhaustible. This is also the model of culture without which modern knowledge and institutions would be impossible.

But this is likewise the cultural model that has ceased to be hegemonic and that has proven itself inadequate in describing or critiquing contemporary culture production, which has been dubbed "recycling." The current modes of cultural production express a radically diverse temporality, not based on continuity, and do not generate inert artifacts whose sense undergoes constant renewal and replenishment. Bound up with actuality to the same degree as material goods, immaterial goods—that is, culture—are subject to the same pressures as any other product; while cultural productions may nonetheless reappear in subsequent actualities, their appearance or "recycling" is discontinuous and owes nothing to linearity. Contrary to the cultural model deriving from the written text, which presupposes a continuity of mind, tradition, and social consciousness produced through access to a shared culture, the culture of recycling produces disjunctures, and the collective consciousness it fosters is at best fluctuating and temporary.

Moreover, as a phenomenon tied to cultural production itself and its economic circulation, it undermines distinctions central to modern institutions of culture; as Baudrillard remarks with disdain, there is no longer any "difference between 'avant-garde' creations and 'mass culture'" (152). There is no sphere immune to the logic of cultural recycling in what Benjamin called the epoch of mechanical reproducibility. An entire media vocabulary has emerged to represent a complex series of discontinuous interrelationships—terms such as *spin-off* (recycling of stories or figures "borrowed" from a particular cultural artifact) and *tie-in* (simultaneous recycling into another medium of a given cultural product or figure). For example, current recyclings of the Shakespeare figure and his cultural artifacts have only an incidental relationship to whatever meaning might be or might have been realized in conjunction with their inclusion in a cultural patrimony. Driven by the perceived needs, concerns, interests, or simply the economics of contemporaneity, any given artifact produced by the figure Shakespeare might be recycled at any moment, whether it be in the form of a reprinted story for children, first retold over a hundred years ago; a play staged in modern costume; a play converted into a screenplay; a staged play that is filmed; a play used as a prototype for other plots in diverse media; and so on to infinity. This recycling, whether it refers to Shakespeare productions and motifs or to vampire figures that are no more than hinted at in some distant past, belongs to a different order of cultural logic, far removed from the presuppositions founding the cultural configuration of modernity and its concomitant print economy.

In this context of an emergent cultural and political economy, the notion of the human being inescapably becomes an issue, along with its attendant historical implications. Baudrillard's account offers an incisive characterization of the human being of consumerism: "The man of consumerism never stands face to face with his own needs any more than with the product of his own work; nor is he ever confronted with his own image: *he is immanent to the signs that he orders*. There is no longer any transcendence, any finality, any objective" (309; emphasis in the original). Predictably, Baudrillard draws the conclusion that, consequently, "what characterizes this society is the absence of 'reflection,' of perspective on itself" (309). From a critical perspective that relies on a trascendental notion of culture, this judgment is inescapable, if overly predictable. In effect, in the face of proliferating contemporaneity, the partially secular discourses of modernity, which profoundly rely on universals untarnished by the flux of history, tend toward the mourning of a superseded past (nostalgia) or the seeking of a renewed universal (utopia), two specular refractions of the same transhistorical vision.

These transhistorical visions and claims collapse as rapidly as they are uttered, for consumer society, with its multimedia proliferation and rampant globalization, brings universal claims down to size, renders immanent all efforts at transcendence. Nevertheless, it is far from certain that critical thought requires a transcendental fiction to be sustained and that knowledge and institutions achieve stability only by resting on ideas of human essence. The premise of universalism itself may be faulty. In fact, the real stakes of contemporaneity, in which immaterial culture and knowledge answer to the same forces as material artifacts, derive from the possibility of elaborating a truly secular historical vision. In the age of contemporaneity, critical perspectives, the anthropos figure from which they emanate, and their accompanying organization of knowledge, can no longer dispense with reflection on their own emergence and, at the same time, their programmed obsolescence.

7

Collective Culture of Print

Thinking about culture, specifically in terms of its material underpinnings, is fraught with numerous obstacles. In accord with our media-based global society, the discussion of culture as a concept and an issue pervades all arenas, ranging from economics to the human sciences to straightforward news reporting, and it has become truly transnational in scope. Yet the daunting quantity of material on the issue of culture, which in the academic and the media industries increases on a daily basis, tends to mask the more necessary challenge of coming to terms with culture and its workings, which remain enmeshed in understandings of tradition, linguistic autonomy, and the institutions of social stability, both material and immaterial, as well as in questions of power, nationhood, and statehood. Moreover, culture in modernity has inevitably been thought and conceived on the basis of the written—or, better, the printed—word as the privileged means of preserving, handing down, and interpreting cultural phenomena. To analyze the notion of culture means examining it in relationship to the web of interests that constitute and police it. Only then can one begin to envision an understanding of culture that does not rest squarely on the supremacy of print.

Though infrequently acknowledged, Antonio Gramsci is one of the twentieth century's few political philosophers to have a comprehensive theory of culture. The broad implications of his writings on culture have been ignored for many reasons: because his work was written in specific prison conditions, it generally takes the form of fragments (similar in some respects to those of Wittgenstein or Benjamin); because he was a Marxist, non-Marxists rarely read his work, yet among many Marxists

189

his work is not considered central to the tradition, possibly because he was very quick to challenge orthodoxy, especially economism. Nonetheless, this resistance to Gramsci's contribution perhaps relates more to his materialist understanding of culture, in which culture could not easily be reduced to an isolated category but rather had meaning only in carefully interpreted social, political, and historical contexts.

From our perspective, separated from his by a gulf of economic growth and technological transformation, Gramsci's recommendations about what course of action to take may seem at times anachronistic; yet his analyses of the sociopolitical role of culture in establishing and perpetuating the modern state remain pertinent and would almost seem to prefigure recent debates about culture. Nowhere is the pertinence of his analysis more apparent than in the slim prison notebook entitled "On the Margins of History (The History of Subaltern Social Groups),"[1] which dates from 1934 and contains only sixteen printed pages. This notebook's theme is related to Italy's well-known southern question, an issue that served as the point of departure for all of Gramsci's prison writings and for their reflection on culture and the state;[2] in translating the southern question into a global context, as Pasolini would later do, it comes to refer to the Third World or, in a more current description, the "north-south problem." Concerned explicitly with how one proceeds to represent the history of those groups who have not held power, who have been dominated economically and culturally, the notebook immediately demonstrates both the explanatory power of Gramsci's analyses and the assumptions that produce his interpretations. As often occurred with the later notebooks, Gramsci created the notebook by bringing together earlier notebook entries around a specific theme that was to be elaborated further.

Embedded in a series of remarks about Italian historical figures and discussions of various books, the notebook's principal theme concerns constituting and reclaiming the history of subaltern groups in the service of the present. The subaltern historian in this sense operates according to an explicit and unambiguous theory of history: subaltern histories are necessarily fragmentary, because by definition they are subaltern to the history that accompanies and maintains the state. Yet history is without exception powered by struggle, and all groups move toward a unifying group identity; one result of the conflictual nature of history is that the group or groups who have achieved unity, who in effect control the state, move to divide subaltern groups, to perpetuate their fragmentariness. In the terms of this historical conception, then, the subaltern historian combs the past to identify moments of "autonomous initiative" on the part of subaltern groups; one might almost say, to identify inklings of a self-consciousness that according to the underlying understanding of history will later emerge in full force. Knowingly or unknowingly, much of so-called oppositional history, history of the "people," or the empirical histories of daily life, dating from the past fifty years, shares the basic assumptions of this theory of history, which has profoundly marked the cultural understanding implicit in the modern worldview.

Against this backdrop, the notebook offers a brief characterization of what a subaltern group is, specifically with regard to Roman society, but the passage's implications are relevant to the later argument: "Often subaltern groups are originally of a different race (different culture and different religion) from the dominant groups, and often they are a mixture of various races, as in the case of slaves. The question of women's importance in Roman history is similar to that of subaltern groups, but only to a certain point" ("Quaderno 25," 2286). Originally, subaltern groups bore the mark of difference, which was based on ethnicity, race, culture, and religion; the implication is, of course, that these differences became institutionalized as the groups were folded into the state and given a distinct social and political space that excluded them, as groups, from the exercise of power. That is the condition of subalternity. The mention of women in this context proves suggestive for discussions of culture in the early twenty-first century, although for Gramsci, women did not constitute a class that in the then-prevalent Marxist notion of history powered the historical process. In effect, subaltern groups represent the pool of dominated groups that would furnish the makings of class and class consciousness in the epoch of the modern state.

As in all of Gramsci's writings, the historical analysis is driven by a need to conceive the present historically and to devise an appropriate mode of intervention. Thus, to underscore the innovation of the modern state, he briefly describes what the classical and medieval states had in common: "The state was in a certain sense a mechanical bloc of social groups, often of various races: within the circle of political and military pressure, which was acutely exerted only in certain moments, subaltern groups had an autonomous life of their own, had their own institutions and so forth, and these institutions sometimes had state functions, which made the state into a federation of social groups with various functions that were not subordinate" ("Quaderno 25," 2287). This passage presents the basic description of the state: a social, political, economic, and military mechanism to produce stability over generations. And as one might expect, the coalescence of these elements seems to form the barest skeleton of the state structure that would emerge most fully in the twentieth century. The state is centralized especially, though not exclusively, in military and political affairs, yet also decentralized, in that the subaltern groups it dominates have a limited autonomy in the sphere of civil society, including culture and its institutions of reproduction, institutions that the state can call on when necessary to act in its name.

With the advent of the modern state, these series of relationships were completely remapped. The sociopolitical components of the classical and medieval state, meshed to form an effective if cumbersome unity, gave way to a fluid unity that was based on state penetration in previous spheres of relative autonomy: "The modern state replaces the mechanical bloc of social groups by subordinating them to the active hegemony of the ruling and dominant group, thus abolishing some autonomies that however are reborn in another form, as parties, unions, associations of culture" ("Quaderno 25," 2287). From this description, it is not difficult to understand why the transformation to the so-called modern state is accompanied by the emergence of codified languages, by enormous efforts to renew and expand social institutions such as universities, and by controlled support for print technology and all its material and immaterial products. This new state depends on establishing and maintaining different channels of power that do not stop at the borders of semi-autonomous communities. The autonomy, however, does not disappear but is dispersed into other social forms that would take centuries to develop.

In the modern state as Gramsci depicts it, the community, a delimited civil society within a larger state and alongside other communities, could no longer play a crucial role as guarantor of state power. Its inclusiveness and self-definition, the very reasons for its existence, were based on notions of birth, physical proximity, language, and shared culture, all of which would be taken over as categories for determining one's belonging to the state. These categories, of course, do not all bear the same weight in the modern state any more than they did in all traditional communities; physical proximity, for example, inevitably means less when technology allows for both qualitative and quantitative communication over large distances, a possibility opened up by mechanical publishing, to cite an instance crucial to the consolidation of the state. In the same vein, physical proximity means almost as little for communities resting on a text and its interpretive tradition; this was true even in the Middle Ages (among the Jewish communities, for example).

Although aspects of this interpretation of the modern European state are familiar and date back at least to Spinoza's *Theologico-Political Treatise,* Gramsci's primary concern resides in the potential collectivity that becomes possible in the diffusion of the community's autonomy. This perspective furnishes the context for Gramsci's writings on Machiavelli and is especially significant for his references to the *prince* and the *modern prince,* two terms whose supposed meanings have become clichés along with *hegemony* and *organic intellectual,* among others. Machiavelli's prince, a concept that came to be in the attempt to understand the transformed nature of state power, is, for Gramsci, linked to the potential collectivity; he describes the prince as a "condottiere, who represents plastically and 'anthropomorphically' the symbol of the 'collective will.'"[3] The prince as representation does not refer to some model of governmental representation; it is, in Gramsci's reading, a rhetorical necessity that permits discussion of a new conception of state power that can be reached only by interpretation, because a collectivity, or a "collective will," is not an empirical object. Interestingly, Gramsci chooses to underscore this interpretation of the prince as a figure of thought by naming it a personification, a prosopopoeia that occupies a central position in rhetorical theories of language and action. This figure of thought, because it allows for devising a critical strategy of action, lies at the base of Gramsci's theory of history.

Although the concept and historical significance of the prince and its modern elaboration both relate to the postmedieval state, Gramsci reflected at length on how to render the figure of thought it incarnates, how "to translate the notion 'Prince' as it is used in Machiavelli's book into modern political language . . .: 'Prince' could be a head of state or head of government, but 'Prince' could also be a political leader who wants to conquer a state or establish a new type of state; in this sense, 'Prince' could be translated in modern terms as 'political party.'"[4] This interest in thinking a "Prince" in the completely transformed political landscape of modernity leads to another understanding of the way figures project and motivate historical action. In this perspective, Gramsci's formulation of the modern prince was a response to the specific social, historical, and cultural situation of the twentieth century. In the words of Notebook 13, on Machiavelli's politics, "The modern prince, the myth-prince, cannot be a real person, a concrete individual. It can only be an organism, a complex element of society in which a collective will, which has already been recognized and has to some extent asserted itself in action, begins to take concrete form. The unfolding of history has already provided this organism, and it is the political party" (*SPN*, 129; "Quaderno 13," 1558).

The linguistic parallels between the prince and the modern prince are exact, but the precision of the latter's description is striking, all the more so given Gramsci's renowned concern for philological detail. Like the prince, the modern prince is also a prosopopoeia, which belongs to the realm of allegory and therefore to history; in Gramsci's conception, however, the prince figure also functions as a symbol, which in rhetoric has traditionally had an "organic," nontemporal relationship to what it represents. As an "organism," the political party is in a state of constant transition, is constantly reestablishing itself, and in Gramsci's political theory it remains the center through which political activity is channeled. Yet this organicism, a widely criticized concept especially today, does not exemplify the important insight repeatedly developed in the notebooks, which is the necessity of a historical figure of thought to understand and counter the state of the first half of the twentieth century.

In effect, since in this view of history the self-affirming action of a collective will can come about only partially, the ongoing action, which is for Gramsci ultimately aimed toward the constitution or conquest of the state, is what powers history itself. This activity, however, represents a long-term intervention, not a momentary seizure of power: "In the modern world, only a historical and political action that is immediate and imminent, characterized by the necessity to proceed with lightning speed, can be mythically incarnated in a concrete individual . . . But an immediate action of this kind, by its very nature, cannot have a wide-ranging and organic character: it will almost always be of the restoration and reorganization type and not appropriate for founding new states and new national and social structures" (*SPN*, 129; "Quaderno 13," 1558). This careful elaboration leads to an understanding of politics that cannot be reduced to executive action; in this context, the concern with civil society, with culture, becomes preeminent, and the focus on achieving a state takes on a very different meaning. The resulting concern with what one might call symbolic action, historical intervention not calculated or expected to have immediate effects, leads back to the issue of subaltern groups.

Although the notebook on subaltern groups deals with many aspects of historical understanding, including references to historical detail, the larger historical process, and the political significance of history for the then current situation, the self-proclaimed task of the notebook is methodological. It intends to demonstrate the groups' significance for historical practice and to explain how the historian might proceed to produce their history. In precise historical terms, the subaltern groups' lack of autonomy results from the peculiar relationship between state and civil society: "Basic historical unity, in its concreteness, is the result of organic relations between the state or political society and 'civil society.' Subaltern classes, by definition, are not and cannot be unified until they can become a 'state': their history is therefore bound up with that of civil society, is a 'disaggregated' and discontinuous function of the history of civil society and, by this means, of the history of states or groups of states" ("Quaderno 25," 2288).

The notion of integral history, which comes about through a binding relationship between a state and the institutions that buttress it, highlights the disjunctive, discontinuous, or partial history of subaltern groups. In a sense, this confrontation between historical unity and historical disjunction is the powerful contradiction that enables the practice Gramsci outlines and intimates its own historical limitations. His theory of history, which fundamentally relies on Marx's interpretation of Hegel, posits a close, unifying relationship between state and civil society. In this conception, every excluded group, every subaltern group that is prevented from achieving this state of unifying equilibrium, is potentially on the way to achieving this status. That is the transformative power of Gramsci's historical understanding: it is simultaneously descriptive of a prevailing situation, the historical ascendancy and maintenance of a specific group or class, and an operative conception of how that domination is countered and overturned. Apart from questions about the accuracy of this conception's analysis for its own time, its relevance as an overarching historical theory cannot be separated from the historical efficacy of its enabling assumption that establishes a necessary unity between state and civil society.

The history of subaltern groups is, therefore, intertwined with the dominant groups served most directly by the state, but only through the mediation of civil society, the institutions supporting the state directly and indirectly. Thus emerges the crucial significance of the modern prince as the figure of collective will: it permits a historical account of the subaltern group in terms of the future self-consciousness that the figure of thought will help produce: "And a definition must be given of collective will, and of political will in general, in the modern sense: will as operative awareness [*coscienza*] of historical necessity, as protagonist of a real and effective historical drama" (*SPN*, 130; "Quaderno 13," 1559). The party, in this instance, takes on human form, can be ascribed a consciousness, and acts historically. This history has to be recuperated, however, and with respect to subaltern groups, the task of recounting this history appropriately falls to the historian, who "must take note of and justify the development leading to integral autonomy, from its most primitive phases" ("Quaderno 25," 2288). Although much of today's debate regarding so-called revisionist history would indicate that this activist view of the historian's role is a twentieth-century phenomenon, this view is deeply woven into the fabric of modern statehood and nationhood. For example, Claude de Seyssel, a contemporary of Machiavelli, succinctly summarized the agency of the historian: "Historians are the ones who create nations," and "without a national history there is no nation."[5] By drawing on what transpired in the Italian Risorgimento, the remainder of this entry in the notebook on subaltern groups outlines the willful transition from subalternity to "statehood." It describes in shorthand the way a specific subaltern group will achieve ascendance with relation to other groups, thereby constituting an autonomous bloc capable of historical action.

This concept is the spine that holds together the skeletal fragments of Gramsci's prison writings as a whole. The finite understanding of culture and civil society that emerges against this backdrop cannot be grasped in isolation from this historical perspective of the modern state. Moreover, this historical conception requires an active and critical engagement with the mental, physical, economic, and cultural spheres of domination. In Notebook 16 (on cultural topics), which contains another of the few explicit references to subalternity, Gramsci makes clear what is entailed in this historical transformation. Departing from the historical and finite significance of what is called "natural," the discussion expands into a network of interrelated forces and modes of existence:

> Because of subaltern groups' lack of autonomy in historical initiative, their disaggregation is more profound, and harder is their struggle to throw off principles that are imposed rather than proposed in achieving an autonomous historical consciousness . . . But how should this autonomously proposed historical consciousness be formed? . . . [O]ne needs to refer to technical relations of production, to a specific type of economic civilization that, to be developed, requires a specific mode of living, rules of conduct, and certain habits. One must be convinced that not only a certain tool is "objective" and necessary but also a certain mode of behavior, a certain education, a certain mode of coexistence, etc. ("Quaderno 16," 1875–1876)

This reflective passage, like many passages in the notebooks, puts forth a number of considerations that impinge on historical understanding. At the same time, it contains subtle hints of Gramsci's forceful polemic against economism. Even if statehood is recognized as the necessary prerequisite for unity and, therefore, social, political, and historical action, the question of consciousness, of how to throw off the condition of subalternity, ultimately remains unanswered. Yet Gramsci's approach to this question is novel, because it indicates the political nature of human existence and refuses to relegate any element of the human to some sphere outside of history. Thus the transformation must occur not simply in the realm of ideas, because of some ideology, or through the invention and utilization of some new form of technology. What is "objective" is historical, and it involves all of human existence, from standards of individual behavior to collective relations, education, and customs. This view is far from proposing any form of economic determinism: "economic civilization" is an aspect of human existence that includes as an integral component economic production in all its connectedness to other aspects of historical existence. In other words, individual and collective action does not take place mechanically, with the subject grasping a different tool to accomplish a new task. Subjectivity itself is also a crucial part of the historical equation. This radical historical conception permits culture to emerge into the foreground.

Retrospectively, it seems ironic that the existing state, the object of

Gramsci's critical analysis, was rejected even as its form was to be duplicated. Again, with regard to subaltern groups, "How should everyone select and combine the elements for constituting such an autonomous consciousness? Will every 'imposed' element have to be rejected a priori? It will have to be rejected insofar as it is imposed, but not in itself; that is, it must be given a new form appropriate to the respective group" ("Quaderno 16," 1875). What has been imposed must be repeated in a new form to support the group seeking unification, historical autonomy. The need to repeat what is historically given, even if given as imposition, represents the limits of historical understanding and action. In sum, Gramsci's notion of subalternity, of constructing a historical movement and providing for its self-awareness as a historical protagonist, operates according to the same economy of hegemony as the state. That is the historical limitation circumscribing Gramsci's recommendations for historical intervention, but this does not detract from the power of its analysis.

In effect, the reference to the prince and its reformulation in the present both underscores this reliance on the state and inscribes it in yet another set of issues and power relations. Just as the state maintains the equilibrium of disparate forces ranging from the economic to the cultural, the modern prince anchors what Gramsci calls "cultural reform" and "intellectual and moral reform," in necessary conjunction with concrete economic reform. It becomes the primary mediator of a new conception of history and action, accruing hegemonic power to itself:

> The modern Prince, as it develops, upsets the whole system of intellectual and moral relations, in that its development means precisely that any given act is conceived as useful or harmful, as virtuous or wicked, only insofar as it has as its point of reference the modern Prince itself, and serves to increase its power or oppose it. In individual consciences, the Prince takes the place of the divinity or the categorical imperative and becomes the basis for a modern secularism and for a complete secularization of all aspects of life and of all relationships of custom. (*SPN*, 133; "Quaderno 13," 1561)

From the very beginning, the monarchic state borrowed the trappings of spirituality for the purposes of legitimation, but the reference to secularization, especially in the twentieth century, is of a very different order. Culture in its new status emerges at the moment when the principal arbiter, the central authority, is no longer viewed as outside of history. Gramsci is describing not only a shift in the social order—its reconstitution—and a shift in consciousness but also a shift in their relationship. To be precise, a state-governed secularism signals a new form of mediation. For Gramsci this situation, in its early twentieth-century rendition, opens up the possibility of a conflicting series of mediators vying for a central position that has to be perpetually enforced. Religion and those who speak for the deity become historical players like any other, with the exception of their long-standing history, which is an advantage in the struggle over legitimacy. In this conception, power takes a form that requires constant attention: in regard to the modern prince, for instance, it accrues to a figure of thought. The modern prince, which is always directed toward statehood, becomes the point of reference for achieving social identity. This understanding provides the barest glimpse of what will later become consumerism, when one's individual actions realize their meanings in a seemingly haphazard way, without reference to a social and historical anchor. Gramsci's further elaboration of this new realm of mediation, while remaining bound up with the notion of statehood, only hints at the more radical transformations that will to a certain extent verify his analysis. Two terms that are often discussed, for example, *Fordism,* which describes production characterized by a specific market form and deployment of capital, and *Americanism,* a precise notion of Fordism's accompanying cultural production, are limit-terms of this conception of history that emphasize the necessarily global nature of the modern historical enterprise.

The close links Gramsci perceives between modern cultural economy and secularization are apparent in his ongoing concerns about the church as a threat to statehood generally and in respect to particular states: "If the state renounces being the permanently active center of its own, autonomous, culture, the Church cannot help but triumph in substance" ("Quaderno 16," 1872). In other words, despite the spiritual power the church as social structure represents, in the epoch of the modern state it has no privileged place as guarantor of temporal power. And the state occupies the position of guarantor only to the extent that it controls culture. Thus state and culture go hand in hand, so closely, in effect, that neither is the condition of the other. One immediately implies the other in the prevailing political economy of the modern state. Building a cultural identity also builds the "state," and not simply its foundations, just as seizing state power entails establishing control of cultural institutions along with the rest of civil society. By choosing to base his concept of intervention on a cultural politics, a pragmatic, and perhaps necessary, decision in view of the physical resources of the state, Gramsci essentially anchored his political action in his belief in, and understanding of, the historical process. Cultural politics, within the confines of a political economy based on statehood, mimics the dynamics of tradition building:

> Affirming that the philosophy of praxis is a new, independent, original conception, though a moment of world historical development, is to affirm the independence and originality of a new culture in incubation that will be developed with the development of social relations. What exists from one moment to the next is a variable combination of old and new, a momentary equilibrium of cultural relations corresponding to the equilibrium of social relations. The cultural problem is imposed in all its complexity and tends toward a consistent solution only after the creation of the state. In any event, the attitude preceding the state formation cannot but be critical-polemical and never dogmatic, it should be a romantic attitude, whose romanticism consciously aspires to its composed classicism.[6]

The philosophy of praxis, a set phrase used in the notebooks to convey Marxism, draws on the past for which it is the historical future and views the moment of statehood as the future outcome of its present activity. This future projection comes to exist in the present by virtue of the modern prince, a figure of thought that mobilizes a conception of history and historical action.

Because of the twists and turns of history, the cultural sphere holds the key to the future, to the modern prince's ascension to power. Prior to the creation of the state, however, cultural intervention operates differently than it will once the state is in place. Instead of consolidating power, it creates possibilities, conditions for future configurations of stability. In a sense, it means negotiating the historical present with a conceptual agenda that includes dismantling the past by reinterpreting it. As with any notion of so-called organic history, a history that evolves toward ever more complex, higher stages of development, it requires a moment of romanticism, or the recognition of incompleteness, fragmentariness;

yet in Gramsci's schema, this "romantic" perspective is the basis for consciously striving for completeness.

This very detailed conception of history, with the correlative understanding of the state as essential for controlling the social order, lends a coherence to what might be called the Gramscian project. Although the term *historical materialism* has often been used euphemistically to describe Marxism, Gramsci's materialist notion of history is less formulaic because of the historical role it assigns to culture. It is materialist in the sense that no category of thought and culture is exempt from the force of history; those that claim to originate outside of history—religion or aesthetics, for example—are highly suspect.

The notebooks, fragmentary as they are, thus represent a wide-ranging attempt to remap the categories of culture and knowledge. Because the role of culture is so critical to the notebooks' overall political project, their remapping of cultural categories simultaneously addresses how to translate this historical conception into practice and political action. The notebook on subaltern groups and the role of the historian most explicitly aims to redirect and redefine critical history, but other notebooks proceed in similar fashion with other objects of analysis. Because of the integrated and overlapping spheres of cultural mediation, one object of analysis leads to another, and recommendations for reconceiving and motivating the new culture abound. The notebooks' recurring themes, which undergo massive expansion because of Gramsci's propensity to think by elaborating on his reading, only to be regrouped and organized according to select subjects, constitute a vast network that lays the groundwork for enacting a cultural and political agenda. These reflections represent an attentiveness to issues ranging from the smallest detail to the broadest abstraction.

In the much discussed Notebook 12, "Notes and Loose Jottings for a Group of Essays on the History of Intellectuals," history, the ever present point of departure, is once again in the foreground. Yet the focus is on the sociopolitical significance of education and the intellectuals' role within a new social order; its topics include questions about how to reshape education according to an appropriate "organization of culture" (1538), in contrast to the prevailing organization of culture that survives as "cemeteries of culture" (1539)—a characterization that would undoubtedly find contemporary supporters. Squabbles about literary canons and national traditions, however, seem particularly tame when compared with the thoroughgoing transformations sketched out in the notebooks. In conjunction with formulating a new system of education appropriate to the historical moment and to disseminating a new culture that would in turn eventually support a new state, Notebook 12 affirms the historicity of even the intellectual's physiology, not simply the ideas the intellectual is to reproduce:

> The problem of creating a new stratum of intellectuals consists there-fore in the critical elaboration of the intellectual activity that exists in everyone at a certain degree of development, modifying its relationship with the muscular-nervous effort towards a new equilibrium, and en-suring that the muscular-nervous itself, insofar as it is an element of a general practical activity, which is perpetually innovating the physical and social world, becomes the foundation of a new and integral con-ception of the world. (*GR*, 321; "Quaderno 12," 1551)

This represents materialism at its most basic level: those characteristics we would identify as human are themselves no less historical than the accompanying consciousness that is modified through time. Intellec-tually, the ability to think critically, which exists potentially in all indi-viduals, no longer refers only to the self-enclosed mind but also to phys-ical action. This reference to the physical is not gratuitous but signals a change in the social role of the intellectual, in the production of knowl-edge accompanying the contemporary state, and in the worldview gen-erally. (The advent of the computer, along with notions of cyberspace and virtual reality, underscores the relevance of speculation about the historical character of physiology.) Integrality, a notion that appears again and again in the subaltern notebook and elsewhere, refers both to the relationship between the physical and mental and to a conception based on necessary links between state and civil society. In the same way that Gramsci opposes a new culture, which integrates a critical faculty with what he sometimes calls "life," to the traditional notion of culture that lays out the cemeteries and determines the bodies that will lie there, the new intellectual is opposed to the traditional humanist who speaks for a very specific cultural heritage:

> The traditional and vulgarized type of the intellectual is represented by the man of letters, the philosopher, the artist . . . The new intellectual's mode of being can no longer consist in eloquence, which is an external and momentary mover of feelings and passions, but in being actively

intermingled with practical life, as constructor, organizer, "permanent persuader" and not just a mere orator . . . ; from technique-as-work one proceeds to technique-as-science and to the humanist historical conception without which one remains a "specialist" and does not become a "leader" [*dirigente*] (specialist + politician). (*GR*, 321–22; "Quaderno 12," 1551)

Despite his own rigorous philological training, which had been the backbone of secular humanism since the nineteenth century, Gramsci predicted the end of the traditional humanist, because the intellectual's social function was becoming altered with respect to the changes in media, mass production, and socioeconomic needs of the state. The new intellectual emerges against the background of industrial labor and all it entails technologically and socially; although the description suggests what we would today call a "technocrat," having a specialization or being an "expert" is not sufficient for the purpose of political action. While this analysis scarcely prefigures the tumultuous technological, economic, and social upheavals of the last half of the twentieth century, it points to the ways that those incipient changes were already disrupting the stability of the social order. Nonetheless, humanism, or at least those aspects of humanism that merit preserving, remains important to any future culture because it is the repository of history. Humanism, because it emerged alongside the modern state and helped to establish it, preserves a necessary historical bond between the "new" state and the state it would replace.

This brief glimpse at the role of humanism hints at the disturbing complexity that results from conceiving culture as the sphere of social mediation generally and as the point of entry for building a critical movement. One issue leads to another, and another, and another, on to infinity, and no concept, category, or plan of action can be taken for granted; all have to be rethought, for they are no longer adequate to the reality they supposedly explain or describe. This is partly due to the materialist enterprise and partly due to the ambition of the historical conception. Comparing these two sorts of intellectual juxtaposes the oral economy of the traditional intellectual, which depends on a greater degree of immediacy, with the less immediate, more repetitive forms of action available to the new intellectual.[7] In this context, it is no accident that the common denominator of the humanist intellectual and the emergence of the state resides in the effectiveness of print culture, its

technological and commercial development. All of Gramsci's formulations, even the concern with culture itself, owe much to recognizing
print as coextensive with, and a necessary companion to, modern statehood.

Gramsci's endeavors to create new print venues for his ideas and analyses are well known and are reflected in his work as a journalist on *Il
grido del popolo, Avanti!, L'Ordine nuovo,* and *L'Unità.* Yet even apparently
unrelated concerns, such as parenthetical descriptions about what constitutes opinion in modern society, cannot be understood without an
implicit awareness that the publishing economy brought about an ex-
panded and radically transformed sphere of mediation: "Ideas and opinions are not 'born' spontaneously in each individual brain: they have had
a center of formation, of irradiation, of dissemination, of persuasion"
(*SPN*, 192; "Quaderno 13," 1625). Not surprisingly, this description of
opinion rests upon the state notion so clearly articulated in the notebook on subaltern groups. Contrary to unilinear notions of state control
that supposedly steals away subjectivity, this passage merely warns
against the belief that ideas and opinions originate in the subject, the individual; in view of Gramsci's overriding concern with social change,
with political agency, this affirmation is better understood as describing
the sphere of mediation, the prevailing conditions that inform one's actions.

In fact, since publishing is the primary means for preserving and disseminating culture, it has a crucial role to play in fostering the growth
and diffusion of a new culture. "Integral" journalism, which again harks
back to the goal of integrated state and civil society, is

> one that seeks not only to satisfy all the needs (of a certain category) of
> its public, but also to create and develop these needs—in a certain
> sense, to arouse its public and progressively expand it . . . [One needs
> to presuppose] that there exists, as a point of departure, a more or less
> homogeneous cultural grouping (in the broad sense) of a certain type,
> of a certain level, and especially with a certain general orientation; and
> that one wants to use such a grouping to construct an autarkic and
> complete cultural edifice, beginning directly with . . . language, that is
> with the means of expression and reciprocal contact.[8]

In the same way that opinions do not spring into existence in solitary
isolation, modern publics are not born spontaneously in a rhapsodic

moment of self-awareness. They are produced on the basis of assumptions about a cohesive cultural agenda. As so often occurs in the notebooks, this analysis both describes the way journalism functions and provides the logic for constructing a new integrated culture. This description accords with the often unacknowledged philosophy behind most critical publications, whether they have specialized or mass-market ambitions; whether the accuracy of this philosophy continues to hold may serve as an index to the continued relevance of Gramsci's explicit recommendations for contemporary critical movements. Moreover, this notion of cultural production and mass audience applies just as well to the marketing philosophy of any new commercial product, although, of course, the relationship between capital investment and return on investment is governed by a different set of expectations.[9] As always, the predominance of the state concept is apparent in the reference to a common language. Just as those consolidating the state move quickly to adopt a state language, devise vernacular grammars, and suppress the languages of rival groups, the mechanisms of culture structurally depend on the foundation of linguistic commonality.

While Gramsci endorsed the statist notion of social organization, his rigorous historicism prevented any illusions about repeating modes of the past in the present: "The unitary national elaboration of a homogeneous collective consciousness demands a wide range of conditions and initiatives. Diffusion from a homogeneous center of a homogeneous way of thinking and operating is the principal condition, but it must not and cannot be the only one. A widely held error consists in thinking that every social stratum elaborates its consciousness and its culture in the same way, with the same methods" (*CW*, 416–417; "Quaderno 24," 2267). This specific historical understanding separates Gramsci from cultural commentators as diverse as Matthew Arnold, György Lukács, Theodor Adorno, and Dwight Macdonald; his theory of culture, because it is based not on aesthetic principles but on sociohistorical analysis of culture in relationship to the state, refrains from preemptive dismissals of mass production. Literature, a central cultural category for humanism, remains for him exemplary for forming critical culture; but the new formulation no longer works according to traditional strategies of preservation and, in a second moment, of dissemination by culture's legitimate inheritors. An unadulterated notion of humanistic literature and literary production gives way to one that derives from the techniques of mass production, which Gramsci refers to as "the question of the so-called 'popular literature,' that is, with the success of serial literature (adventure stories, detective stories, mysteries, and so forth) among the national masses, a success that is assisted by cinema and newspapers" (*CW*, 101; "Quaderno 15," 1821).

Although Gramsci's conception remains tied to the national sphere in a way that has diminished its explanatory power today, it acknowledges that the technology of publishing had fundamentally reconfigured the cultural terrain. This active stance regarding present, past, and—ulti-mately—future history leaves little room for nostalgia or utopia, the twin categories often serving to consolidate most theories grounded in an understanding of historical process. The "new culture" emerges as a response to the cultural situation providing the very means for its exis-tence: "Only from the readers of serial literature can one select a suf-ficient and necessary public for creating the cultural base of the new lit-erature . . . The premise of the new literature cannot but be historical and political, popular. It must aim at elaborating what already exists, whether polemically or in some other way does not matter; what does matter, though, is that it sink its roots into the humus of popular culture as it is" (*CW*, 102; "Quaderno 15," 1821–1822).

Just as the impetus for cultural and political action departs from the present—the more intrusive state, the maturing of a mass public, the breakdown of timeworn institutions of hegemony—it aims toward in-tervention in that present. Yet what Gramsci's analyses suggest is not simply a new form of action superimposed on centuries-old social, polit-ical, and cultural relationships: this form of action necessarily devolves from the economy of modern culture in the early twentieth century. The qualitative shift in the economy of culture meant that it had become truly secularized, revealing itself to be produced in the confrontation of conflicting historical forces. The sociohistorical situation had uncovered a new understanding of culture in its political role and consequences: culture became recognized as an issue in its own right, and today's strug-gles, knowingly or not, grow out of the transformed situation Gramsci describes. Gramsci's often very practical recommendations, of course, retain more than mere vestiges of traditional humanism, yet in coming to terms with the contemporary state, his historical perspective shifts the conceptual grounds for understanding culture.

The sense of urgency that runs through the notebooks is not tangential to the historical vision that underlies them. The necessary emergence of new collectivities—new possibilities for historical organization and new figures of thought to launch them—serves as the basis for the project sketched out in the notebooks, but these possibilities also inform the most immediate context for the oppressive potential that Gramsci glimpsed and worked to stave off. The concrete operation of the state, particularly as it evolved between the twentieth century's two world wars, represented a different sort of historical confrontation. Whereas the modern state corresponded to the decline of traditional forms of community and to new forms of social and cultural autonomy, the eventual collapse of the old social order, accompanied by ever more refined means of mass production, paved the way for a potential reduction in social autonomy itself. This subordination of civil society to the state was a principal characteristic of fascism, which Gramsci was to know firsthand. The subaltern notebook, with its interest in linking the historian's practice to the subaltern groups' achievement of self-consciousness, pinpoints the historical significance of the totalitarian state, the notebooks' much-used synonym for fascism: "Contemporary dictatorships legally abolish even these new forms of autonomy and force their incorporation into the activity of the state: the legal centralization of the entirety of national life in the hands of the dominant group becomes 'totalitarian'" ("Quaderno 25," 2287). In this characterization, the institutions of civil society become identified with the state itself instead of working indirectly to maintain state stability; the sphere of mediation is greatly reduced, and executive action becomes more pronounced, at the expense of symbolic action that most often characterizes so-called democratic states.

Gramsci's incarceration afforded him the motive, the time, and the opportunity for unceasing reflection on state, civil society, and culture. Yet while his considerations on the workings of culture present the most comprehensive view of its social and political significance, he was obviously not the sole thinker to recognize the quantitative and qualitative transformations taking place in the realm of cultural production and the novel historical conceptions they required. Interestingly, the notebooks' careful and detailed analyses, which force a new perspective on the terms and concepts of traditional cultural understanding, offer a productive configuration for considering other efforts to interpret this series of transformations. Most prominent among these other efforts, and certainly the most provocative if one is to judge by subsequent commentary, is Walter Benjamin's "The Work of Art in the Age of Mechanical Reproducibility," an essay that belongs to the same critical and historical context as Gramsci's notebooks. Because of Benjamin's specific set of concerns, however, the essay opens up a different dimension of the question.

Apart from the obvious similarities between the historical fate of Benjamin's and Gramsci's work in general, with questions about establishing the various texts and fragments and with diverse schools of interpretation, of sometimes contradictory political inclination, vying for supremacy, Benjamin's essay on mechanical reproducibility duplicates in microcosm the objective conditions of Gramsci's notebooks. Benjamin's essay, perhaps the most philosophical and certainly the most compressed statement on the issue, nonetheless complicates matters even further because of its original publication in a French version that cannot be reduced to any of Benjamin's three German-language versions. In addition, therefore, to its significance as an interpretive gloss to the second German version, a gloss that Benjamin to a certain extent endorsed, the French version has an independent status alongside the German-language drafts, the numerous manuscript pages that were recast or discarded, and pertinent correspondence on the essay. And it is precisely the French text's independent status, established in large part because of pressures from Max Horkheimer and those working with the *Zeitschrift für Sozialforschung,* where it was published, that initially points to the common concerns of this essay and the recurring themes of Gramsci's notebooks. Not unlike Gramsci's own practice, which often substitutes abstract locutions for more explicit Marxist terminology, Benjamin's essay was rigorously edited to eliminate any concept that smacked of Marxism. To cite a few examples: "fascism" became "totalitarian state" or "authoritarian regime"; "imperialist" became "modern"; and "communism" became "the constructive forces of humanity."[10] In sum, this essay, inherently difficult merely in its formulations, exists in uncensored versions—that is, three different German texts, none of which was published during Benjamin's lifetime—and in an altered version that permits a contrasting perspective on the project as a whole.

In his letters, Benjamin is very clear about the essay's ambitious aims. In a letter to Horkheimer, he describes it as "making a thrust in the direction of a materialist theory of art"; in effect, the letter continues, it strove "to give questions of art theory a truly contemporary form." In a letter to Gershom Scholem written two weeks later, Benjamin is more explicit about the motivation of the essay; its ruminations "anchor the history of nineteenth-century art in the recognition of their situation as experienced by us in the present."[11] This essay, like so many of Gramsci's remarks, draws its impetus from the present without sacrificing the goals of historical understanding dependent on a theoretical perspective that Benjamin calls "universal history." Whereas Gramsci's analysis departs from the terms of political economy to arrive at issues of culture, Benjamin's essay structures its argument around the question of symbolic production and its corresponding social, epistemological, and economic significance. On the basis of this formulation, which the essay often refers to under the rubric of aesthetics, Benjamin makes specific claims about the nature of fascism or what the French version characterizes as the totalitarian state.[12] Benjamin's much-cited conclusions echo those of Gramsci: "Fascism [or, in the French version, the totalitarian state] attempts to organize the newly created proletarian masses . . . Fascism sees its salvation in giving these masses not their right, but instead a chance to express themselves. The masses have a right to change property relations; Fascism seeks to give them an expression while preserving property. The logical result of Fascism is the introduction of aesthetics into political life."[13]

Within the terms of its own argument, this passage characterizes the workings of the fascist, or totalitarian, state, specifically with regard to the emerging masses and the new sociopolitical relations their emergence entails. This formulation of the aestheticization of the political sphere, which is simultaneously a politicization of the so-called aesthetic sphere, exhibits the dialectical character that runs through all of Benjamin's work. The state openly intervenes in aesthetic production to give the masses expression while preserving the realm of law and right for itself, yet at the same time this aesthetic intervention extends the domain of state power and control. This is precisely what Gramsci designates in asserting that "the legal centralization of the entirety of national life in the hands of the dominant group becomes 'totalitarian'"—that is, the totalitarian state openly intrudes into areas of autonomous or semi-autonomous activity.

Unpredictability in the social order translates into instability and, consequently, undermines what society exists to maintain. In the modern state, stability is often expressed in terms of property and ownership; for Benjamin, as for Gramsci, the questioning of property relations is a consequence of a newly emerging mass consciousness and the social and cultural means that create its possibility. Benjamin's concern with mechanical reproducibility, and with film as its most striking contemporary manifestation, relates to the overriding historical interest in the social and epistemological role of culture, art, and tradition. Thus the essay has a twofold purpose: on the one hand, it seeks to assess the social possibilities that accompany the technological and cultural changes; on the other, it condemns the state manipulation of these new media and the cultural economy they foster, a manipulation dedicated to defusing forces the media unleashed. These divergent tendencies confront each other in the constitution of the masses, in the degree of their self-awareness: the cult of the film star has as its complement "the cult of the public, [which] furthers the masses' corrupt state of mind that Fascism seeks to substitute for their class consciousness."[14] These observations about public versus class consciousness seem necessarily incomplete today, when in fact the "public" has achieved a global cohesiveness at the same time that it has fragmented into numerous unequal "publics," alternately created and abolished by market forces. Nonetheless, the essay's power and continuing relevance derive from its treatment of film as exemplary of the mass media that produced new economies of mass agency and awareness.

The state's attempt to master and channel the potentially disruptive masses took the form of subordinating culture and technology to its own ends. This is a commonsensical notion today, especially in regard to fascism and the totalitarian state in general. Yet the most straightforward description of this process, in a sentence that appears in only the third and final German version of the essay, leads one to suspect that the significance for the epoch of "mechanical reproducibility" lies elsewhere: "The violation of the masses, whom Fascism, with its Führer cult, forces to their knees, has its counterpart in the violation of an apparatus which is pressed into the production of ritual values [Kultwerten]" ("Work of Art," 241; GS, 1: 506). What happens in the sphere of executive action has its counterpart in the symbolic or "cultural" sphere. As it does throughout the essay, the apparatus refers here to the system of technological reproduction embodied in and represented by film. More striking, however, are the means by which fascism strove to "violate the

masses," in Benjamin's words. It sought to usurp the mechanism of technological reproducibility in order to produce ritual, cult values that hark
back to the epoch of the so-called aura and to another form of collective
existence.[15] In sum, this is fascism's great anachronism: it attempted to
inject the forms of a superseded cultural economy into a logic of culture
and technology that was antithetical to it.

While it goes without saying that the new technologies and emergent
forms of mass consciousness did not develop in isolation from the flow
of capital and political economy generally, the essay's immediate context
is the new accommodation required between politics, aesthetics, and the
masses. Nowhere is this context more unadorned than in Benjamin's
first efforts to express the notions that would later appear reformulated
in the epilogue:

> The most far-reaching changes in the two realms—in the aesthetic as
> well as in the political—are bound up with that large-scale mass move-
> ment, in the course of which the masses occupy the foreground of the
> historical stage with a previously unknown insistence and with a previ-
> ously unknown direct-indirect consciousness. This has its drastic ex-
> pression in two of this epoch's most important turning points, whose
> common and undisguised manifestation is fascism. They are the de-
> cline of democracy and the preparation for war. (*GS*, 7: 669)

In the essay's subsequent versions, this mass adherence to fascism translates into the notion of the public, which becomes further qualified in
the final version. In terms of Marxist categories, the crux of the issue resides in the reference to "direct-indirect" consciousness, a partial self-
consciousness that impedes the proletariat's understanding of itself as a
historical protagonist. Yet these categories express only abbreviated aspects of the historical transformation taking place. As Benjamin's focus
on technology reveals, mass consciousness and altered forms of subjective agency are inherent in the logic of modern capitalism and its concomitant culture; the conflict over consciousness and its eventual forms
was, and to a large extent remains today, the terrain for discussing implications of the new technology that increasingly governs modern society.
The rupture, gradual as it was, between a society resting on a culture of
tradition-bound certainty and a society characterized by rapid and unpredictable, almost vertiginous change, concerns all subsequent political and cultural economies.

In this broad context, aesthetics, understood historically, along with its links to the concept of tradition and sociopolitical authority, becomes the means for relating state, culture, and history in an interpretive framework. The decay of the "aura," for example, a commonplace from Benjamin's work circulated on a par with Gramscian hegemony, is closely tied to the emerging masses. The circumstances of the "contemporary decay of the aura," made possible by mass production, "are related to the increasing consciousness of the masses and the increasing intensity of their movements."[16] The loss of the aura indicates a greater danger for the social order than simply political upheaval, for aura has a strong epistemological charge. Introduction of aura into the analysis emphasizes the radical nature of the mass transformation taking place—a mass transformation in terms of both production and reception. This section introducing the aura concludes with a sentence that remained unchanged throughout all drafts of the essay: "The effect of reality on the masses and of the masses on reality is a process of unlimited scope, as much for thinking as for perception [*Anschauung*]" ("Work of Art," 223; *GS*, 1: 480). While on the surface this statement integrates the discussion of aura into philosophical discourse, it also claims that thought and perception are subject to historical change, an assertion that runs counter to the traditional precepts of knowledge.[17] These historical claims, in fact, constitute the basis for understanding aura's significance: "And if the changes in the medium of contemporary perception can be comprehended as the decay of the aura, it is possible to show its social causes" ("Work of Art," 222; *GS*, 1: 479). "Aura," with its decay and attendant sociopolitical effects, points to the historicity not only of knowledge but also of the faculties of knowledge.

In addition to, and not despite, claims of universalism, Benjamin's statements about the historicity of thought and knowing are rooted in contemporary historical concerns. The disruption—historical, social, cultural—occasioned by the advent of mass production called attention to the historicity of knowledge, because traditional concepts no longer proved adequate to the phenomena they would express. Much of the conceptual resistance in Benjamin's essay derives from the difficulties inherent in describing a historical process that becomes manifest as epistemological change. The intertwining of history and knowledge, of consciousness and epistemology, underlies the need for the "aura" concept and accounts for the essay's constant return to the notion of perception. Historically, the notion of a qualitative rupture with the past, thus constituting the contemporary "epoch" as different in unprecedented ways, enables a more concrete history to be recounted. Although this brief essay, itself more of a theoretical think piece, does not flesh out this history, its argument hinges on specified historical moments of the aura's transformation and ultimate collapse.

These moments can readily be summarized and, perhaps not entirely by happenstance, approximate Gramsci's schema of the development of state and civil society. In Benjamin's cryptic history that contextualizes an analysis of the present, the aura is originally identified with its function in tradition; aura and the perception of uniqueness, which Benjamin chooses to emphasize, characterize knowledge when symbolic production, or "art," as we might retrospectively designate its artifacts, partake directly of the structure of authority and power. This depicts the epoch when hegemony was exercised by magic and religion, and the collective reception of these cultural products was based on ritual. The second key moment in Benjamin's history concerns the incipient secularization of art, its separation from religion and therefore a shift in its collective significance; this moment, located in the Renaissance, corresponds to the establishment of a self-conscious cultural program, growth of secular institutions such as the university, the codification of vernacular languages, the emergence of the printing press—in Gramsci's terminology, this refers to the early constitution of the modern state. Ultimately, however, the changes inhering in this second moment represent a secularization only in a certain sense. The cult of beauty, with its retention of the ritualizing aspect, takes the products of art from the religious hegemony by duplicating religion's structure of cultural authority. Aura remains central to the concept of beauty because art or culture preserves its ritual function. The third moment of historical rupture is, of course, the essay's principal concern. In Benjamin's words, "For the first time in world history, mechanical reproduction emancipates the work of art from its parasitical dependence on ritual" ("Work of Art," 223; *GS*, 1: 482). This historical sketch, which places into relief the radical shift provoked by mass production, leads to the essay's forceful conclusion that art production, becoming detached from ritual, enters the political domain.

The essay refers to this shift repeatedly, often in different but related realms; the ripple effect of this series of confrontations between the collapsing hegemony and the drive to establish a new one is discussed in terms of aura, tradition, aesthetics, mass consciousness, mass production, and so on. "Doing justice to these relationships" is the essay's complex, self-proclaimed goal. Film, which unites these disruptive elements into an object of analysis, becomes the vehicle, the point of reference for the unbridgeable break with past modes of cultural production. Standing irrevocably on this side of the rupture, it does not lend itself to ritual values, despite the state's attempts to promote the cult of communal legitimacy. Thus, because of its precise location in twentieth-century culture and economy, film becomes the "most powerful agent" of historical transformation. Benjamin remarks: "Its social significance, particularly in its most positive form, is inconceivable without its destructive, cathartic aspect, that is, the liquidation of the traditional value of the cultural heritage" ("Work of Art," 221; *GS*, 1: 478). The shift, or rupture, described here goes beyond merely modifying the cultural tradition or what constitutes it. It strips culture of its traditional value, liquidates it, resulting in a transformation of culture's social function, of the way it is produced and consumed. Not least of all, it calls for reconsideration of culture's political significance, the implications of which are even more pertinent today.

In this respect, Gramsci's remarks about culture and art wrestle with similar historical concerns. Although Benjamin and Gramsci have different, almost opposed intellectual orientations, dissimilar criteria of judgment, critical methodologies, and literary inclinations, each approaches the specificity of contemporary history and politics through extensive reflection on the relationship between culture and state, between culture and historical change. Yet Gramsci's ongoing concern with culture and, by extension, with art derives from an acute interest in culture's role in supporting an eventual state structure. Thus, every discussion of culture takes place in the context of intervening in the making of culture. At the same time, Benjamin's philosophical and epistemological analysis helps situate the historical intervention conceived by Gramsci. The nature of intervention has changed in the age of mass production. Gramsci opposes "culture" to "art" and endorses culture as the more inclusive, operative concept in conjunction with the emergence of mass consciousness. As in the subaltern notebook, the following passage refers to "a new social group that enters historical life with a hegemonic attitude":

> It seems evident that, to be precise, one should speak of a struggle for a "new culture" and not for a "new art" (in the immediate sense). To be

precise, perhaps it cannot even be said that the struggle is for a new artistic content apart from form because content cannot be considered abstractly, in separation from form. To fight for a new art would mean to fight to create new individual artists, which is absurd since artists cannot be created artificially. One must speak of a struggle for a new culture, that is, for a new moral life that cannot but be intimately connected to a new intuition of life, until it becomes a new way of perceiving [*sentire*] and seeing reality and, therefore, a world intimately ingrained in "possible artists" and "possible works of art." (*CW*, 98; "Quaderno 23 [Critica letteraria]," 2192)

Culture's move into the foreground not only calls for a new form of politics but also reveals that the notion of art and its links to the individual creator belong to another hegemony, one incommensurate with the twentieth-century state and mass society. "Art," in the sense this passage critiques, is tied to immediacy, a notion necessarily accompanying a view of the individual as the originator of art, a view that ignores art's social function and the social mediation providing for its conception and realization. The emphasis on culture—that is, on the production of culture and its social origins—reintroduces the question of mediation. The focus on culture and mass consciousness, as opposed to art and the individual artist, opens up the previously unquestioned domains to conscious struggle for historical change, including perception in all senses (*sentire*) and new relationships to reality. It is not gratuitous that this assertion bears more than a casual resemblance to Benjamin's claims about the aura's dissolution. In fact, Benjamin's discussion of aura's secularization, the cult of beauty that formed in the Renaissance, is inextricably tied to the emergence of the individual creator: "To the extent to which the cult value of the painting is secularized the ideas of its fundamental uniqueness lose distinctness. In the imagination of the beholder the uniqueness of the phenomena which hold sway in the cult image is more and more displaced by the empirical uniqueness of the creator or of his creative achievement" ("Work of Art," 244 n. 6; *GS*, 1: 481 n. 8).

If one takes the terms of Benjamin's essay as a point of reference, Gramsci's notion of culture unambiguously dispenses with aura as an operative concept; with the "liquidation" of this more rigid and limited understanding of auratic culture, culture itself becomes the domain for building new historical protagonists. Moreover, the section from Gramsci's notebook on art and culture concludes with an additional paragraph that is not part of the original text (which first appeared in

Notebook 9, on the Italian Risorgimento, before being recopied into the 1934 notebook on literary criticism). The new paragraph reads:

> Therefore, one cannot talk about a new "poetic aura" being formed—to use a phrase that was in favor a few years ago. "Poetic aura" is only a metaphor to express the ensemble of those artists who have already been formed and have emerged, or at least the process of formation and emergence [that is] under way and already consolidated. (*CW,* 98; "Quaderno 23," 2193)

Whatever mystery aura might have had, whether in the context of its cult value or of the ideology of an individual creator, it has now been dispelled. Aura, specifically "poetic aura," has become only a term of historical expediency to express the group of those individuals who have come forth to produce the culture appropriate to the subaltern group in the process of being consolidated. For Gramsci, aura becomes another notion, alongside "art" and the "individual creator," that is emptied of its traditional meaning as it is historicized.

The process of secularization embodied in the modern state was fundamental for both Benjamin and Gramsci in their attempts to grasp the specificity of the twentieth-century state and culture, although where they placed their emphasis has relevant consequences. For Benjamin, the advent of the state and the secularization it signaled corresponded to, on the one hand, the separation of aura from religion, and on the other, the incipient development of mechanical reproduction in the printing press. Film, and the cultural economy it represents, carries forward in a radical fashion the cultural transformation wrought by mass-produced publishing. Moreover, the Renaissance would have been inconceivable without Gutenberg and his legacy; this conceptual understanding of printing is essential for Benjamin's argument and underlies the very notion of history his essay advances: "The enormous changes which printing, the mechanical reproduction of writing, has brought about in literature are well known. However, within the phenomenon which we are here examining from the perspective of world history, print is merely a special, though particularly important, case" ("Work of Art," 218–219; *GS,* 1: 474).

The essay's entire theory of historical understanding is generated in the tension between the print form of mechanical reproduction and its most recent visual form, which is of a different order, even if film and print are linked in Benjamin's particular perspective of universal history. Mass production, when it extends beyond the primitive mass production of printing to annex and determine other cultural domains, is infinitely more than a simple progression and continuation of mass-produced print culture. Print serves as a reference point for twentieth-century mass production only in terms of the historical understanding that attempts to outline the consequences for thought, society, and consciousness of the explosion of mass production. The specificity of Benjamin's understanding of this phenomenon, which culminated in his efforts to reappropriate the analytical and cultural categories that emerged as the agents of mass production in the age of printing, has proved to be his most far-reaching insight.

The publishing revolution, in its technical and ideological aspects, also lies at the base of Gramsci's theory of history and goals of cultural intervention. In contrast to Benjamin, the humanist cast to Gramsci's historical enterprise, with its unshakable reliance on the state concept, becomes apparent in the historical role he assigns to the emergence and ongoing impact of printing. Print ushered in a new mode of thinking and permitted the development of logic and argumentation, necessary components in "creating a new culture on a new social base, which does not have traditions like the old class of intellectuals."[18] The section "Oratory, Conversation, Culture" openly reveals the humanist orientation of Gramsci's understanding of history. Print, in contrast to speech, provides the social and intellectual means for the new social group to challenge the dominant cultural order. Over against culture reproduced according to an oral economy, the art of printing "revolutionized the whole world of culture, giving to memory an aid of inestimable value and allowing an unprecedented extension of educational activity. Another kind of extension is thus implicit in this study, that of the qualitative as well as quantitative changes (mass extension) that the technical and mechanical [*strumentale*] development of the organization of culture brought to the way of thinking" (*CW,* 382; "Quaderno 16," 1891). While this passage indisputably echoes Benjamin's formulation, the ultimate divergences between Gramsci's and Benjamin's views derive from more than simply a question of contrasting sensibilities. As always in Gramsci's thought, the core of his understanding concerns the social, political, and cultural possibilities of marginalized, or subaltern, groups, particularly how these groups move from the condition of being dominated, to forming a coherent unity through cultural means, to achieving some sort of state power.

In Gramsci's conception, print culture, in addition to sparking the emergence of a multitude of new institutions and new forms of social consciousness, provides—for the first time—access to the dominant means of cultural production. For those who have been excluded, speech, or the oral economy in general, which because of this exclusion is not based on a prior legitimized knowledge, represents a dead end and the continuation of domination. Gramsci's example for this condition is to the point. The so-called traditional intellectual, who by virtue of social position and all it entails has automatic access to the dominant culture, learns almost by osmosis: "The children of educated families [*famiglie colte*] learn to speak 'grammatically,' in other words they learn the language of educated people [*persone colte:* persons who have achieved a certain level of culture], without ever having to go through specific and tiring grammatical exercises, unlike the children of parents who speak a dialect or Italian mixed with a dialect" (*CW,* 384; "Quaderno 16," 1892). In this sense, Gramsci's larger conception of history and social change is based on print culture, which for the first time extracts the means of cultural production—knowledge spanning centuries and the potential for developing oppositional interpretive strategies, alternative history, and theoretical reasoning—from the absolute monopoly of the dominant groups. Although Gramsci brings a radical perspective to bear on the question of culture, his views of print culture accord with the fundamental precepts of humanist understanding. These views, however, determine the moral imperatives he reiterates in the notebooks, which often relate to questions of bodily and mental discipline, of concentration, all of which have to do with training oneself to obtain and internalize knowledge that was not readily part of one's psychosocial makeup. While one might be tempted to make an analogy between this philosophical and political position and Gramsci's biography, more pertinent is the fact that this model of social and cultural change, along with the institutions to promote it, represented a theory of knowledge and history on which a movement could be founded.

Against this background, Benjamin's and Gramsci's differences in regard to print culture and the state can be pinpointed in their respective views of contemporary journalism and, by extension, film, for they both draw analogies between journalism and film. Before radio and television developed to complement, or even usurp, many of its social functions, journalism played a major role in consolidating and maintaining the polity. Despite Gramsci's own project for an "integral" journalism to build a new culture, he maintained that existing journalism operated according to an oral economy that did not measure up to the reflective thought characterizing the written economy. This view is almost prescient, for the competitors of today's print journalism are all media that clearly belong to orality, whether television, radio, or electronic communication. In Gramsci's words, "The newspaper is very close to oratory and conversation. Newspaper articles are usually written in a hurry, are improvised, and are for the most part like speeches made at public meetings because of the speed with which they are conceived and argued" (*CW*, 381; "Quaderno 16," 1890). Although journalism is obviously part of print culture, it is not on a par with books or journals; in considering the "solidity of a culture," a phrase Gramsci often uses in depicting the historical staying power of a developed culture, journalism poses only a rudimentary and unreliable stability. Journalism is a necessary component of national culture, but it cannot provide the basis for cultural tradition; like a conversation, it seldom stands the test of time, and a cultural tradition, which serves as the guarantor of, and means for, producing historical self-consciousness, is at the same time history and access to that history.

For Benjamin, especially in the context of his concern with the technological means of cultural production and the correlative effects on the sociopolitical order, journalism has a significant role more because it is a mass medium than because it mimics conversation. In fact, journalism is the mass medium that most urgently introduces the question of social, political, and cultural agency, and on that basis, it is paradigmatic for film: "With the increasing extension of the press, which kept placing new political, religious, scientific, professional, local organs before the readers, an increasing number of readers became writers . . . Thus, the distinction between author and public is about to lose its basic character. The difference becomes merely functional; it may vary from case to case. At any moment the reader is ready to turn into a writer" ("Work of Art," 232; *GS*, 1: 493).

Twentieth-century mass media, which Benjamin knew in their incipient form, always subject to control by an overzealous state, reconfigured individual and mass consciousness. The transformed nature of subjectivity, which is briefly described in the fluctuating interaction between individual and public, denies any unilinear notion of "mass communication": the mass is, in a way, communicating with itself, with each interlocutor occupying alternately diverging poles of an ongoing dialogue. Benjamin would, of course, deal with this hybrid form of subjectivity in many of his other writings, ranging from the dynamics of tradition and orality in "The Storyteller" to his analysis of Edgar Allan Poe's "The Man of the Crowd" and the concept of the flaneur. According to the logic of technological reproduction, this unstable form of mass agency poses problems for state attempts to mediate and, therefore, regulate the content and the nature of the mass's communication with itself. Against the totalitarian drive to master and contain this instability with state models inappropriate to the task, Benjamin argued from the perspective of world history and focused on the logic of technology that underlay mass media. Film, the implications of which were only becoming apparent when Benjamin was writing, represented the future of that logic, and today one could extend it to technological media scarcely imaginable in the 1930s, even in the annals of science fiction.

As for Gramsci, his underestimation of film and the mass media it exemplifies derives from his historical allegiance to the precepts of humanism, to the necessary relationship it endorses between culture and state in particular. Gramsci's own organized efforts to counter the state had a decisive impact on his understanding of how that opposition should take place; although he resolutely fought to reformulate culture in the context of this struggle, his conception of mass consciousness and the role of culture owes much to the contemporary state that was the object of his analysis and that determined the terrain of his opposition. Gramsci's brief consideration of film, in addition to bringing into focus important aspects of Benjamin's essay, highlights the terms of state-based theories of culture. For Gramsci, film, like journalism, not only simulates but also belongs to an oral economy: "Even today, spoken communication is a means of ideological diffusion which has a speed, field of action, and an emotional simultaneity far greater than written communication (theatre, cinema and radio, with its loudspeakers in public squares, beat all forms of written communication, including books, periodicals, newspapers and notices pasted on walls)—but superficially, not in depth" (CW, 382–383; "Quaderno 16," 1891).

Although the argument seems to be a conceptual one, aligning cinema with speech precisely because it is not the medium for in-depth analysis and criticism, for building a new culture, it also represents a political position drawn from the immediate historical situation. Speech, in the form of oratory, and the mass media that extended its range, was a primary means for fascist consolidation of the state. This aspect of fascist practice is, of course, vigorously critiqued in Benjamin as well; in this instance, however, the reference to speech has to do not with speech itself, not with language, but with nonwritten forms of communication. Unlike the case of journalism versus more reflective and enduring forms of print culture, in which forms of written communication are themselves hierarchized according to their "cultural solidity" or suitability for forming the basis of a new culture, spoken communication belongs to a different order altogether, partly because of its immediacy, partly because of its appeal to emotion.[19]

In other words, Gramsci's political understanding of humanism signals endorsement of the state conception as a model for political and cultural action and determines the scant attention he gives to the sociopolitical implications of mass technology, including cinema. Given Gramsci's unusually progressive views of so-called popular, or mass, culture, cinema's unheralded role in culture has to do with this conceptual framework of humanism. Superficially, since writing serves as the foundation of national-cultural tradition, cinema cannot be readily identified as nation-specific because it is not written. Cinema's peculiar status, however, seems to depend more on its relationship to its potential audience. This becomes apparent in the way Gramsci defines literary culture, which he refers to as literary art in distinction to other forms of art or culture: "From the viewpoint of cultural history, and thus also of cultural 'creation' . . ., there exists a difference between literary art and other forms of artistic expression (figurative, musical, orchestral) . . . [In reference to literary art,] 'verbal' expression has a strictly national-popular-cultural character" (*CW*, 122; "Quaderno 23," 2194). Here verbal expression does not mean speech, or oral communication, but rather means verbalization of a text written in a specific national language; the examples offered are reading original texts by Goethe or Dante, which represent literary, as opposed to nonliterary, culture. Nonliterary culture refers to "art" in the form of a Michelangelo sculpture or a Verdi musical composition, cultural artifacts that admit of experience by those not sharing the culture where they originate. Understanding Goethe in the original German means being German, although Gramsci specifies that this has no racial or ethnic implications: it means simply that one participates, or is able to participate, in German culture. Moreover, while those nonliterary arts may have a national-cultural substratum, they also "travel," in the contemporary language of commercial trade, and as a result, they are not intrinsically national-popular-cultural, a designation that has an exclusivity built into it.

The precepts of humanism are well known if not often discussed. Language, which is central to culture and to the collectivity whose togetherness is produced and maintained by that culture, represents the medium for establishing collective unity. While modern culture, which emerged in conjunction with the modern state, requires that the unifying language be written, written language is a necessary, but not sufficient, condition for state or national culture. Journalism, for example, fulfills the necessary condition—it is written, but it plays only a supportive role in disseminating culture because of its temporal limitations, its inability to transcend its historical moment. In addition to a repository of texts that are language-specific yet not historically limited, the idea of modern cultural unity requires historical justification and a class of intellectuals to determine the course of that history and to adjudicate claims against it; when such a body of texts does not exist, intellectuals must craft them or cobble them together, a charge that in the nineteenth century fell to the philologists. Departing from this historical, political, social, and cultural understanding, Gramsci rightly evolved a model for achieving state power that began with a subaltern group, which for him was the proletariat, that assumed what he termed a "hegemonic attitude" and set out to consolidate a culture designed to provide the group with an awareness of itself as a historical protagonist. This understanding, historically determined, in that state and culture have operated in collusion from the outset, a collusion always more blatant in totalitarian regimes, led to predictable conclusions.

Forms of culture that are not anchored in language, specifically written language, exceed the configuration of nation and culture. While in Gramsci's notebooks this is obviously the case for cinema, it is also the case for the so-called figurative arts and for oratory. In effect, oratory provides the paradigm for all nonwritten culture, as for example, when Italians, because of shared historical experience, can follow a non-Italian speaker who speaks in a language other than Italian. For Gramsci, the predominance of nonlinguistic elements affects both the mode of reception and the potential size of the public:

> In oratory speech is not the only element: there are also gestures, tone of voice and so on . . .: gesture in the broad sense, which scans and articulates the wave of feeling and passion.
>
> These observations are indispensable for establishing a cultural politics and they are fundamental for a cultural politics of the popular masses. They explain the international "success" of cinema and, earlier, of opera and music in general. (*CW,* 123; "Quaderno 23," 2194–2195)

As is customary from the perspective of print culture, nonlinguistic elements of representation are identified with sentiment, emotion, with aspects of experience that cannot be objectively registered in writing. Cinema is a form of mass culture that speaks to masses both inside and outside the national border; it cannot be wholly grasped by the category of national culture. By contrast, a truly national culture necessarily operates along the axis of inclusion and exclusion; one has to share it in order to have access to it. In terms of the epoch of print hegemony, with all the institutions of life and law that accompany it, Gramsci's views of culture and state are accurate and unassailable. The question remains, however, whether cinema, as a drastically different form of mechanical reproduction, can be appropriately evaluated according to the paradigm of print hegemony, and whether it does not signal the advent of an incompatible logic of reproduction.

Although Gramsci relegated cinema to a secondary role in the constitution of cultural hegemony, listing it alongside music, opera, and so on, cinema has a distinction that the other arts cannot replicate: it cannot be separated from the mass production that creates it. This difference, which Gramsci did not remark, becomes the central motif in Benjamin's study precisely because his discussion of film is really an analysis of an entirely new economy of culture: "In the case of films, mechanical reproduction is not, as with literature and painting, an external condition for mass distribution. Mechanical reproduction is inherent in the very technique of film production. This technique not only permits in the most direct way but virtually causes mass distribution" ("Work of Art," 244 n. 7; *GS,* 1: 481–482 n. 9). Many analogies could be drawn between film and painting, on the one hand, and film and printing, on the other. Film, silent film in particular, shares with painting the potential for a transnational audience, whereas with printed material it shares the built-in necessity for a mass audience. But the significance of film, and the mass production it exemplifies, resides elsewhere. Despite attempts by subsequent film criticism to import into film print concepts such as director-auteur, film on the level of creation remains as anonymous as the mass it addresses. The reasons for this, as Benjamin suggests, are as much economic as inherent in the process of making a film. Individuals cannot supply the extensive capital required to produce a film, a situation that is even truer today than in the 1930s; the extraordinary capital investment in film reflects the needs of mass production generally, although film was arguably the first and most blatantly ideological, because it openly challenged the precepts of print culture. Film causes mass distribution in its very logic, because mass replication and distribution are necessary for a return on the enormous investment. Just as a film cannot be made without investment in the mechanical means of reproduction, it cannot be viewed without the mediation of technology. Consequently, reception of the film is not based on the customary notion of material possession. Even today, with the widespread availability of videocassettes, there is no access to the film, to its series of images, without massive technological mediation; its existence as an object that can be purchased and possessed cannot be equated with that of a painting or book, even though contemporary book production itself has more and more adopted the logic of mass production and distribution.

The introduction of speech in film, in the first instance, seemed to reassert the power of the state in the new economy of culture and mechanical reproduction. As Benjamin remarks: "With the sound film, to be sure, a setback in its international distribution occurred at first: audiences became limited by language barriers. This coincided with the Fascist emphasis on national interests. It is more important to focus on this connection with Fascism than on this setback, which was soon minimized by synchronization" ("Work of Art," 244 n. 7; GS, 1: 481–482 n. 9). In Benjamin's conception, technology, by virtue of the further development of its own logic, countered attempts to reimpose national interests. Synchronization, which allowed for repackaging and making accessible the nonlinguistic visual image that is the vehicle of film, created the basis for an even larger mass audience, thereby further challenging hegemonic notions of national culture. This view, coupled with Benjamin's materialist understanding of history, helps explain assertions that his essay would resist appropriation by those who endorsed fascism or the totalitarian state: history was moving inexorably in the opposite direction.

Nevertheless, the new disposition of capital is the aspect of synchronization that is most important for subsequent developments of mass production: the sound film "merged new capital from the electrical industry with that of the film industry. Thus, viewed from the outside, the sound film promoted national interests, but seen from the inside it helped to internationalize film production even more than previously" ("Work of Art," 244 n. 7; *GS*, 1: 481–482 n. 9). Even though language, with all its national differences, emerged to play a role in film, in the global cultural network it led to a de-emphasis of the nation, because it represented a shift in the center of gravity from the nation to industries, themselves not necessarily based in the same nations or in nations with wholly compatible interests. The intertwined industries and global interests of today are unfathomable even in the terms of Benjamin's own analyses.

Although Benjamin's later comments indicate a more concretely political understanding of the sound film, the global perspective remained the point of departure. In a letter to Adorno of 9 December 1938, Benjamin writes: "I see more and more clearly that the launching of the sound film must be regarded as an operation of the cinema industry designed to break the revolutionary primacy of the silent film, which generated reactions that were hard to control and hence politically dangerous."[20] As in the essay on mechanical reproduction, mass production and film signaled the breakup of cultural and political hegemony based on print culture and accompanying nationhood. At the same time, however, since culture functions to stabilize potential disruptions in the social and economic order, a new cultural hegemony has been in the making, one that corresponds to the new importance of industry apart from its national provenance and to new forms of global capital. In an interesting parallel, the journal *The Economist* describes this transition as it relates to print culture: "In Gutenberg's day, the output from printing presses was both rare and potentially subversive; church and state sought to own the presses, or at least to control what they published. As the technology spread, control became more difficult and was deemed less necessary. Today publishing is as easily and suitably dealt with by private markets as light bulbs are."[21]

In the twentieth century, the transition to mass production was abrupt and surprisingly complete in its historically rapid expansion to all sectors of economic, social, and political life. Today this shift to the transnational arena is accelerating at an ever faster pace; fewer and fewer companies and products are really national. And just as Benjamin treated film as an early emblem of this transformation, one could make a similar series of historical claims about the automobile, no less an index of mass production and virtually omnipresent in twentieth-century economy and culture. Yet, as *The Economist* indicates concerning printing, the decline in overt state intervention corresponds to a growth in the force of the market, an agent no less anonymous than the masses it is claimed to serve. And the market itself, geared to a mass scale, whether in terms of production, circulation, distribution, or capital of socially unmarked provenance, requires a controlled, but voracious, consumerism, which has become the engine of this new political and cultural economy.

Contemporary cultural production, which simultaneously projects collective images and disperses them into disparate consumers, has shattered the aura of tradition, fostered a transformed political economy. The multiple matter of contemporary cultural artifacts, including their diverse media and necessary global circulation, has set in motion a new institutional logic that is no longer immediately accessible to the quaint concepts and figures of modern historical understanding. This logic of cultural production, which runs counter to ideas of national patrimony, humanist ideals, and the literary domination of culture, has irrevocably transformed the relationship between culture and collectivity, a founding amalgam of modernity.

8

Reflections on the Force of the Figure

Engaging the notions of figuration, the way that seemingly nonmaterial ideas produce material effects, involves historical issues that stress the overlap between literary concerns and political interests. Although concern with figures of thought has traditionally been inseparable from thinking about written texts, the conceptual tools of literary understanding are not only applicable to other cultural domains and productions but also are necessary for coming to terms with their emergence, historical significance, and political economy. This realization has begun to transform the study of literature and language, rendering it more self-critical and more oriented toward the societal forces that impinge on it and to which it contributes. In this critical context, for example, Edward W. Said straightforwardly proposes a conceptual model that involves thinking "both in political and above all theoretical terms."[1] Theoretical reflection on culture at large incorporates and draws its impetus from literary thinking, which since the invention of writing has been central to forming political hegemonies and to the unfolding of human traditions, as well as to the historical continuity they provide. Ultimately, yoking the theories of literary and linguistic production to analyses of political interests inevitably leads to questions about potential materialist understandings of history.

Before broaching these implications for critical thinking, the reference to literature and literary understanding requires further comment. Elaborating a materialist understanding of written culture, including its ideas, concepts, and linguistic presuppositions, necessarily departs from the operative notions of literature in modernity. The term *literature* bears the burden of its institutionalization in the epoch of modernity and, in its nationalist versions (for example, French literature, Spanish literature, and so on), has been the glue of cultural hegemony since the beginnings of literary history in the late eighteenth century. In the modern structure of the university, literary disciplines and, later, departments have been identified with ahistorical humanist values, universal qualities to which all human beings in all historical times should aspire.[2] In virtually all present-day literary histories, the Renaissance marks the moment when literature—that is, secular writing—became the vehicle both of abstract universal values and of the national or communal identities that claim to share them. Consequently, every cultural group striving for national or communal hegemony in the epoch of modernity has elaborated a secular literary tradition, complete with historical account, grammars of the literary language, and dictionaries. Inescapably in the service of a given collectivity, literary scholars—who have gone under many names, ranging from philologist to humanist, from intellectual to literary critic—reinforced the institutional scaffolding of literature by creating critical editions of canonical works, reinterpreting their meanings and generally underscoring their importance for universal values (thus the category of *Weltliteratur*) and for the evolving collective consciousness of a people. In sum, the claim of literature as the bearer of universals effaced its political aspect and veiled its hegemonic role, just as the amalgamation of humanism with literature (the backbone of the "humanities") served to isolate it from political economy and epistemological claims.[3]

Questioning the historicity of writing or literature is not an idle task. Across diverse historical epochs, the terms, concerns, and objects of (literary) reflection or interpretation seem to vary greatly according to social, political, and material factors. For example, the fundamental historical conditions of biblical times certainly moved particular textual problems into the foreground and had an obvious effect on the means, procedures, and outcomes of interpretation. The elements determining the parameters of reflection are undeniably distinct if the text exists as words baked in clay, carved in stone, written on parchment, or printed on paper; if the words are deemed to originate in a deity's voice, an emperor's court, or the activity of an autonomous individual; if the text is recognized as belonging to a homegrown or foreign tradition. The way in which these factors are combined, in conjunction with others including the size of the potential public and the institutions that produce, preserve, and perpetuate the respective text's meaning, help configure the historical limits of interpretation in addition to the hegemony they institute.

At the same time, however, the general questions that underlie literary reflection, that is, reflection on writing (or, more generally, on inscriptions resulting from human intervention), are always of the same order. They derive from a fundamental, almost scientific formulation that has been frequently evoked throughout this book: how does one determine the meanings of an object (in this instance, a written text) that exceeds the empirical moment of its origin? It was produced, and its existence as a material object (and the kind of material is important if only because it defines its period of empirical accessibility, if not legibility) outlasts its author or creator. A number of concerns and categories of thought have emerged to come to grips with this massive question: concerns such as the inscription's (text's) relationship to the collectivity sharing its language, its pertinence to the present, its place in the network of other extant writings, both similar and dissimilar, and its contribution to human understanding at large. Despite superficial differences, these concerns have—aside from the evident historical divergences—remained constant since the advent of writing and attest to the daunting difficulties of any literary reflection as well as to its continued relevance. Just as the physicist uses "idealized experiments"[4] to describe and understand the workings of what has come to be called "nature," the (literary) theorist constructs discursive models to depict the polyvalent relationships between language, the interactions of human consciousness, and the world. In contrast with theoretical physics, however, acknowledging the idealizing or even ideological aspect of literary understanding as an object of reflection necessarily introduces questions about extraneous interference; this interference, which in shorthand can be called the "political," encompasses constraints such as force, power, and the implementing dictates of an institutional or individual agent.

A relative awareness of the historical production of ideas has been an essential component of critical thought since the nineteenth century, particularly with the rise of literary hermeneutics. This awareness constitutes the backdrop of contemporary literary thought and the landscape within which any critical project is necessarily inscribed. Said's efforts to merge theoretical concerns with political reflection are no exception. In elucidating the historical bases of ideas, for example, Said sketches the paradigmatic nature of the literary tradition and its concomitant critical framework:

> Each age, for instance, re-interprets Shakespeare, not because Shakespeare changes, but because despite the existence of numerous and reliable editions of Shakespeare, there is no such fixed and non-trivial object as Shakespeare independent of his editors, the actors who played his roles, the translators who put him in other languages, the hundreds of millions of readers who have read him or watched performances of his plays since the late sixteenth century.[5]

This passage advances various notions that bear closer inspection and that run counter to the universalist or ahistorical bias of modern literature. Furthermore, elaborating the stakes bound up with the name and interpretation of Shakespeare offers an important glimpse into the interweaving of linguistic and historical perspectives that orient much contemporary critical thinking.

In the terms of literary thought that has dominated for centuries, "Shakespeare" is a figure that happens to be a proper name. The figure of personification, a theme that preceding chapters have broached in other contexts, has long been an object of consideration in the tradition of literary reflection, beginning with classical manuals of rhetoric (such as those by Aristotle, Cicero, Quintilian); often described by the term *prosopopoeia,* it took its place alongside a host of other very technical terms of signification, the majority of which have today become archaic.[6] Understanding personification as a technical or formal linguistic element is deeply ensconced in the literary tradition, both in theory and in practice, and typically follows the dictates of commonsense realism. On coming across a proper name, marked in English with a capital letter because of its conceptual singularity, readers immediately personify it by assimilating it to personal experience and to empirical individuals they have actually met. "Shakespeare," a group of letters printed on a two-dimensional page, suddenly has arms, legs, a point of view, and so on. Most literary debates, whether among specialists, in the popular press, or in the classroom, tend to turn on what kind of attributes—attitudes, actions, creations—can be justifiably assigned to a figure of this sort.

Yet rather than pursuing the formalist aspects of personification, this passage evokes how the figure—in this case, Shakespeare's name—

comes to be and how it is deployed in time. The presuppositions of this historical transmission are as easy to enumerate as the repercussions are far-reaching. As a name whose object rests out of reach, whose meaning can be grasped only through the mediation of countless descriptions and qualifications that are themselves no less linguistic than the name itself, Shakespeare and whatever its reference participate in a very precise linguistic economy. Its primary characteristic can best be grasped in contrast to an idealized referential situation. In a straightforward act of referentiality that takes place in an ideal present, a living individual points to an object and utters "Shakespeare." Referentiality is seemingly complete and utterly realized: it is guaranteed by the individual who serves as a relay for the one-to-one correspondence. This classic model of referentiality lays out the elements but displays little communality with the complex discursive networks that give a semblance of life to historical and literary figures. Moreover, in returning specifically to the Shakespeare figure, the presumed empirical moment when the name William Shakespeare was bestowed upon a newborn adds nothing whatsoever to our understanding of the figure and can be rendered present only by yet another layer of language (and, in any event, Shakespearean scholars continue to discuss the empirical identity of Shakespeare, including his authorship of various literary productions). For a figure to signify as a figure, for it to take on the trappings of existence, that from which it derives must be absent—preferably for good.

Though less palpable, historical reality, which is given substance between the lines of written texts, is just as real as the most mundane of physical objects, and this notion of the figure extends reality rather than truncating or diminishing it. On the contrary, maintaining that language operates according to figurations, it presents a model of the way that language intervenes temporally and spatially (given that absence connotes both aspects) to mediate between understanding and the empirical. This basic linguistic model sustains even the most rudimentary historical interpretation of literary texts and has been institutionalized in the form of hermeneutics.

This passage on the Shakespeare figure implicitly describes this hermeneutic version of literary understanding. The "object" of the Shakespeare figure has no fixed identity, no inert existence cut off from Shakespeare's multiple receptions that vary geographically and chronologically, in space and in time. At the same time, however, the characterization underscores the empirical presupposition that provides a methodological framework for interpretation: Shakespeare doesn't change, but his identity is inexhaustible and never ceases becoming manifest in new facets. Whatever Shakespeare's empirical existence, it can never be known directly and is dependent on the amorphous collective idea that historical actors and discourses make of it. Although this basic theory of literary understanding may no longer do justice to the bloated idea of Shakespeare that is today in uncontrollable expansion, spreading throughout the globe and traversing all media, its conceptual and methodological reign in the epoch of scriptural dominance has been incontrovertible. In this sense, it constitutes the foundation of literary—and, by extension, cultural—critique in all its present splendor.

Whereas Said's comments on Shakespeare succinctly summarize the traditional model of literary understanding, the continuation of the passage extends that model to include institutional—and, implicitly, political—aspects: "On the other hand, it is too much to say that Shakespeare has no independent existence at all, and that he is completely reconstituted every time someone reads, acts, or writes about him. In fact, Shakespeare leads an institutional or cultural life that among other things has guaranteed his eminence."[7] In other words, the Shakespeare figure exists beyond the individual realizations that accrue historically. From this perspective, the point of reference for Shakespeare is not a fictional and unreachable place somewhere in the distant past; instead, the institutions of knowledge and culture guide, however unobtrusively, the figure's ongoing realizations, the multiple meanings that can legitimately be attributed to it. Shakespeare's life is *real* and can never be reduced to some form of arbitrariness: there is no *mere* interpretation. The immaterial figure, the idealized Shakespeare, comes about and subsists in conjunction with material interests fueled, channeled, and guaranteed by institutions that go from the micro level of textual debate, to reigning interpretations in the respective disciplines of knowledge, to macro views of historical understanding and potential interpretation.

The institutionalized residue that coats the proper noun of *Shakespeare* covers a much wider literary, cultural, and conceptual terrain. In the preceding chapters, I have repeatedly stressed the peculiar relationship between history and writing (that is, literature in the broadest sense). In the perspective as elaborated in this book, writing constitutes a synthesis of the material and immaterial tensions between historical understanding and contemporary transformation, individual action and collective intransigence, the political status quo and revolution. Other means of recording the sediments of human thought and deed—means spanning the gamut of twentieth-century media—operate along the same axes as writing, but scrutiny of those processes of marking the world has for obvious technological and historical reasons been intertwined with literary understanding, as Schlegel's efforts to fashion literary history suggest. In attempting to render an account of these tensions, thinkers who treat questions of literary theory inevitably touch on concerns more readily identifiable with the political sphere. Nonetheless, very few works confront head-on the conjunction between the literary and the political ramifications of its institutions. In this context, Said's *Orientalism* occupies an important place in critical thought of the late twentieth-century and is without doubt among the most widely read and influential reflections on the intersection between literary and political institutions. A work of ongoing relevance to understanding the underside of literary traditions, the project of analyzing "orientalism" results from important deliberation on the historical capacities of language and on the political force of its deployment in institutions and knowledge production. As such, the book's fundamental argument offers a concise point of entry into questions concerning the entwinement of language and institution.

Instead of simply presenting a counterstory of the "Orient," *Orientalism* analyzes the idea of the Orient as it was linguistically asserted and historically elaborated. There are evident parallels between characterizations of the Shakespeare figure and the idea of the Orient, initially a vague notion that is given body through numberless supporting texts that describe, personify, and endow it with intention. As with all knowledge, figures or ideas clasp together material and immaterial aspects; they undergird all historical understanding or interpretation. Without the material—for example, writing—the idea dies with the mind that thinks it; without the possibility of thinking beyond the material, it is impossible to actuate past legacies, to render them pertinent to any given present. In regard to the Orient, *Orientalism* attempts to lay out the parameters of this complex but absolutely necessary interaction between the material and the immaterial: "The Orient was almost a European invention."[8] Volumes could be appended to this qualification, this "almost," without ever exhausting the subject. Because it emerges from historical awareness, it is not merely an invention or phantasmatic projection, nor is it an unambiguous, objective portrayal of what it names.

Like any linguistic figure, the idea of the Orient possesses historical dimensions that exceed the ideal referential model I sketched out earlier. *Orientalism*'s introductory chapter elucidates the author's presuppositions: "I have begun with the assumption that the Orient is not an inert fact of nature. It is not merely *there*, just as the Occident itself is not just *there* either" (4). Informed by an understanding of writing's specific linguistic character, the figural model *Orientalism* endorses, no matter how scientifically rigorous its application, contrasts with a model construed on the basis of an empirical knowledge of nature. The Orient, whether idea or referent, is not "there," the object of a pointing finger that indicates it for a present and discerning public. Although the "nature" model of knowledge may have useful applications in specific contexts, its potential for explaining the figuration of written language is severely limited owing to the infinite variables involved and to their immateriality. In the case of the figure (of the Orient, for example), understanding is not a matter of clear and transparent perception, as if one were present before an object and had the power and voice to express it unequivocally.

Grasping the workings of this figuration, whose implications for historical understanding go well beyond the sense of any particular figure, is fraught with difficulties. These obstacles come less from the enormous quantity of material than from the intricacy of analyzing historical figures that provide the very means of thinking. *Orientalism* hints at the historical magnitude of the problem: "Therefore as much as the West itself, the Orient is an idea that has a history and a tradition of thought, imagery, and vocabulary that have given it reality and presence in and for the West" (5). As an idea that takes form in time, the Orient is a product of historical accretion; once transcribed, it serves as a virtual point of reference for competing and coalescing discourses that flesh out its skeletal figure. The reality of that Western Orient is that of institutions whose domain is largely immaterial, even if the authoritative actions that reveal its reach have visible consequences. Yet not unlike the figure of Shakespeare, which both channels and derives from countless institutional—and, today, commercial—forces and structures, its historical existence is unassailable. Although *Orientalism*'s object of analysis is specifically defined, the economy of signification it delineates extends beyond any specific object. The "West" no less than the "East" (as well as any personified collectivity so common in literary and historical discourse) necessarily participates in the same circulation and production of meaning. From the perspective of institutionalized knowledge, the figure belongs to a configuration merging multiple series of interwoven vocabulary, a plethora of images, and historical accounts to marshal them into coherence. Moreover, the figures tend to be defined in conjunction with other figures, supplementing, opposing, and becoming assimilated to them, thus increasing the labyrinths of signification and the convoluted imbrication. Therefore, to read, interpret, and explicate this institutionalization, the process whereby a figure comes into existence, involves deciphering the "whole network of interests" (3), coming to terms with the concomitant "constellation of ideas" (5), and confronting the "sheer knitted-together strength" (6) of discourses holding the figure in place.

While repetition of this figure of thought undeniably substantiates the proverb that "history is written by the victors," its force is more epistemological than physical. In the proverb's encapsulated view, control of the past, its sequential unfolding and meaning, follows bodily subjugation. The figural understanding of history, on the contrary, places struggle at the heart of the signifying process, which cannot exist in isolation from its respective medium. The most controversial upshot of this way of perceiving struggle in language revolves around affirmations of historical truth. Cultural discourse circulates "not 'truth' but representations" (21). Injecting reflection on language into the historical equation indicates to what extent the Orient, even as a historically delimited category, becomes an epistemological question, just as knowing and knowledge reveal their political significance.

The nature of language, its ephemeral orality and its inability as writing to transport to succeeding epochs whatever empirical meaning it might have expressed, imposes strong limitations on notions of historical truth. In this sense, grappling with the question of orientalism cannot be separated from this larger investigation of the historical and linguistic sediment of knowledge. Applied to the figure of the Orient, *Orientalism's* assertions constitute a general commentary on this tangle of conceptual relationships: "Its objective discoveries—the work of innumerable devoted scholars who edited texts and translated them, codified grammars, wrote dictionaries, reconstructed dead epochs, produced positivistically verifiable learning—are and always have been conditioned by the fact that its truths, like any truths delivered by language, are embodied in language" (203). History involves institutions, ideal projections, and a complement of presuppositions, but its economy is determined by linguistic process and the material of its inscription (printed words, for example). Without this rigorous scaffolding, historical truth is a meaningless concept, and the scaffolding is bound into form by language. Language, inseparable from its materiality, is the common denominator for these disparate elements that extend from the political to the theoretical. Ultimately, the entire edifice of historical understanding rests on the efficacy of the model of signification attributed to language.

Although such fundamental reflection on language has far from dominated historical thought in the West, it has been a recurring theme among theorists at least since Dante, who addressed issues of language's political repercussions. In evoking this tradition, Said in *Orientalism* cites briefly Nietzsche's "Truth and Lie in an Extramoral Sense" (203); although Said does not dwell on this text, mention of Nietzsche's essay has become de rigueur for both critics and supporters of *Orientalism*'s claims.[9] In effect, Nietzsche's text advances a surprisingly complete hypothesis about the historical and political workings of language; in addition to summarizing one of the principal critical themes of orientalism, it renders explicit the entangled political and epistemological ramifications of critical practice that I have analyzed in this book's preceding pages.

Circulating judgments about Nietzsche display such tenacity that they frequently replace reading of texts attributed to him. Evoking the "Nietzsche" name in describing individuals or their writings suffices to demean their motivation or challenge the validity of their analyses. Nietzsche's essay on truth and lying, which examines language's representational capacity in isolation from the historical contingency of moral judgments, is often cited precisely in this context. For example, Habermas considers Nietzsche (along with the Marquis de Sade) as one of "the really nihilistic *dark* writers of the bourgeoisie."[10] The italicized *dark*ness summons images of the closed room where nefarious events occur, as well as the opposite of "enlightenment," the eighteenth-century ascendancy of reason. In a similar vein, as one of *Orientalism*'s critics affirms in referring to this essay to prove the author's irrationalism, antihumanism, and antihistoricism: "In a Nietzschean world, virtually anything is possible."[11] Although the grounds for this boundless possibility are not rendered explicit, this sentence accurately iterates the standard allegory attached to Nietzsche's name.

However, before writing Nietzsche off as an irrational thinker of mythic proportions, it is essential to consider the text on truth and lying in its entirety (the essay to which the two extant sections belong remains unfinished). This partial essay, which Nietzsche elaborated in the context of teaching classical rhetoric and pre-Platonic philosophy, presents a coherent hypothesis about the way language functions as a means for producing knowledge. Although all interpretation—whether of history or of the empirical world—depends on hypothetical presuppositions, the assumptions leading to understandings or interpretations of human culture (writing or other material forms) are of a different order than those of experimental science. Whereas the latter must by definition admit of empirical verification, no matter how idealized the hypothesis and how tenuous or refracted the link established between the idea and its experimental realization, the presuppositions of cultural interpretation can be judged only according to the efficacy in producing a framework for further interpretation. Unlike scientific understanding, which has a built-in linearity running from relative human ignorance to greater magnitudes of human knowledge, cultural understanding (which encompasses all thought relating to historical artifacts, products of human activity and inscription) exhibits less fixity in projecting the origins and finalities of the collective human species. Presuppositions about historical knowledge (and, therefore, literary and cultural understanding) are distinguished by how they conjecture the relationship between a human origin and its projected end, whether as divine creation awaiting its conclusion in a final judgment, human consciousness moving toward absolute knowledge by virtue of its own efforts, or successive social formations marching inexorably toward classless society. This larger set of concerns forms the context for Nietzsche's comments on the veracity of language, which propose a novel hypothesis about its epistemological role.

For all its supposed irrationality, Nietzsche's essay proceeds methodically and analytically, staking out a series of philosophical positions by referring to the assumptions underlying Western views about the role that language plays in engendering human knowledge. In this sense, the essay's basic elements are not new; its novelty results rather from taking those observations drawn largely from political thinkers and placing them into an immanent model of historical explanation. The essay's ironic opening, which recounts a fable about how "clever beasts invented knowing" and thus paved the way for their subsequent death, underscores the fictional, narrative nature of all conceptions of the emergence of human consciousness.[12] This beginning, no less than the first gurglings of language itself, can be recaptured only in the form of a story; in any subsequent historical moment, humans are unavoidably left with nothing more than a process of institutionalization already under way. Nevertheless, how one thinks of this "origin," even if one denies it entirely, has a decisive impact on the historical, linguistic, and cognitive potential of the human agent. For Nietzsche, that moment of emergence is irrevocably and, in fact, structurally lost, and all recuperations that claim a simultaneity for language, human consciousness, and subjective intention can only be ideological, subordinate to and supportive of historical interests. In offering a different hypothesis of the eruption of language, Nietzsche provides the backbone for an immanent historical understanding that draws its impetus from the disparity between an unknowable origin, without an identifiable author, and a full-blown human reason enjoying the unacknowledged benefits of sociopolitical institutions. This historical conception rests squarely on Nietzsche's materialist view of language that stands opposed both to the positivist belief in history as a homogeneous continuum and to Heidegger's philosophy of history characterized by efforts to catch glimpses of an overlooked Being.

In Nietzsche's hypothetical reasoning, the contrast between truth and lie, which has been at the core of moral critiques of the essay, comes to be as a by-product of sociolinguistic institutions. Laws of truth emerge alongside linguistic legislations. At this point in the argument, Nietzsche reformulates the themes of the essay in a more precise fashion: "And besides, what about these linguistic conventions themselves? Are they perhaps products of knowledge, that is, of the sense of truth? Are designations congruent with things? Is language the adequate expression of all realities?" (81; 878). In the logic of the essay, the upshot is that language, knowledge, and the sociopolitical are inseparable, and no single element enjoys even relative priority. Examining these questions in reference to their historical import occupies the remainder of the essay. In the context of contemporary critique, this batch of questions can be restated somewhat differently: what theory of language would enable one to account for the role that language itself plays in producing knowledge, on the one hand, and in setting up the sociopolitical institutions that monitor such knowledge, on the other?

To address this issue, the essay posits that at the heart of human society lies a basic forgetfulness of the epistemological situation in which language evolved. A far cry from Heidegger's dire warnings about the forgetfulness of Being, this assertion is nonetheless commonplace among Western thinkers whose concerns combine political and linguistic deliberation. For example, as I discussed at some length from a different angle in chapter 1, Dante and Machiavelli are prominent in this tradition, although they stress opposing aspects of the question. For Dante, whose philosophical role in providing arguments for modern national languages has long been recognized, this original forgetfulness (*oblivio*) anchors the secular process of human action and linguistic change: "All our language—besides that which God created at the same time as man—is subject to the reworkings of our free will [*beneplacito*], after that confusion which was no more than a forgetting of previous language."[13] In the post-Babel world, after the divine gift of language that could only be the perfect expression of reality, language is as unstable as human action is fickle; Dante's well-known proposal to counter this deleterious tendency calls for instituting a grammar of an idealized Italian language belonging to no particular community. In this way, an (institutionalized) sphere of collective culture and sociopolitical writing could be demarcated.

For Machiavelli, "forgetfulness" occurs as a result of active struggle between societies or between human beings and the elements of nature. Thus instead of a passive forgetting, the inability to ascertain, much less to represent past plenitude with any certainty, results from an active effacement or annihilation, something like the historical rewriting that took place in twentieth-century dictatorships. When a new religion emerges—a new cultural hegemony, as we would say it today—the first task is to eliminate the preceding religion, a goal easier to accomplish if it is simply a matter of substituting a new language. In this way, Machiavelli concludes, human and natural events (like floods, the plague, and so on), "wipe out the memories of things," "extinguish" the old institutions in favor of the new.[14] As is customary in Machiavelli's straightforward analyses, historical outcomes are determined by relations of force in which the struggling actors can be readily identified.

Despite obvious distinctions between Machiavelli's and Dante's orientations, their shared historical conception, as well as its political implications, are specifically modern; the questions they raise about culture, it social and conceptual institutions, and the need for a collective written language have furnished the parameters for modern political thought. Writing in the shadows of this tradition, however, Nietzsche expands the historical conception to include the notion of *knowing*, that is, that language is an institutionalized process of knowing, which is consequently also subject to historical transformation, rather than just a means to record history. This contrast between Nietzsche and the tradition from which his considerations emerge succinctly illustrates the point of contention between interpreters who endorse Nietzsche's materialist view of language and those who exempt the faculty of human knowing from the forces of history. In its simplest terms, Nietzsche's view of language is summed up in his definition of the word: "What is a word? It is the copy in sound of a nerve stimulus" (81; 878). Words are not initially products of a masterful consciousness but are born out of interactions and result from nerve stimuli, out of the purview of a controlling human mind. This hypothesis is obviously unverifiable to the same extent as any other story about the origin of language, even those based on the most rigid belief in a one-to-one correspondence between word and thing.

Once again, though, Nietzsche's hypothetical discourse on language and knowing does not appear out of nowhere, and, as in the case of forgetfulness, his particular inflection is significant. Jean-Jacques Rousseau, another thinker whose writings traverse many domains along the literary-political axis, pursues a similar series of conjectures. Rousseau's *Essai sur l'origine des langues* tells the story of what he calls the figural origin of language.[15] This much debated text offers an example of Rousseau's hypothesis of language formation, and the components of his account are easily summarized: one human being sees another and, having no inkling of their resemblance, names him a "giant" (because his apprehension at seeing someone else for the first time leads him to believe that the other was much larger, stronger, and so on, than himself); after recurring sightings of the other, however, he realizes their similarity and invents a new name to describe them both; at this point, human beings have a word, "giant," with no referent, even though it was the first word.[16] After elaborating this example, Rousseau makes the following observations: "This is how the figural word is born before the proper word, when passion leaves us starry-eyed and the first idea it offers us is not that of truth . . . With the illusory image offered by passion being the first to show itself, the language corresponding to it was also the first invented; then it became metaphorical when the enlightened mind, recognizing its prior error, employed its expressions only for the same reasons that produced it" (381–382).

Despite its being heavily marked by eighteenth-century notions of language and signification,[17] the fundamental components of Rousseau's linguistic understanding differ only slightly from those of Nietzsche (even if Nietzsche might have been shocked to see this affinity, given his constant ridicule of Rousseau). What for Nietzsche is an utterance provoked by a nerve stimulus, becomes in Rousseau's description the result of an involuntary passion. Just as with Nietzsche's nerve stimulus, inciting a reaction akin to a protozoon's response to an electric shock, the passion depicted by Rousseau takes place spontaneously, gratuitously, without the intervention of thought. This intense reaction of passion transpires according to an unpredictable logic of its own, not reducible to an economy of truthful representation. In Rousseau's account, with the engagement of reason (that is, the enlightened mind: *l'esprit éclairé*), the linguistic irruptions of passion, along with the resulting idea and the experience prompting it, are deemed erroneous or flawed. At that moment, subsequent to the mindlessness of passion, all enters into order: truth opposes error, and proper meaning wins precedence over the figural. Redressing this disjuncture, which is recognized only as it is established, creates the linguistic space of metaphor.

In paring away the divergent dramatization, Nietzsche's version seems to endorse similar conclusions: for reasons that become clear as its argument unfolds, Nietzsche's essay stresses that the very distinction between truth and error comes from the legislated regulation of reference. But Rousseau's portrayal of figural languages as error that an enlightened mind will later correct privileges individual consciousness and experience, no matter how much a traumatic experience and the resulting expression might disrupt its placid serenity. In tracing the further implications of this involuntary model of linguistic emergence, Nietzsche assigns the production of concepts to the linguistic process itself rather than to individual consciousness alone, thus dispelling any ambiguity about the absolute privilege of individual reason. As part of linguistic process, any utterance is caught up in the formation of concepts: "Every word instantly becomes a concept precisely insofar as it is not supposed to serve as a reminder of the unique and entirely individual original experience to which it owes its emergence; but rather, a word becomes a concept insofar as it simultaneously has to fit countless more or less similar cases—which means, purely and simply, cases which are never like and thus altogether unlike" (83; 879–880). In addition to echoing Rousseau's account of the repeated experiences necessary (*"après beaucoup d'expériences"* [381]) to realize the error of the word *giant* and invent the category of *man,* Nietzsche's analysis takes up the terms of Aristotle's logical conception of language, which forms the basis of Western linguistic thought.[18]

Contrary to Aristotelian logic, however, which derives language from assumptions about the essences of things and about its capacity to absorb and represent them, the conceptualization inherent to language in Nietzsche's essay does not owe its existence to the presumed essence of things. As the essay continues, even the "contrast between individual and species is something anthropomorphic and does not stem from the essence of things" (83; 880). This anthropomorphism, the figural dimension of language that creates an interface between consciousness and reality, is closely intertwined with the conceptual categories of human thought that build on the individual's particularizing experiences. This anthropomorphic impulse permeates language as a network of meaning production and surfaces repeatedly as obligatory for linguistic analysis (a tendency reflected in both Aristotle's and Rousseau's use of the human figure in analyzing the links between thought and language). Rather than attributing human specificity to the ability to use language, a historically common assertion, Nietzsche emphasizes the capacity to manufacture concepts, a by-product of the amalgam between thought and language: "Everything which distinguishes man from the animals depends upon this ability to volatilize perceptual metaphors [*die anschaulichen Metaphern*] in a schema, and thus to dissolve a figure [*Bild*] into a concept."[19] Ultimately, this human penchant to conceptualize operates by virtue of language, which is of a wholly different order than what it expresses. Nietzsche characterizes this disjuncture as mimicking a "suggestive transference, a stammering translation into a completely foreign tongue."[20] Language, and the thought it permits, dissipates this incommensurability, just as the translation replaces the original it can never equal.

In its own highly original way, the essay on truth and lying presents a model of historical and linguistic knowing with a defined set of presuppositions. This insistence on a model does not signal the relative interchangeability of historical models and their consequent interpretations. All models or groups of assumptions cohere with compatible interests and historical constraints, including socioeconomic and cultural formations, even if the dominance or hegemony of certain models is not wholly arbitrary. In this sense, the Aristotelian idea that essences—by definition intangible and invisible—underlie appearances, a model that requires a reinforced and extensive network of institutions to guarantee the proper correspondence between essences and appearances, meanings and expressions, tends to produce regular and stable views of history that proceed in orderly fashion toward an orderly and fulfilling end. In the same way, Nietzsche's model also has a highly charged historical component, even if it stops far short of identifying the historical with the breezy narrative claiming to represent it.

The extreme importance of this fragmentary essay for contemporary critical thought generally derives more from the consequences of Nietzsche's formulations than from the formulations themselves. As Nietzsche's essay makes clear, in stretching this linguistic model along a time line, history—and, no less significantly, concomitant human consciousness—becomes a never-ending process of sedimentation:

> Even the relationship of a nerve stimulus to the generated figure is not in itself a necessary one. But when the same figure has been generated millions of times and has been handed down for many generations and finally appears on the same occasion every time for all humankind, then it acquires at last the same meaning for human beings it would have if it were the sole necessary figure and if the relationship of the original nerve stimulus to the generated figure were a strictly causal one. (87; 884)

This description contains the nucleus of a theory of history that resembles more a radical materialism than an empty denial of external reality. What is arbitrary at some long lost beginning, what is not necessary in itself *(an sich)*, takes on a historical necessity through time. Historical necessities exist, but only as the result of history itself. The figure—of thought, of expression—cannot be divested of its history any more than a language can be freed of its meanings and still remain a language. The gradual naturalization of these figures, that is, the (tools of) thought they render natural, makes human consciousness possible; at the same time, they pose formidable obstacles for any theory of history that would not place human consciousness at its conceptual center. A rigorous materialist theory of history would inevitably have to take into account the matter of thought, which means integrating consideration of language while refusing to grant absolute primacy to human consciousness and to the theories of representation and causality that such primacy involves.

This theory of language, what I have called Nietzsche's model of historical understanding, surrounds and traverses the passage *Orientalism* cites to indicate the theoretical underpinnings of its investigation into the figure or idea of the Orient. This passage, certainly the best known paragraph of the essay and perhaps of Nietzsche's work as a whole, both summarizes the essay and, because it is torn from the carefully constructed argument, misrepresents it:

> What then is truth? A mobile army of metaphors, metonymies, and anthropomorphisms: in short, a sum of human relations which have been poetically and rhetorically intensified, transferred, and embellished, and which, after long usage, seem to a people to be fixed, canonical, and binding. Truths are illusions which we have forgotten are illusions; they are metaphors that have become worn out and have been drained of sensuous force, coins which have lost their figure [*Bild*] and are now considered as metal and no longer as coins.[21]

The problem with truth is that it is inextricably tangled up with language, but the result of this observation is to historicize rather than relativize truth. Language and the concepts that feed on it definitely establish truths; but truths are also the product of historical forces and live on by virtue of social, political, and linguistic institutions, among others, whose longevity masks the figuration at the basis of all language. This model of language and consciousness, which presupposes that the economy of language is fundamentally metaphorical and figural, opens up new avenues of historical critique that extend to the concepts themselves. Institutions—understood in the broadest sense—efface that figuration into invisibility, just as time erodes the face of a coin; in this perspective, historical understanding calls for recovering those figures and deciphering the forces that promoted their disappearance.

Since the publication of *Orientalism*, the theory of history put forth in Nietzsche's essay has had significant reverberations in contemporary criticism. Whatever their ultimate goals, however, these reactions end up at the very least nodding to the political implications of this materialist view of language. In an important essay on anthropomorphism, for example, Paul de Man remarks on Nietzsche's definition of truth: "Tropes are neither true nor false but are both at once. To call them an army is however to imply that their effect and their effectiveness is not a matter of judgment but of power. What characterizes a good army, as distinct for instance from a good cause, is that its success has little to do with immanent justice and a great deal with the proper economic use of its power."[22] Although de Man primarily seeks to read the figures of Nietzsche's text and show how the anthropomorphism of its language plays out its assertions, his comments are revealing of the dual power that inhabits language. De Man refers to this power as "epistemological" and "strategic" (243), tied simultaneously to the production of knowledge and to persuading, to convincing, to provoking actions. In other words, as a product of ongoing institutionalization, language enforces, cajoles, and convinces, but its more insidious power lurks in its concepts, in the very matter of thought. Conceptually, this power is an antecedent to judgment, which acts in the name of that power even as judges can do little more than assert their impartiality.

Power has an intimate relationship with what I have throughout this book called figuration or figures of thought, if only because figures embody, refer to, or indicate something else not immediately accessible. Whether executive or symbolic, power concerns the capacity to determine, establish, and enforce specific meanings that facilitate or mobilize given worldviews or historical understandings. That "something else," whether "behind," "above," or simply generically "hidden," resides somewhere beyond the obvious, the visible. Since this unveiled sense or meaning never appears on its own, never shows itself for all to see, the potentiality of proclaiming it and convincing others of its veracity belongs properly to the domain of power, whether rhetorical or executive, and figuration in this context is its precondition. This peculiarity of figuration, of materializing meanings that can be tentatively determined with only a modicum of certainty, if any at all, goes a long way toward explaining why language has historically played a decisive role in setting up and perpetuating figures of thought and expression. The nature of language incorporates this evocation of "elsewhere" into its workings. At the same time, this particularity also suggests why the sixteenth and seventeenth centuries, which laid the foundations of modern secular institutions at the expense of a historical vision based on ongoing divine intervention and regulation, are so crucial to understanding the figural constellation of modernity; the shift from a theological to a secular understanding entails a different, though not entirely unrelated, management of this "elsewhere," above and beyond the necessity to rethink the organization of knowledge in the wake of print reproduction.

This "elsewhere," the basis for all interpretation that would render inscriptions from the past explicable or pertinent in view of any present, does not emerge simply from literary debates and is not restricted to the sphere of literary phenomena, a fact already suggested by the tenor of the disputes surrounding Nietzsche's various assertions. Moreover, what Nietzsche proposes, in a way not unlike that of Rousseau, does not present a historical account of how sociopolitical and linguistic institutions came to be. On the contrary, his remarks offer a set of presuppositions that enable, to the limited degree possible, a detached look at the institutions, values, and unquestioned material assumptions of the overarching worldview of modernity. Reflection on the question of power, the extent of its presence and deployment, constitutes an essential component of this critical model, and anyone undertaking a fundamental engagement with linguistic and historical figuration necessarily confronts that question. For example, in Paul de Man's extrapolations on Nietzsche's fragmentary essay, passing reference to the concept of power belongs to this line of reasoning and hints at how power is bound up with the issue of figuration, at least in Nietzsche's formulations.

In fact, de Man's largely unfinished reflections in this direction furnish an important basis for coming to understand the political and institutional stakes inherent in theories of language. De Man, generally regarded as a brilliant but excessively literary critic of so-called high theory, came to pose the question of power and figure only in his later writings. While his concern with power in a linguistic perspective follows from his untangling of Nietzsche's theories, its most pertinent, if still incomplete, expression is found in his project titled *Aesthetic Ideology*, which was published posthumously. At the heart of this skeletal project, de Man's most direct engagement with power and language deals not with Nietzsche but with Pascal. His essay on various texts and fragments of the seventeenth-century thinker, "Pascal's Allegory of Persuasion," has become a classic statement of de Man's later theories of figuration.[23] Nonetheless, the essay's conclusion turns around the issue of "power"—or, in various other renderings of Pascal's discussion of the theme, of "force" or "might." The essay's critical argument brings together a number of elements, including Pascal's attempts to link the reasonableness of linguistic representation to number theory (and, in particular, to the conception of infinity), but for my purposes, its crucial aspects can be readily summarized.[24] In a series of detailed readings that have become his particular signature, de Man shows how Pascal's language interacts with his logical assertions. This axis between supposed truth and the presumed capacity to represent that truth in language has been fundamental for theorists of rhetoric at least since Aristotle. In the essay, this opposition—that is, the two opposing poles of this axis—is evoked in a number of different ways: for example, epistemology (what is or can be known) versus persuasion (52); truth versus narrative (or allegory) (52); propositional logic (what is the case) versus modal logic (what should or ought to be the case) (64); cognition (and the tropes of representation) versus the performative (69); and so on. Rather than considering Pascal's reflections from a transcendental perspective, that is, taking his notion of infinity or of the role of zero in the number system as referring to some ineffable divine, de Man examines the effects in Pascal's language itself (59). In this general framework, de Man identifies and succinctly explicates how Pascal's thought proceeds dialectically, through the rigorous use of rhetorical figures and their qualities, to pose a contradiction and resolve it beyond logical challenge.

But in de Man's reading, the question of power, which bears directly on the institutions of knowledge, emerges at the moment when Pascal's airtight reasoning collapses. More precisely, the reference to power moves the discussion from the domain of abstract, logical assertion to that of the potential expression of physical power and constraint. Although de Man's essay does not pursue this path of reflection, it overtly recognizes the sociopolitical implications of this shift in Pascal's discourse: "The transition from self-knowledge and anthropological knowledge to teleological knowledge often passes, in Pascal, through the dimension of the political" (65). In this sense, Pascal's formulations, however concerned with theories of knowledge and resolving contradictions, ultimately confront the realm of executive action. While evolving a theory of discourse profoundly laced with rhetorical strategy, with the linguistic powers of figuration, Pascal inevitably brings his discourse down to earth, to the political. In other words, Pascal's reflections tend to join the logical, the capacity to reason through dialectically resolving or domesticating contradiction, with an understanding of knowledge as a product of institutional forces.

Although this tendency runs through all of Pascal's nonscientific writings, one of the most direct expressions of this mélange of concerns is the *Pensées'* fragment titled "Justice, Power." This fragment, on which de Man's essay grounds its conclusion, has been repeatedly scrutinized by interpreters of Pascal's thought. It runs as follows:

> It is just that what is just should be followed; it is necessary that what has the most power should be followed.
>
> Justice without power is impotent, power without justice is tyrannical.
>
> Justice without power is open to contradiction, because there always are wrongdoers. Power without justice stands accused. Justice and power must therefore be brought together, by making the just strong and the strong just.
>
> Justice is subject to dispute. Power is easily recognizable and without dispute. Thus it has been impossible to give power to justice, because power has contradicted justice and said that it is unjust, and said that it is itself just.
>
> And thus, not being able to make the just strong, one has made the strong to be just.[25]

Justifiably adopting a "linguistic point of view" (69), de Man's analysis of this passage is impeccably reasoned and argued. In referring to the series of oppositions evoked above, he meticulously elucidates how this representation of justice in opposition to power remains asymmetrical. Justice and power simply do not occupy the same plane of existence, with power taking precedence over justice to the extent that power makes and defines what is just. In de Man's reading, which explicitly concentrates on how language is simultaneously cognitive and performative, the intermingling registers make an important statement about the rhetorical operation of figures and, in particular, about the allegorical basis of narrative.

But what about power, which produces effects in what de Man's essay calls in passing "the realm of practical and political justice" (69)? While Pascal unquestionably projects a theory of rhetoric, of language and its figuration, his understanding of the political and of the force that inhabits it extends beyond a banal notion of literary criticism and the relatively anodyne rhetorical effects that are its object. What Pascal attempts to bring together in his lopsided dialectic, that is, justice and power, presents a model of historical and political comprehension, a conception of what might today be called the ideological. This view of historical or political understanding relies heavily on a theory of rhetorical figuration from which it is inseparable. Similarly, Pascal's reflections on the deployment of force in society suggest that the concept of figuration has its greatest resonance precisely in the political and ideological domain.

The tradition against which de Man elaborates his own specifically rhetorical interpretation more than hinted at this link between the figural and the political. For example, de Man states (without further comment) that a well-known interpreter of Pascal and Port-Royal, Louis Marin, "is right to insist on the close interconnection between epistemology, political criticism, and theology" (66). Marin, who has his own critical agenda that entails characterizing the broader theory of discourse in Pascal's texts, delineates the more straightforwardly political aspects of Pascal's dialectic of figures. In describing the section of the *Pensées* in which the fragment on justice and power appears, Marin specifically engages what he considers the sociopolitical relation of opposition in Pascal's fragments, an opposition that cannot be reduced to its rhetorical or linguistic expression:

> The people are opposed to the rich, the nobles, the upper echelons, the king, to all who, in one way or another, directly or indirectly, use institutional power [*force*], whether in the realm of imagination, custom, or deed. The people are therefore those who are subjected very directly to the effects of naked power or power that is manifestly assimilated into a system of signs and that the people's language reproduces in behavioral forms of respect, obedience, and passivity or in discourse generalizing this behavior in propositions that are its justification. From this point of view, ordinary discourse entirely derives, in language, from the meaning effect of institutional power; this is so clear that Pascalian dis-

course discovers in this oppositional relationship the paradigm of ordinary discourse at large.[26]

The people in this relationship of opposition are not those of the nation-state, but the commoners who wield no power and are not privy to the culture of privilege. In this sense, "the people" is a figure that appears frequently in Pascal's writings and represents resistance to the institutions that traverse society and monitor the flow of ideas and comportment. Power, therefore, inevitably exceeds its external manifestation, that is, when a sanctioned agent of the polity physically seizes a wrong-doer; in addition to dominating justice, which can never have the last word in a conflict with force, power also permeates customs, habits, and the imagination. From the perspective of meaning, interpretation, and behavior, what Marin includes under the general rubric of "discourse," this relation of power fundamentally marks thought, its products and practices, because it is entwined with all forms of social codification. Figures of thought belong to this sociopolitical configuration, along with the institutions that regulate them even while repressing or concealing the naked power that shows itself only when the regulation breaks down. As Pascal's asymmetrical opposition between force and justice indicates, de facto and de jure power share the same circuit, even if their means are different.

In another *Pensées* fragment that expands on the more rhetorical juxtaposition of justice and power, Pascal explicitly addresses these two aspects of power through a more revealing opposition: "Had it been possible, power would have been placed in the hands of justice, but since power does not let itself be manipulated as one wants because it is a tangible quality, whereas justice is a mental quality that can be used as one wants, justice was placed in the hands of power and thus we call just what power leaves us no choice but to follow."[27] Here the contrast between justice and power revolves around the materiality of power, its external manifestation, and the more ideal or immaterial nature of justice. Power has a necessarily physical element that cannot be entirely dispensed with; it is the restraining hand, the bolted door, the clasped straitjacket, as well as the peasant's obligatory salute to the reigning noble or the recitation of the pledge of allegiance in some distant American grammar school. Power is present even in its absence because it remains, as bottom, a physical guarantor that punishes noncompliance. Justice, however, resides in the domain of interpretation, of belief, reason, or understanding; disputes regarding what is just cannot be resolved by justice itself, which is why power has absolute primacy over justice. As palpable, tangible force, power lurks in the background of any and every claim of justice.

As Erich Auerbach has pointed out, Pascal's exposition of his theory of justice and power relies extensively on the figure of the people. Auerbach, whose analysis of medieval *figura* (presented above in chapter 2) has served as a significant backdrop to my ongoing argument, contributed an important essay on Pascal's political thinking and, specifically, on his view of justice and power (interestingly, Auerbach's point of departure is the same fragment that becomes central to de Man's later rhetorical argument). In the context of power's material element, Auerbach's observation offers a succinct characterization of Pascal's notions: "In their respect for power and its outward signs, the people show a sound instinct though their motives are mistaken; they believe that they must respect power because it is just, and that is a fallacy. Power should be respected not because it is just but for its own sake, because it exists."[28] Despite their unavoidable entanglement, power and justice are not to be confused. Power compels respect because it is the imperative of the stronger. Considering power to be *in any way* just is to misunderstand both the nature of power, which has definitively subjugated justice, and that of justice, which has no possibility to become universal and remains subject to the vagaries of human temporality. While power's existence implies its application, a potentiality always on the verge of being actualized, justice can be rendered effective only by power itself.

Although Pascal proposes a model for understanding the workings of power and justice, it is not even superficially a plea for implementing a new justice claiming to be less unjust. In this world, profoundly marked by power, justice belongs to the domain of sociopolitical institutions of thought and comportment. As such, power inescapably determines the most just justice. In a series of short discourses on the "condition of royalty," Pascal remarks that "[t]itles and nobility are in this category. In one country, nobles are respected, in another, commoners; the elders in this one, the youngest in that one. Why is that the case? Because men found it agreeable. The thing was insignificant before being established [*avant l'établissement*]: after being established it becomes just because it is unjust to disturb it."[29] Justice is therefore linked to the institutions of

society, which codify relations of power, including even social disparities. Institutions, which always have been established at some earlier
point in time, constitute the backdrop for all human action and thought.
There is no way to wipe the slate clean, to return to a state of tabula rasa,
before the establishment of institutions. It is possible to tell stories about
some preinstitutional time, in the vein of Nietzsche's or Rousseau's fa-
bles of the presumed origins of thought and language, but such stories
offer only a means to think those institutions without aiming to deny
their evident power. For Pascal, the moment that institutions become established is crucial for drawing the line between what is just and what is
unjust. Pascal reiterates this perspective in yet another *Pensées* fragment:
"Justice is what is established; and thus all our established laws will be
necessarily held to be just without being examined, since they are established."[30] In this sense, after the parameters—of behavior, of social status, of speech, and so on—are institutionally established, in the realm of
action one's hands are tied.

At first glance, it appears that Pascal calls for unquestioning acceptance of the status quo, the epitome of conservatism. Once established,
injustice, inequality, and oppression—all of which power systematically
renames as "justice"—would seem to brook no challenge, and the individual seems to have no alternative but to follow. In his comments on
this aspect of Pascal's thought, Auerbach introduces a complementary
series of concerns intimately interlaced with this historical view of institutions:

> Through reason and experience Pascal infers that the institutions and
> the whole process of this world are based on chance and arbitrary
> power; that our whole earthly order is sheer folly. He believed he was
> serving the faith by demonstrating, forcefully and convincingly, that
> misery and injustice, arbitrariness and folly, are the foundations of our
> life; and then he goes on to say that Christians, fully cognizant [*in
> voller und detaillierter Kenntnis*] of these follies, should obey them, not
> because they respect folly, but because they respect the will of God
> who, in order to punish human beings and open the road of salvation
> to them while at the same time making it more arduous, has subjected
> them to these follies; because, accordingly, they are the just law, the
> only law we deserve.[31]

On a superficial level, this Pascalian view has more than a little whiff of
fatalism, much in accord with the anachronistic conservatism of medi-

eval Christianity: the order of this world has nothing to do with the next, where compensation will be granted according to real and just merits. But Pascal's picture of the world serves as a model of knowledge, of understanding in which judgment is absolute, even if it does not necessarily lead to action or to the exercise of power. Nor is worldly justice relative—it is just unjust. In this perspective, a vast fissure opens between, on the one hand, understanding or recognizing the world's inevitable injustice and, on the other, the obedience commanded by the powers that be. Recourse to the transcendental vision of god, who reduces immanent justice to its role as handmaiden of power, permits a critical understanding of the status quo even while it militates against any action to transform it. In this conservative logic of immanence, of the boundaries of the possible in this world, overpowering the established order and its false claims to justice would only install yet another injustice no less subservient to the power that backs it.

Nevertheless, the space that opens up between the interior and the exterior, between what one knows or understands and one's cognizant obedience, houses the potential of a new critical awareness. There is no ambiguity in Pascal about the difference between external action, that is, the realm of material power, and immaterial thought: "It is not necessary for me to hold you in high esteem because you are a duke; but it is necessary that I salute you . . . But if you were a duke without being a gentleman [*honnête homme*], I would still do you justice [*je vous ferais encore justice*]; because in granting you the external obligations that the order of men has attached to your birth, within myself I would still hold you in the contempt that the baseness of your spirit deserved."[32] In this example, the disparities "of birth," of privilege and power, are at the heart of sociopolitical institutions that exist to maintain an immanent order through the course of time. External trappings, however, which require not only obedience but also acts of submission determined by whichever justice is in power, cannot wholly dictate the thought underlying subservient acquiescence. This discrepancy between thought and deed creates the basis for a critical awareness that became fundamental for modernity and for the political and historical struggles it entailed. In the words of Auerbach, Pascal's thought constituted "a framework which despite its appearance of radical Christianity, contained many elements of secular knowledge and even the germs of a revolutionary social criticism."[33] This framework merely plants the seeds of revolutionary thinking because it does not endorse—and, in fact, forecloses—action leading to revolution. In the Christian view elaborated by Pascal, revolution, no matter how great its claims or accomplishments, proves useless: it fails to advance the divine scheme that ordains human injustice as the modus operandi of the sociohistorical domain.

While this futility of revolution signals the limits of Pascal's historical understanding in the executive realm, it simultaneously designates a new point of departure for considering the immaterial workings of power. In fact, significant portions of the *Pensées,* not to mention Pascal's writings on the interplay between grace and free will, among others, are devoted to elaborating a critical thought not wholly identifiable with the institutions of power. For Pascal, this critical reflection is deeply buried within oneself, where only the divine has access; as he states it in one of the various "Reason of effects" fragments, "One must have a counter-thinking [*pensée de derrière*], and judge everything in that perspective, while speaking like the people."[34] This duplicity, political in nature while stopping short of revolutionary action, emulates the people who are the object of institutional power and adopts a critical stance vis-à-vis that power. Although in Pascal this counterthinking never translates explicitly into counteraction, it constitutes a reflection on the way in which power permeates thought itself, renders itself immaterial in the historical practice of institutions. In this sense, Pascal's thinking against the established order proposes a model for considering the figures of thought that repeatedly operate in conjunction with institutionalized power. This ongoing process of figuration, so eloquently enunciated in the fragment on the figural entwinement of power and justice, goes hand in hand with power always willing to act in its own name.

Despite assertions of veiled or critical thought, thinking never takes place in pristine seclusion, separate from the figures of thought that necessarily channel it. No matter how developed an individual's critical awareness, thinking remains marked by institutional power, by the conditions that render it possible and by the interpretations that demarcate the tolerated limits of divergence. In effect, by definition critical thinking results from the struggle to detach thought from the means of thinking; that is, it is the sediment from the effort to think the figures of thought. In this sense, striving to articulate and mobilize critical understanding displays an irrepressible linguistic component. For example, Nietzsche's text "On Truth and Lie in an Extramoral Sense," which shows more than a trace of Pascal's notions in its evoking the fundamental duplicity of thought, presents a view of historical understanding that is grounded in the linguistic matter of concepts. In Nietzsche's text, the mechanism of critique embedded in this theory of history has to do with metaphors, those figures always caught up in the process leading to concepts: "The drive toward the formation of metaphors is the fundamental human drive, which one cannot for a single instant dispense with in thought, for one would thereby dispense with man himself. This drive is not truly vanquished and scarcely subdued by the fact that a regular and rigid new world is constructed as a prison from its own ephemeral products, the concepts" (88–89; 887). At bottom, the human linguistic process portrayed here, certainly anti-Aristotelian and contrary to beliefs in mystical essence, exceeds the concepts that would channel and master it. In this sense, it is a theory concerned with production cutting across concepts that accrue to themselves universality while denying—or forgetting—the historical force necessary for them to come into being. Because figuration belongs fundamentally to language and, consequently, to human thought, the social and cognitive power of institutions lives by the same process that enables unmasking, however fleetingly, the power they conceal.

This conception of historical and linguistic matter acknowledges a wholly different form of power and no longer relegates discursive and cultural expression to simply a secondary role vis-à-vis executive power. This basic force of linguistic figuration, of the formation of metaphors, underscores the importance of the matter of history—inscribed almost exclusively on paper prior to the late nineteenth century—and of literary reflection. It is not happenstance that Nietzsche was trained as a classical philologist, the nineteenth-century equivalent of a literary critic; nor should it be surprising that Antonio Gramsci, the twentieth-century thinker who has most deeply analyzed the historical ramifications of cultural production and who has also become a fundamental reference for institutional critique, was a university student of literature who concentrated on linguistics. Gramsci's view of metaphor displays interesting affinities with that of Nietzsche, despite their wide differences of historical vision. In clarifying the use of the term *immanence* in materialist theory, Gramsci characterizes the status of metaphor: "All language is a continuous process of metaphors, and the history of semantics is an aspect of the history of culture: language is both a living

thing and a museum of fossils of past life and civilizations."[35] This historical layering, inscribed and reinscribed in the ongoing elaboration of
figures, provides the stuff of thought, of its hegemonic force, and of the
critique that sifts out the interests that cover up their figural nature.

In Gramsci's speculations, the overlapping effects of the linguistic and
the political receive greatest emphasis. Gramsci links these disjunctures
between reigning metaphorical languages to the emergence of new
worldviews (or new world conceptions: he refers to a *nuova concezione
del mondo* ["Quaderno 11," 1438]), thereby placing into the foreground
the historical question. Contrary to Nietzsche, whose concern with the
power of ideas and concepts took a largely epistemological turn, in his
work Gramsci focused on the significance of historical transformation
and of the ideologies in subsequent world orders. Language is "always
metaphorical. Although one may not be able to say exactly that every
discourse is metaphorical with respect to the thing or material object indicated (or to the abstract concept), so as not to enlarge too much the
concept of metaphor, one can nonetheless say that present-day language
is metaphorical with respect to the meanings and ideological content
that the words have had in prior periods of civilization" ("Quaderno
11," 1427).

Despite Gramsci's hesitation about putting into question the empirical
model of language deriving from Aristotle, the unfolding trajectory he
describes clearly operates according to a historical model of meaning
production: there is no pure essence hiding and waiting only to be discovered. The explicit recognition that metaphor is also a concept un-
comfortably dovetails with language's ineluctable production of concepts and introduces an irony that Nietzsche would have no doubt
appreciated. But Gramsci's notion of succeeding worldviews, with their
concomitant hegemonies and supporting constellations of ideas, gives
this theory of history an overtly political face. While the primary outcome may be to radicalize historical understanding, to question universals presumed to continue unscathed by history, in practice this linguistic materialism hints at a new approach to historical intervention.

At the onset of the twenty-first century, the question of historical intervention takes on unforeseen meanings, largely because of the historical conjuncture itself, the clash in worldviews and the technological
means that diffuse them. At this juncture, figures plot new trajectories
for materialist history. Recognition that truth and its mobilizing figures

are not discovered but made, products of an unsteady evolution whose linguistic and ideological foundations have been forgotten or suppressed, brings thought down from the heavens and shows thinking's porousness to sociopolitical institutions. Even in terrestrial paradise, cut off from transcendental illusions, institutions are more than simply the buildings that have doors, locks, fenced-in lawns, and local police. They are also nonempirical institutions composed of language, concepts, and figures—figures that serve as protagonists of worldviews, galactic or merely planetary.

Notes

Unless otherwise noted, translations are my own.

Introduction

1. Michel de Montaigne, "De l'expérience," *Oeuvres complètes*, ed. Albert Thibaudet and Maurice Rat (Paris: Gallimard [La Pléiade], 1962), 1059. English is cited from John Florio's translation of 1603: *The Essays of Montaigne* (New York: Modern Library, 1933), 978.

2. Gottfried Leibniz, "Leibniz Bemühungen um ein kaiserlich Privileg für den Plan seiner *Semestria*," *Oeuvres de Leibniz, publiées pour la première fois d'après les manuscrits originaux*, vol. 7, ed. A. Foucher de Careil (Darmstadt: Fotokop Wilhelm Weihert, 1969, facs.; orig. Paris: Librairie de Firmin Dido frères, fils et cie, 1875), 7. Hereinafter cited as "Privilege."

3. Leibniz, "Von nützlicher Einrichtung eines Archivi," ibid., vol. 7, 126–137.

4. Leibniz, "Repraesentanda," ibid., vol. 7, 140.

5. Leibniz, "Semestria literaria," ibid., vol. 7, 157. Hereafter cited in the text as "Semestria."

6. "Histoire," *L'encyclopédie ou dictionnaire raisonné des sciences, des arts et des métiers*, ed. Denis Diderot and Jean d'Alembert, vol. 8 (Neufchastel: Samuel Faulche, 1765), 223 ; emphasis in original.

7. "Livre," ibid., vol. 9, 601, 605; emphasis in original.

8. "Imprimerie en taille douce," ibid., vol. 8, 620.

9. "Imprimerie," vol. 8, 608–609.

10. See, for example, Pierre Lévy, *L'intelligence collective: Pour une anthropologie du cyberspace* (Paris: Éditions La Découverte, 1994).

11. Immanuel Kant, "What Is Enlightenment?" *On History*, trans. L. W. Beck (Indianapolis: Bobbs-Merrill, 1963), 5; translation modified. "Beantwortung der Frage: Was ist Aufklärung?" *Schriften zur Anthropologie, Geschichtsphilosophie, Politik und Pädagogik*, vol. 1, ed. W. Weischedel (Frankfurt: Suhrkamp, 1977), 55–56. Subsequent references to this essay appear in the text, indicating first the English translation and then the German original.

12. Immanuel Kant, *Metaphysiche Anfangsgründe der Rechtslehre,* ¶31, II, cited in G. S. A. Mellin, "Buch," *Encyclopädisches Wörterbuch der kritischen Philosophie,* vol. 1 (Züllichau and Leipzig: bei Friedrich Frommann, 1798), 736.
13. Immanuel Kant, "Von der Unrechtmäßigkeit des Büchernachdrucks," *Abhandlungen nach 1781,* vol. 8 of *Kant's Gesammelte Schriften,* ed. Prussian Academy of Sciences (Berlin and Leipzig: Walter de Gruyter and Co., 1923), 81n.
14. Michel Foucault, "Qu'est-ce que les Lumières?" *Dits et écrits: 1954–1988,* vol. 4: 1980–1988 (Paris: Gallimard, 1994), 568.
15. Kant, "Von der Unrechtmäßigkeit des Büchernachdrucks," 87.
16. Antonio Gramsci, "Quaderno 23 (Critica letteraria)," *Quaderni del carcere,* ed. Valentino Gerratana (Turin: Einaudi, 1975), 2194. Gramsci's view of the media is discussed in greater detail in chapter 7 below.
17. This has given rise to numerous theories about the new hegemony of the image; see, for example, Mitchell Stephens, *The Rise of the Image and the Fall of the Word* (New York: Oxford University Press, 1998).
18. Walter Benjamin, "Eduard Fuchs, Collector and Historian," *One-Way Street and Other Writings,* trans. Edmund Jephcott and Kingsley Shorter (London: New Left Books, 1979), 357.
19. Antonio Gramsci, *Selections from the Prison Notebooks,* trans. Quintin Hoare and Geoffrey Nowell Smith (New York: International Publishers, 1971), 324, translation modified; "Quaderno 11 (Introduzione allo studio della filosofia)," *Quaderni del carcere,* ed. Valentino Gerratana (Turin: Einaudi, 1975), 1377.

1. Hegemony of the Vernacular

1. Marcelle Padovani, "Les 'chemises vertes' de Padanie," *Le nouvel observateur,* 12–18 Sept. 1996, 36.
2. Nino Sunseri, "Svizzera, allarme Padania," *La Repubblica,* 2 Nov. 1996, 6.
3. Padovani, "Les 'chemises vertes' de Padanie," 36.
4. Nino Sunseri, "Indipendentisti d'Europa unitevi," *La Repubblica,* 2 Nov. 1996, 6.
5. Sunseri, "Svizzera, allarme Padania."
6. Antonio Gramsci, *Lettere dal carcere, 1926–37,* vol. 2, ed. Antonio A. Santucci (Palermo: Sellerio, 1996), 458–459.
7. Niccolo Machiavelli, "Che la variazione delle sètte e delle lingue, insieme con l'accidente de' diluvii o della peste, spegne le memorie delle cose" (book 2, chap. 5), *Discorsi sopra la prima Deca di Tito Livio,* vol. 2 of *Le grandi opere politiche,* ed. Gian Mario Anselmi and Carlo Varotti (Turin: Bollati Boringhieri, 1993), 250–254.

8. Carlo Prandi, "Tradizioni," *Enciclopedia Einaudi,* vol. 14 (Turin: Einaudi, 1981), 414.

9. See, for example, Eric A. Havelock, *Preface to Plato* (Cambridge, Mass.: Harvard University Press, 1963), Albert B. Lord, *The Singer of Tales* (Cambridge, Mass.: Harvard University Press, 1960), and Walter J. Ong, *Orality and Literacy: The Technologizing of the Word* (London: Methuen, 1982). This avenue of research was opened up by classicists reflecting on the peculiar textuality and socioliterary production of Homeric texts. The theme of orality and textual production rapidly developed into a specialized field of research with important historical implications.

10. Antonio Gramsci, "Quaderno 13 (Noterelle sulla politica del Machiavelli)," *Quaderni del carcere,* ed. Valentino Gerratana, (Turin: Einaudi, 1975), 1618. Other references to the notebooks are to this edition.

11. Jacques Le Goff, *Les intellectuels au Moyen Age* (Paris: Seuil, 1957, 1985), ii.

12. Pier Vincenzo Mengaldo, "Introduzione al *De vulgari eloquentia,*" *Linguistica e retorica di Dante* (Pisa: Nistri-Lischi, 1978), 118.

13. Gramsci, "Quaderno 29 (La così detta 'quistione della lingua')," *Quaderni,* 2350.

14. Dante, *De vulgari eloquentia,* bilingual ed. (Latin-Italian), ed. and trans. Sergio Cecchin (Turin: Tea, 1988), IX.6–7.

15. Antonio Nebrija, *Gramática de la lengua castellana,* ed. Antonio Quilis (Madrid: Editora Nacional, 1980), 97–102.

16. Leo Spitzer, "The 'Ideal Typology' in Dante's *De vulgari eloquentia,*" *Italica* 32, no. 2 (1955): 75–94.

17. See Dante, *De vulgari eloquentia,* 52n, and also the French translation: "De l'éloquence en langue vulgaire," *Oeuvres complètes,* ed. and trans. André Pézard (Paris: Gallimard [La Pléiade], 1965), 21n.

18. Spitzer, "The 'Ideal Typology,'" 94.

19. Dante, *Vita nuova,* ed. Manuela Colombo (Milan: Feltrinelli, 1993), XXV.1–3.

20. Dante, *De vulgari eloquentia,* 81n.

21. Personification is of course a literary or rhetorical term; in the chapters that follow, it will often be discussed as a principal figure of literary understanding. At the same time, however, it is a figure of understanding generally and has played a major role in conceiving collective political action. For Machiavelli's prince figure, in particular for Gramsci's interpretation of the prince figure in the twentieth-century context, see chapter 7 below.

22. Niccolò Machiavelli, "Discorso o dialogo intorno alla nostra lingua," *Tutte le opere,* ed. Mario Martelli (Florence: Sansoni Editore, 1971), 926.

23. Machiavel, *Oeuvres,* ed. and trans. Christian Bec (Paris: Robert Laffont, 1996), 1006.

24. Gramsci, "Quaderno 6 (Miscellanea)," *Quaderni,* 789.

25. Benedict Anderson, *Imagined Communities,* 2nd ed. (London: Verso, 1983, 1991), 133–134; emphasis in original.

26. Gramsci, "Quaderno 6," 748.

2. Figural Economy of the Worldview

1. Erwin Panofsky, *Perspective as Symbolic Form,* trans. Christopher S. Wood (New York: Zone Books, 1991), 72.

2. Rousseau makes this notion—and the word, which he apparently coins in French *(perfectibilité)*—the primary characteristic distinguishing human beings from animals; see Rousseau's *Discours sur l'origine et les fondemens de l'inegalité parmi les hommes: Oeuvres complètes,* vol. 3 of *Du contrat social: Écrits politiques,* ed. Bernard Gagnebin and Marcel Raymond (Paris: Gallimard [La Pléiade], 1964), 142. After Rousseau this notion underlies virtually all views of (secular) human history.

3. Erich Auerbach, *Mimesis: The Representation of Reality in Western Literature,* trans. Willard R. Trask (Princeton: Princeton University Press, 1953), 318; *Mimesis: Dargestellte Wirklichkeit in der abendländischen Literatur,* 4th ed. (Bern: Francke Verlag, 1967), 302.

4. Lucien Goldmann, in *Le dieu caché: Étude sur la vision tragique dans les Pensées de Pascal et dans le théâtre de Racine* (Paris: Gallimard, 1959), also equates the tragic with a new historical moment and its accompanying forms of subjectivity.

5. Martin Heidegger, "The Age of the World Picture," in *The Question concerning Technology and Other Essays,* trans. William Lovitt (New York: Harper and Row, 1977), 117; "Die Zeit des Weltbildes," *Holzwege,* 4th ed. (Frankfurt am Main: Vittorio Klostermann, 1963), 70.

6. Eric Auerbach, "Figura," *Scenes from the Drama of European Literature,* trans. Ralph Mannheim (Minneapolis: University of Minnesota Press, 1984), 76, translation modified here and in subsequent passages; "Figura," *Gesammelte Aufsätze zur romanischen Philosophie* (Bern: Francke Verlag, 1967), 92.

7. See Hans-Georg Gadamer, *Truth and Method,* trans. Joel Weinsheimer and Donald G. Marshall, 2nd rev. ed. (New York: Continuum, 1994), 70–81.

8. Charles Sanders Peirce and Victoria Lady Welby, *Semiotics and Significs: The Correspondence between Charles S. Peirce and Victoria Lady Welby,* ed. Charles S. Hardwick (Bloomington: Indiana University Press, 1977), 24. (See also page 29: "If you take any ordinary triadic relation, you will always find a *mental* element in it. Brute action is secondness, any mentality involves thirdness.) Peirce's historical views are discussed below in chapter 3.

9. Reflections on modern science often demonstrate a profound awareness of a

conceptual mode's implications for thought. For example, in recounting the epistemological rupture provoked by the theory of relativity, Albert Einstein and his coauthor Leopold Infeld stress that the origin of the theory's possibility derives from a turn away from direct experiment (intuitive reasoning) toward the "idealized experiment" that "can never actually be performed," in *The Evolution of Physics: From Early Concepts to Relativity and Quanta* (New York: Simon and Schuster, 1938, 1966), 7. This leads, as the authors state, to a "different picture of the universe" (35).

10. Marvin Minsky, *The Society of Mind* (New York: Simon and Schuster, 1986), 65.

11. Antonio Gramsci, letter of 5 Oct. 1931, *Lettere dal carcere, 1926–1937*, ed. Antonio A. Santucci, vol. 2 (Palermo: Sellerio, 1996), 475.

12. For discussion of this prince figure, see chapter 7 below.

13. See, for example, Marc Augé, *Pour une anthropologie des mondes contemporains* (Paris: Aubier, 1994), especially chap. 5, "Nouveaux mondes," 127–175.

14. The difference between concepts and figures evoked here can be seen in *Enciclopedia Einaudi*'s (Turin: Einaudi, 1977–1984) highly laudable project of mapping the concepts of modernity, which is a twentieth-century version of the eighteenth-century *Encyclopédie,* with an evident inclination toward positivism rather than materialism. Its concepts are treated as objects, even when their historical genesis is recounted, and their discursive aspects and linguistic underpinnings are ignored.

15. These essays and their numerous versions are discussed below in conjunction with Benjamin's theory of the figure and culture. See chapters 3 and 7.

16. Considered from a commercial perspective, the book's publishing history reflects the strangeness of this combination; its original printing was 500 copies, and some stock remained even after ten years (in 1933); see the critical commentary in *Gesammelte Schriften,* vol. 4 (Frankfurt am Main: Suhrkamp, 1980), 893. In his correspondence, Benjamin remarked that he received no honorarium and a reduced number of complimentary copies (letters to Scholem, 5 Dec. 1923, and Christian Rang, 9 Dec. 1923).

17. Benjamin's 1921 letter to Scholem, cited in *Gesammelte Schriften,* 4: 891.

18. Charles Baudelaire, *Oeuvres complètes,* ed. Claude Pichois, vol. 1 (Paris: La Pléiade, 1975), 993.

19. Benjamin's translation, far from literal, sometimes (but not always) renders the *tableau* of Baudelaire's poems by some form of *Bild:* for example, in "Le jeu" or "Le rêve parisien." In an early translation of "Le cygne," Benjamin makes recourse to *Bild* to translate "image" as well; this line however does not make it into the published version (*Gesammelte Schriften,* 4: 899). The fundamental issue, though, is that Baudelaire's "Tableaux" poems concen-

trate on how consciousness interacts with representations through the intermediary of language; this will be the point of departure and theme of Benjamin's introductory essay.

20. Walter Benjamin, "Die Aufgabe des Übersetzers," *Gesammelte Schriften,* 4: 9; hereafter cited as *GS.* English translation: "The Task of the Translator," trans. Harry Zohn, *Illuminations* (New York: Schocken, 1969), 69, translation slightly modified; hereinafter cited as "Task."

21. In this regard, Paul de Man's discussion of the essay's allegory of the vessel's "broken fragments" is pertinent; see "Conclusions: Walter Benjamin's 'The Task of the Translator,'" *The Resistance to Theory* (Minneapolis: University of Minnesota Press, 1986), 89–93.

3. Illusions of Unfolding Time

1. Alain Touraine, *Critique de la modernité* (Paris: Librairie Arthème Fayard, 1992), 244.

2. In Charles Sanders Peirce, *Scientific Metaphysics,* vol. 6 of *Collected Papers* (Cambridge, Mass.: Harvard University Press, 1935), 190–215. Subsequent references to this essay are to this edition. This essay also appears in *The Essential Peirce: Selected Philosophical Writings,* vol. 1, ed. Nathan Houser and Christian Kloesel (Bloomington: Indiana University Press, 1992), 352–371.

3. In Claude Allègre, *Introduction à une Histoire naturelle: Du big bang à la disparition de l'Homme* (Paris: Fayard, 1992).

4. Pierre Lévy, *Les technologies de l'intelligence: L'avenir de la pensée à l'ère informatique* (Paris: Editions La Découverte, 1990), 17.

5. Alain Finkielkraut, *La sagesse de l'amour* (Paris: Gallimard, 1984).

6. Pierre Missac, in "Walter Benjamin: From Rupture to Shipwreck," in *On Walter Benjamin: Critical Essays and Recollections,* ed. Gary Smith (Cambridge, Mass.: MIT Press, 1988), gives a brief overview of these divergent views of Benjamin's work on history. These differences in interpretation (and in the interpreters' agendas) are most visible with regard to efforts to understand the historical status of the "aura." In *Marxism and Form* (Princeton: Princeton University Press, 1971), for example, Fredric Jameson identifies the aura as a "Utopian component of Benjamin's thought" (77) to link it to Benjamin's presumed nostalgia. Gianni Vattimo's *La società transparente* (Milan: Garzanti Editore, 1989) interprets the aura as proof that the mass media have simply changed the way in which "art" reveals itself (64–65). In sum, the interpretation given to aura inevitably serves a theory of history; Jameson reads Benjamin through Lukács's notion of history, whereas Vattimo adopts the ontologizing history of Heidegger. Habermas, Scholem, Adorno, Wohlfarth, and others invest aura with differing meanings, but for each it is the historical question that proves troubling. "Aura" and Ben-

jamin's essay on mechanical reproducibility are discussed in chapter 7 below.

7. These oppositions are so well ensconced that even the most unlikely critics adopt their terms. Jacques Derrida, for example, in his reading of Benjamin's essay "Zur Kritik der Gewalt" (in his *Force de loi* [Paris: Galilée, 1994]), describes the essay as *"révolutionnaire dans un style à la fois marxiste et messianique"* (69); as characterized by *"la greffe du langage de la révolution marxiste sur celui de la révolution messianique"* (70); and as *"une greffe de mystique néo-messianique juive sur un néo-marxisme post-sorelien (ou l'inverse)"* (77).

8. Benjamin, "Über den Begriff der Geschichte," in *Gesammelte Schriften*, vol. 1 (Frankfurt am Main: Suhrkamp Verlag, 1974, 1980), 702; translated as "Theses on the Philosophy of History," in *Illuminations*, ed. Hannah Arendt, trans. Harry Zohn (New York: Schocken Books, 1969), 262. The textual questions about Benjamin's work are endless and frequently permit no definitive answer. In the case of "On the Concept of History," there is a final German text and an almost complete French version that Benjamin himself wrote. Both of these versions are published in volume 1 of Benjamin's *Gesammelte Schriften*, the German text on pages 691–704, and the French text, entitled "Sur le concept d'histoire," on pages 1260–1266. In the discussion that follows, I will generally refer to the Zohn's official English translation (of the German version), often modifying the translation; subsequent page references to this version, which indicate first the German original and then the English translation, will be included in the text. Occasional references to the French version, which offers some productive differences and clarifications of the German text that preceded it, also appear in the text; in these instances, the translations are mine.

9. For a contrast with Gramsci's theory of historical agency, see chapter 7 of this volume.

10. Benjamin, *Das Passagen-Werk*, vol. 5 of *Gesammelte Schriften* (Frankfurt am Main: Suhrkamp Verlag, 1982), 584; my translation. Future references to this work will appear in the text. Benjamin had long considered this conflictual notion of tradition and history; in his *Moskauer Tagebuch*, he wrote that *"die Geschichte der 'Gebildeten' müsse materialistisch als Funktion und im strengen Zusammenhange mit einer 'Geschichte der Unbildung' dargestellt werden"* (in *Gesammelte Schriften*, vol. 6 [Frankfurt am Main: Suhrkamp Verlag, 1986]), 310 (see also the continuation on 311). This particular set of concerns, with the "cultured" versus the "uncultured" layers of society, antedates Benjamin's attempts to dismember historical agency.

11. Stéphane Mosès, *L'ange de l'histoire: Rosenzweig, Benjamin, Scholem* (Paris: Seuil, 1992).

12. Elsewhere in the *Passagen-Werk*, Benjamin will use this notion of totality to

describe how the idea of progress extinguished the possibility of historical critique; see 598–599.

13. Mosès, *L'ange de l'histoire,* 153; author's italics.

14. In fact, this assertion of the ethical permits Mosès to link Benjamin's theory of history to Jewish messianism (155–156) and thereby confirm Scholem's interpretation (180). The tradition of Benjaminian interpretation requires that one adopt a perspective with regard to his lines of intellectual heritage, often at the expense of Benjamin's inconclusive texts.

15. *Bild,* which I render here with "figure," is most often translated by "image"; here, however, the emphasis on reading suggests that "figure" is more appropriate. Moreover, "image" bears a great deal of interpretive baggage that would make it an obstacle for understanding the specificity of Benjamin's theory of history. See chapter 2 for Benjamin's use of *Bild* in regard to the question of translation and Baudelaire's *Les tableaux parisiens.*

16. Quintilian, *Institutio oratoria,* trans. H. E. Butler (Cambridge, Mass.: Harvard University Press, Loeb Library, 1921), V.ix.9.

17. In *Elements of Logic,* vol. 2 of *Collected Papers* (Cambridge, Mass.: Harvard University Press, 1932), 161; subsequent page references appear in the text.

18. See Umberto Eco, *A Theory of Semiotics* (Bloomington: Indiana University Press, 1976), 115–121.

19. 693–694; 254. Much of this passage was omitted in the English translation.

4. The Epic Figure of Literary History

1. Jorge de Sena, "A Poesia de Camões: Ensaio de revelação da dialética camoniana," in *Da poesia portuguesa* (Lisbon: Edições Atica, 1959), 31.

2. Frank Pierce, "Introduction," in *Os Lusíadas,* ed. Pierce (Oxford: Oxford University Press, 1973), xvii.

3. Frank Pierce, "The Place of Mythology in *The Lusiads,*" *Comparative Literature* 6 (1954): 104.

4. Maria Lucília Gonçalves Pires, *A crítica camoniana no século XVII* (Amadora: Livraria Bertrand, 1982), 67.

5. François Marie Arouet de Voltaire, "Essai sur la poésie épique," in *Oeuvres complètes,* vol. 8 (Paris: Garnier Frères, 1877), 332.

6. A. H. de Oliveira Marques, *History of Portugal,* vol. 1 (New York: Columbia University Press, 1972), 304.

7. Cleonice Berardinelli, "Os excursos do poeta n'*Os Lusíadas,*" in *Estudos Camonianos* (Rio de Janeiro: Gráfica Olímpica Editora, 1973), 29.

8. António José Saraiva, *Camões* (Lisbon: Jornal do Fôro, 1963), 187.

9. As one example among many, see Celso Lafer, *Gil Vicente e Camões* (São Paulo: Editora Atica, 1978), 109–150, in which the question of subjectivity

is not explicitly broached, although Lafer's interpretation depends entirely on the notions of "empiricism," "experience," and "epistemology," all emanating from the figure of Camões as a knowing subject.

10. A great deal of the literature has also taken the form of tracing the fortunes of *The Lusiads* through translations that have been made of it. Besides Gonçalves Pires, *A crítica camoniana no século XVII*, see B. Xavier Coutinho, "Camões no mundo do espaço cultural," in *Presença de Portugal no mundo* (Lisbon: Academia Portuguesa da História, 1982), 499–547; William Melczer, "The Place of Camões in the European Cultural Conscience," in *Empire in Transition: The Portuguese World in the Time of Camões*, ed. Alfred Hower and Richard A. Preto-Rodas (Gainesville: University of Florida Press, 1985), 195–203; António Soares Amora, "A crítica feita ao poema no decurso da história literária," in *Actas da I Reunião Internacional de Camonistas* (Lisbon: Oficinas da Neogravura, 1973), 177–206; Jorge Borges de Macedo, *"Os Lusíadas" e a história* (Lisbon: Editorial Verbo, 1979).

11. See Gonçalves Pires, *A crítica camoniana*, 64–66, for her summary of the significance of *The Lusiads* during this period.

12. The original title is "Resposta ao Juízo do Poema dos Lusíadas de Luís de Camões em que se mostra não ter as perfeições que lhe atribui e ter outras conformes a sua invenção e sua matéria," Gonçalves Pires, *A crítica camoniana*, 79–87.

13. Saraiva, *Camões*, has very succinctly noted the difference between the earlier epics and that of Camões, showing how the idealized existence of the state replaces the hero (see 149–150). But Saraiva does not even hint at the consequences that this might have for narration.

14. Luiz Piva, "Os patriarcas da crítica de *Os Lusíadas*," in *Leituras de Camões*, ed. Joseph Maria Luyten et al. (São Paulo: Instituto de Cultura e Ensino Padre Manoel de Nóbrega, 1982), 43–61.

15. *Os Lusíadas* I, 3, 1–6. Citations of Camões's text will be taken from the critical edition edited by Frank Pierce (Oxford: Oxford University Press, 1973), which differs from that of Emanuel Paulo Ramos (3rd ed. [Porto: Porto Editora, 1978]) only concerning capitalization of proper nouns. Because of the nature of my argument, my translation tends to adhere closely to the Portuguese text. *Peito*, which is the term I have rendered by "heart," actually refers to "chest," "bosom," "courage," and so on. By far the finest literary translation of Camões's text in English is *The Lusiads*, translated by Leonard Bacon (New York: Hispanic Society of America, 1950).

16. Frank Pierce, "The Place of Mythology in *The Lusiads*," 97.

17. Saraiva, *Camões*, 181.

18. Voltaire, "Essaie sur la poésie épique," 335–336.

19. In Pierce's edition of *Os Lusíadas*, xlv; my translation.

20. Cited in Artur Anselmo, *Camões e a censura literária inquisitorial* (Braga: Barbosa and Xavier, Editores, 1982), 60.
21. Ibid., between 44 and 45.
22. Melczer, "The Place of Camões in the European Cultural Conscience," 199.
23. Friedrich Schlegel, *Geschichte der Alten und Neuen Literatur,* ed. Hans Eichner, vol. 6 of *Kritische Ausgabe* (Paderborn: Ferdinand Schöningh, 1961); hereinafter referred to as v6. Translations of this and other Schlegel texts are mine.
24. Schlegel, "Portuguesische Dichtkunst," a section in "Beiträge zur Geschichte der modernen Poesie," in *Charakteristiken und Kritiken II,* ed. Hans Eichner, vol. 3 of *Kritische Ausgabe* (Paderborn: Ferdinand Schöningh, 1975), 24–32; hereinafter referred to as v3.
25. Paul de Man, "The Rhetoric of Temporality," in *Blindness and Insight,* 2nd ed. (Minneapolis: University of Minnesota Press, 1983); for a specific example, see 225.
26. Teófilo Braga, for example, cites it (from a French translation of 1829) on 349–350 of *Camões,* vol. 13 of his *História da literatura portuguesa* (Porto: Livraria Chardron, de Lello and Irmão, 1911).
27. João de Barros, *Asia; dos feitos que os portugueses fizeram no descobrimento e conquista dos mares e terras do oriente,* ed. António Baião (Coimbra: Imprensa da Universidade, 1932), 1–2. The passage comes from the *Década I,* first published in 1552.
28. Antonio de Nebrija, *Gramática de la lengua castellana,* ed. Antonio Quilis (Madrid: Editora Nacional, 1980); it was originally published in 1492 and dedicated to Isabella.
29. In his 1803 *Europa* essays, Schlegel goes so far as to say that in *material* terms *("was die Materie betrifft")* the Portuguese and Spanish languages are so similar that it is sometimes difficult to tell them apart. See v3: 25–26.
30. Schlegel, "Die Spanishe-Portuguesische Literatur," in *Wissenschaft der Europäischen Literatur,* vol. 11 of *Kritische Ausgabe,* ed. Ernst Behler (Paderborn: Ferdinand Schöningh, 1958), 158; hereinafter referred to as v11.
31. Schlegel, *Fragmente zur Poesie und Literatur,* vol. 17 of *Kritische Ausgabe,* ed. Ernst Behler (Paderborn: Ferdinand Schöningh, 1991), 426; hereinafter referred to as v17.
32. Schlegel, "An Camoëns," *Dichtungen,* vol. 5 of *Kritische Ausgabe,* ed. Hans Eichner (Paderborn: Ferdinand Schöningh, 1962), 311.

5. Cosmopolitical Grounding of Literature

1. See Roberto Fernández Retamar, *Caliban and Other Essays,* trans. Edward Baker (Minneapolis: University of Minnesota Press, 1989), 6–14.

2. Michel de Montaigne, "Des cannibales," *Oeuvres complètes*, ed. Albert Thibaudet and Maurice Rat (Paris: Gallimard [La Pléiade], 1962), 200; my translation. When possible I will use Donald M. Frame's standard translation, *The Complete Essays of Montaigne* (Stanford: Stanford University Press, 1958), and I will give the page reference to this edition as a matter of course; in this instance, Frame's corresponding translation is on page 150. For "prevailing opinions," the original literally says "vulgar opinions" *(opinions vulgaires)*, but at that time *vulgaire* meant "current," "commonly held," just as vulgar language was only the vernacular.

3. Montaigne, "De l'expérience," in ibid., 1045; Frame, 818.

4. Frank Pierce, "Introduction," in *Os Lusíadas*, ed. Pierce (London: Oxford University Press, 1973), vii.

5. José Agostinho de Macedo, *Reflexões críticas sobre o episódio de Adamastor* (Lisbon: Impressão Regia, 1811).

6. Teófilo Braga, *Camões,* vol. 13 of *História da literatura portuguesa* (Porto: Livraria Chardron, de Lello and Irmão, 1911), 656. Subsequent page references to this work are cited in the text.

7. "Rebattre," in *Dictionnaire de la langue française* (Paris: Pauvert, 1962–1965).

8. More recent acknowledgments of some of these linguistic and conceptual similarities show that Macedo was not entirely wrong in his assessment of Camões's borrowings. See Américo da Costa Ramalho, "Aspectos clássicos do Adamastor," in *Estudos camonianos* (Coimbra: Instituto de Alta Cultura, 1975), 51.

9. *Disparate* is a complex word that merits a study of its own. In addition to being a logical term defined in contradistinction to negation and contradiction, in the Romance languages, *disparate* often means silliness or nonsense. As nonsense, it now names a genre of discourse; see Blanca Periñan, *Poeta Ludens: Disparate, perqué y chiste en los siglos XVI y XVII* (Pisa: Giardini Editori e Stampatori, 1979).

10. Francisco Rodrigues Lôbo, *Corte na aldeia,* ed. Afonso Lopes Vieira, 3rd ed. (Lisbon: Livraria Sá da Costa, 1972), 70.

11. Reis do Brasil, *"Os Lusíadas": Comentários e estudo crítico,* vol. 5 (Lisbon: Editorial Minerva), 294.

12. For a relevant discussion of Ferreira's *Nova arte,* see Maria Lucília Gonçalves Pires, *A crítica camoniana no século XVIII* (Amadora: Livraria Bertrand, 1982), 70–71.

13. Braga, *Camões,* 649.

14. Hernâni Cidade, *A literatura portuguesa e a expansão ultramarina,* vol. 1 (Lisbon: Divisão de publicações e Biblioteca Agência Geral das Colônias, 1943), 282–283. His later work, *Luís de Camões: O épico* (Lisbon, 1950) will

advance this view more programmatically regarding the poem as a whole. For Saraiva's comparable praise of Adamastor, see António José Saraiva, *Camões* (Lisbon: Jornal do Fôro, 1963), 189.

15. François Marie Arouet de Voltaire, "Essai sur la poésie épique," in *Oeuvres complètes,* vol. 8 (Paris: Garnier Frères, 1877), 334.

16. C. M. Bowra, *Heroic Poetry* (London: Macmillan, 1952), 125, 126.

17. Reis do Brasil, *"Os Lusíadas,"* 295.

18. Saraiva, *Camões,* 190–191.

19. João de Barros, *Asia; dos feitos que os portugueses fizeram no descobrimento e conquista dos mares e terras do oriente,* ed. António Baião (Coimbra: Imprensa da Universidade, 1932); Lopes de Castanheda, *Historia do descobrimento & conquista da India pelos portugueses,* ed. Pedro de Azevedo (Coimbra: Imprensa da Universidade, 1924). Both historians were working and publishing roughly at the same time: Barros published *Década I* in 1552, *Década II* in 1553, and *Década III* in 1563, whereas Castanheda published *Book 1* in 1551 and *Book 2* and *Book 3* in 1552.

20. "Padrão," *Novo dicionário da língua portuguesa,* ed. Aurélio Buarque de Holanda Ferreira (Rio: Editora Nova Fronteira, S.A., 1975).

21. Joaquim Ferreira, *História da literatura portuguesa,* 4th ed. (Porto: Editorial Domingos Barreira, n.d.), 378.

22. Barros, *Asia,* 86–87; further references in the text.

23. Castanheda, *História do descobrimento & conquista,* 14; subsequent references in the text.

24. First edited by Diogo Köpke and António da Costa Paiva (1838), then (with Costa Paiva) by Alexandre Herculano, an important figure in Portuguese historical discourse (1861). A facsimile of the handwritten copy (which is not the original and may be in Castanheda's hand), accompanied by a literal transcription, was published as *Diário da viagem de Vasco da Gama,* ed. António Baião, et al. (Porto: Livraria Civilização, 1945). References, however, will be made to the most recent and complete edition, with modernized orthography and detailed notes, published as *Roteiro da primeira viagem de Vasco da Gama,* ed. A. Fontoura da Costa, 2nd ed. (Lisbon: Agência Geral do Ultramar, 1960); English translation: *A Journal of the First Voyage of Vasco da Gama, 1497–1499,* trans. and ed. E. G. Ravenstein (New York: Burt Franklin, 1898).

25. *Roteiro,* 14–15; my translation. The editor adds in a footnote: "What religious and patriotic emotion Vasco da Gama and his men must have felt on glimpsing on land Bartholomeu Dias's Pillar of St. Gregory!" The corresponding passage in the published English translation can be found on pp. 14–16.

26. I am citing Camões's text from Pierce, ed., *Os Lusíadas;* this is from canto V,

stanza 17. Hereafter canto, stanza, and lines are indicated in the text. In the interests of presenting my argument, translations are mine throughout, although in one or two instances I have been able to use lines from Leonard Bacon's excellent translation, *The Lusiads of Luis de Camões* (New York: Hispanic Society of America, 1950).

27. Peirce, ed., *Os Lusíadas,* 118n.

28. Costa Ramalho, "Sobre o nome de Adamastor," *Estudos camonianos,* 33–41.

29. Emanuel Paulo Ramos, ed., *Os Lusíadas de Luís de Camões,* 4th ed. (Porto: Porto Editora, 1978), 468.

30. Hegel, in the second volume of his *Vorlesungen über die Philosophie der Religion* (vol. 17 of *Werke* [Frankfurt am Main: Suhrkamp, 1969]), mentions Thetis in a context that bears on the conceptual relationship between the secular and divine order. After the death of Achilles, the Greeks heard the storming of the sea, which was interpreted as an expression of Thetis's mourning. Hegel then remarks that "this interpretation signifies *forming* the natural phenomenon, giving it the form of a *divine acting*" (*Diese Auslegung heißt eben, die natürliche Erscheinung gestalten, ihr die Gestalt eines göttlichen Tuns geben* [119]). Confronting a threatening phenomenon calls for the assignment of *agency*, of what the passage from Hegel describes as referring to a *deity* as the origin of the event. This *assignment* or idealized reference is repeated not only in the self-consciousness achieved by Adamastor—Thetis continues to circle around the cape, although he no longer has the capacity to grasp her physically—but also in the idealized figurality that defines the relationship between historical experience and discourse.

31. Herman Melville, *Billy Budd, Sailor (An Inside Narrative),* in *Pierre or, The Ambiguities,* et al., ed. Harrison Hayford (New York: The Library of America, 1984), 1375.

32. André Brink, *Cape of Storms: The First Life of Adamastor* (New York: Simon and Schuster, 1993), 13; subsequent page references in the text.

6. The Use and Abuse of the Human

1. This information is summarized from Didier Eribon, "Quand la pensée française voyage sur Internet," *Le nouvel observateur,* 21–27 March 1996, 12.

2. Karl Marx and Friedrich Engels, *Manifesto of the Communist Party,* trans. Samuel Moore (Peking: Foreign Languages Press, 1973), 37, translation modified; *Manifest der kommunistischen Partei,* in vol. 6 of *Werke und Schriften* (Glashütten in Taunus: Verlag Detlev Auvermann K-G, 1970), 529.

3. See, for example, Wilhelm von Humboldt, "Plan einer vergleichenden An-

thropologie," *Schriften zur Anthropologie und Geschichte,* vol. 1 of *Werke in fünf Bänden,* ed. Andreas Flitner and Klaus Giel (Stuttgart: J. G. Cotta'sche Buchhandlung, 1960), 337–375.

4. Immanuel Kant, *Anthropologie in pragmatisches Hinsicht,* vol. 2 of *Schriften zur Anthropologie, Geschichtsphilosophie, Politik und Pädagogik* (Frankfurt am Main: Suhrkamp Verlag, 1977). Page numbers of subsequent citations appearing in the text refer to this edition; translations are mine.

5. In this chapter's discussion of the human figure, I refer to it in a variety of ways, using interchangeably terms such as *idea, figure, notion,* and *the human.* Modernity's projection of "the human" is a figure in the sense used and elaborated in this book. This rhetorical dimension of the human figure is discussed in greater detail later in the chapter.

6. Charles Krauthammer, "Deep Blue Funk," *Time,* 26 February 1996, 50.

7. Paul Davies, "The Harmony of the Spheres," *Time,* 5 February 1996, 52. In these two sentences, Davies summarizes his more detailed analysis of contemporary space explorations, dominant theories of physics, and conceptions of human evolution; see Davies, *Are We Alone? Philosophical Implications of the Discovery of Extraterrestrial Life* (New York: Basic Books, 1995).

8. The debates about the status of the human and its relationship to theories of knowledge and history date back at least to the 1960s, ranging from Michel Foucault's French translation of Kant's *Anthropology* (Paris: J. Vrin, 1970) to the English publication of Marx's so-called humanist manuscripts, with extensive commentary by Erich Fromm, who also relates them to Meister Eckhart's mystical Being, to Louis Althusser's important reflections contained in his various essays on Marx and humanism. See, for example, Fromm, *Marx's Concept of Man,* which includes Marx's *Economic and Philosophical Manuscripts,* trans. T. B. Bottomore (New York: Frederick Unger, 1961, 1966), and Althusser's 1967 essay "La querelle de l'humanisme," *Écrits philosophiques et politiques,* vol. 2 (Paris: Éditions Stock/Imec, 1995), 433–532. Most striking, however, is the present explosion of texts and research projects attempting to ground thought in contemplation of the human. A widely diffused example of this tendency is Luc Ferry's *L'homme-dieu: Le sens de la vie* (Paris: Grasset, 1996), but the list of such efforts is virtually interminable and includes Tzvetan Todorov, *La vie commune: Essai d'anthropologie générale* (Paris: Seuil, 1995); Marc Augé, *Pour une anthropologie des mondes contemporains* (Paris: Aubier, 1994); Pierre Lévy, *L'intelligence collective: Pour une anthropologie du cyberspace* (Paris: Éditions la Découverte, 1994); and Eric Gans's *Anthropoetics* project, an electronic journal (http://www.humnet.ucla.edu/humnet/anthropoetics/home.htm) whose diverse contributors are united in their drive to refurbish humanist ethics by merging anthropological and literary concerns.

9. Martin Heidegger, "The Age of the World Picture," *The Question concerning Technology and Other Essays*, trans. William Lovitt (New York: Harper and Row, 1977), 120; "Die Zeit des Weltbildes," *Holzweg*, 4th ed. (Frankfurt am Main: Vittorio Klostermann, 1963), 73.

10. Erich Auerbach, "Figura," *Gesammelte Aufsätze zur romanischen Philologie* (Bern: Francke, 1967), 55–92; "Figura," *Scenes from the Drama of European Literature*, trans. Ralph Mannheim (Minneapolis: University of Minnesota Press, 1984), 11–76. This text and Auerbach's historical analysis of *figura* have been discussed in detail in chapter 2.

11. See Hendrik Birus, "The Archaeology of 'Humanism,'" *Surfaces* 4 (1994): 1–18.

12. Paul Oskar Kristeller, "The Humanist Movement," *Renaissance Thought: The Classic, Scholastic, and Humanist Strains* (New York: Harper and Row, 1961), 20.

13. Paul Oskar Kristeller, "The Philosophy of Man in the Italian Renaissance," ibid., 138.

14. Niccolò Machiavelli, *The Prince and the Discourses*, trans. Luigi Ricci, E. R. P. Vincent, and Christian E. Detmold (New York: Random House, 1950), 530, translation modified; *Discorsi sopra la prima Deca di Tito Livio*, vol. 2 of *Le grandi opere politiche*, ed. Gian Mario Anselmi and Carlo Varotti (Turin: Bollati Boringhieri, 1993), 527.

15. Cited in Kristeller, "The Philosophy of Man in the Italian Renaissance," 133.

16. Blaise Pascal, "Préface pour le traité du vide," *Oeuvres complètes* (Paris: La Pléiade, 1954), 533.

17. Lucien Goldmann convincingly demonstrates that Pascal's notion of the tragic, which derives from this disjuncture between the human and the divine, gives rise to modernity's view of subjectivity and historical action; according to Goldmann, Pascal's dialectical resolution of this disjuncture introduces a mode of historical understanding that will culminate in Kant's philosophy of history. See Goldmann, *Le dieu caché: Étude sur la vision tragique dans les Pensées de Pascal et dans le théâtre de Racine* (Paris: Gallimard, 1962), especially chaps. 1 and 8–10.

18. Heidegger, "The Age of the World Picture," 152; "Die Zeit des Weltbildes," 102.

19. Emmanuel Lévinas, *À l'heure des nations* (Paris: Minuit, 1988), 146.

20. "Anthropologie," *L'encyclopédie ou dictionnaire raisonné des sciences, des arts et des métiers*, ed. Denis Diderot and Jean d'Alembert, vol. 1 (Neufschastel: Samuel Faulche, 1751), 497; emphasis in the original.

21. Kant, *Anthropologie*, 473n.

22. See "Anthropomorphisme," *Dictionnaire historique de la langue française* (Paris: Dictionnaire le Robert, 1992); Leibniz's use dates from 1710.

23. Immanuel Kant, *Critique of Pure Reason*, trans. Norman Kemp Smith (1929; New York: St. Martin's Press, 1965), 568; *Kritik der reinen Vernunft*, vol. 4 of *Werkausgabe*, ed. Wilhelm Weischedel (Frankfurt am Main: Suhrkamp Verlag, 1981), 603.

24. Spinoza's materialism becomes most evident precisely in this regard; in his *Tractatus theologico-politicus*, for example, *all* historical understanding is necessarily figural and must be interpreted as such, even when that understanding results from divine inspiration. In such a perspective, the non-historical idea, the transcendental, and even the divine have only a relative primacy. See in particular chap. 2 of *Theologico-Political Treatise*, "Of Prophets."

25. Jean Beaudrillard, *La société de consommation* (Paris: Denoël, 1970), 14.

7. Collective Culture of Print

1. Because of the generally haphazard way Gramsci's notebooks have been selected, organized, and rendered into English, attempts to use or refer to English versions are often clumsy. (The integral English translation of Gramsci's prison notebooks, which is currently under way, will alter this situation in the coming years. Thus far two volumes have appeared, containing notebooks one to five and an exhaustive critical commentary by translator and editor Joseph A. Buttigieg.) The Italian edition consists of four volumes, including a volume of notes and critical reference: *Quaderni del carcere*, ed. Valentino Gerratana (Turin: Einaudi, 1975). I will discuss all of Gramsci's texts in English, always citing, and often modifying, published English-language versions when available. Citations refer both to the English translation and to the respective notebook and the page as it appears in the four-volume *Quaderni*, which is paginated consecutively. The full reference to each translation is given when first used and is thereafter abbreviated. When no English-language source is indicated, translations are my own.

2. Joseph A. Buttigieg comments that the southern-question essay "contains embryonically" the elements later to be developed in prison (see Buttigieg's introduction to volume 1 of Gramsci's *Prison Notebooks* [New York: Columbia University Press, 1992], 21); Franco de Felice and Valentino Parlato, in introducing their edition of Gramsci's writings on the southern question, refer to the essay as "Gramsci's most accomplished text" before his arrest (*La questione meridionale* [Rome: Editori Riuniti, 1966], 31).

3. *Selections from the Prison Notebooks*, ed. and trans. Quintin Hoare and Geoffrey Nowell-Smith (New York: International Publishers, 1971), 125, hereinafter cited as *SPN*; "Quaderno 13," (Noterelle sulla politica del Machiavelli)," *Quaderni*, 1555.

4. Notebook 5, *Prison Notebooks*, vol. 2, ed. and trans. Joseph A. Buttigieg (New York: Columbia University Press, 1996), 382; "Quaderno 5 (Miscellanea)," *Quaderni*, 661–662.

5. Claude de Seyssel, *Exorde en la translation de l'histoire de Justin* (1510), cited in Jean-Yves Guiomar, *La nation entre l'histoire et la raison* (Paris: Editions la Découverte, 1990), 17.

6. *An Antonio Gramsci Reader: Selected Writings, 1916–1935*, ed. David Forgacs (New York: Schocken Books, 1988), 353, hereinafter cited as *GR*; "Quaderno 16 (Argomenti di cultura—1°)," *Quaderni*, 1862–1863.

7. For a traditional view of this historical change, which is now widely discussed, see Walter J. Ong's *Rhetoric, Romance, and Technology: Studies in the Interaction of Expression and Culture* (Ithaca, N.Y.: Cornell University Press, 1971).

8. *Selections from Cultural Writings*, ed. David Forgacs and Geoffrey Nowell-Smith, trans. William Boelhower (Cambridge, Mass.: Harvard University Press), 408–409, hereinafter cited as *CW*; "Quaderno 24 (Giornalismo)," *Quaderni*, 2259.

9. The realm of publishing, central to the constitution of state culture, has had, from the very beginning, a curious commercial status. It began with massive subventions, whether from the printers/publishers themselves or other benefactors, and with client relationships with states, which provided licenses and helped create monopolies. (See, for example, Lucien Febvre and Henri-Jean Martin's *The Coming of the Book: The Impact of Printing, 1450–1800*, trans. David Gerard [London: Verso, 1976], 127, 140–141.) Today, the press with a "critical agenda," whether newspaper, newsletter, journal, or book publisher, is gradually disappearing. This situation is due only in part to the fragmentation of every constituted or even potential public; it is accompanied by a decline in the availability of capital offered by investors who would be satisfied with a nonmonetary return. The universities' regimes of fiscal austerity are indicative of this trend.

10. A lengthy commentary about the various versions, including extensive citations of the sometimes heated correspondence regarding the French version, is included in volume 1 of Benjamin's *Gesammelte Schriften* (Frankfurt am Main: Suhrkampf Verlag, 1974), hereinafter cited as *GS*. Four versions of the essay "Das Kunstwerk im Zeitalter seiner technischen Reproduzierbarkeit" have now been published in the *Gesammelte Schriften*. Volume 1 contains the first German-language version (431–469); the French version that was published in 1936 (709–739); and the third and final German-language version, which is listed in this volume as the second version (471–508). The lost German-language text that served as an early starting point for the French version is now available in volume 7 (Frankfurt am Main: Suhrkamp Verlag, 1989), along with additional commentary.

11. Significant parts of these letters are cited in *GS,* 1: 983; both letters are published in their entirety in volume 2 of Benjamin's *Briefe* (Frankfurt am Main, 1966): "An Max Horkheimer" is from 16 October 1935 (688–691), and "An Gerhard Scholem" is from 23 October 1935 (693–696). (The passage quoted from the letter to Scholem comes from *The Correspondence of Walter Benjamin and Gershom Scholem, 1932–1940,* trans. Gary Smith and Andre Lefevere [Cambridge, Mass.: Harvard University Press, 1992], 171, which dates the letter 24 October 1935.)

12. What Benjamin consolidates under the notion of "aesthetics" is firmly rooted in the historical; in the second version of the essay, which became available only in 1989, he takes pains to demonstrate that the epoch of mechanical reproducibility produces a different notion of aesthetics itself. Here, the element of *Spiel* comes to predominate over *Schein,* the traditional dominant element during the hegemony of the so-called aura. Although this lengthy footnote was drastically abbreviated in the final German version, and all references to *Spiel* were eliminated, it goes a long way toward explaining the Frankfurt School's later preoccupation (particularly in the works of Marcuse and Adorno) with recuperating aesthetics based on *Schein.* This digression occurs in version 2, note 10, *GS,* 7: 368–69. Adorno's attempts to rescue a version of the aesthetic are well known; as evidenced in his letter to Benjamin, Adorno understood only too well Benjamin's assertions about the political role of the aesthetic: "I now find it disquieting . . . that you now casually transfer the concept of magical aura to the 'autonomous work of art' and flatly assign to the latter a counter-revolutionary function" (from the letter of 18 March 1936, in *Aesthetics and Politics,* trans. and ed. Ronald Taylor [London: Verso, 1977], 121).

13. From the English translation, "The Work of Art in the Age of Mechanical Reproduction," in *Illuminations,* trans. Harry Zohn (New York: Schocken Books, 1969), 241; from the final version of "Das Kunstwerk im Zeitalter seiner technischen Reproduzierbarkeit," designated the "Zweite Fassung," though now known to be the third, in *GS,* 1: 506. Where possible I will cite from the English translation, sometimes with modifications, which is made from this third version. When citing from this third version, I refer both to the English translation ("Work of Art") and to the original German text in *GS.* In all other cases, the translations are mine. In this instance, the passage is in the French version as well, which is reliable and at times inspired, if only partial, because it does not fully agree with any extant German version; as noted above, its rewritings of the text occur almost exclusively in conjunction with Marxist terminology or Marxist rhetorical gestures. In this passage, for example, in addition to the consistent use of *"état totalitaire"* for "Fascism," where the English translates "The masses have a right to change

property relations," it reads *"Les masses tendent à la transformation des condi-tions de propriété."*

14. This sentence, which appears in the second German version, was sup-pressed in the third version, along with an extensive note that details the dynamics of class consciousness in the context of class struggle, *GS,* 7: 370; an earlier version of this note, which did not make it into any version, is now published in *GS,* 7: 668. The French version of this section is much less detailed in general; this sentence, however, does appear in the translation, although "Fascism" is rendered by *"régimes autoritaires," GS,* 1: 725–726.

15. Recent interpretations of Benjamin's notion of aura tend in this direction. In Samuel Weber's admirable essay on Benjamin's aura, for example, fascism "reinstates the aura of the world-picture by means of the very media that undermine it"; "through the use of the media, above all film, what is in its innermost structure dispersed and distracted is given a form and a shape, a voice and a face," "Art, Aura, and Media in the Work of Walter Benjamin," *Mass Mediauras: Form, Technics, Media,* ed. Alan Cholodenko (Stanford: Stanford University Press, 1996), 102, 103.

16. This sentence, which appears in the second German version (*GS,* 7: 355), is much vaguer in the third version (1: 479). Here I follow the interpretation of the French version, which translates *"mit dem zunehmenden Wachstum von Massen"* as *"avec la prise de conscience accentuée des masses"* (1: 713).

17. Benjamin openly uses Kantian terminology here: *Denken* versus *An-schauung,* "thinking" versus "perception" (although in Kant, *Anschauung* is more commonly translated as "intuition"), is a distinction Kant makes in the *Critique of Pure Reason,* specifically in the section "Transcendental Aesthetic." Interestingly, the French version translates *Anschauung* as *"réceptivité,"* a term Kant uses to describe the capacity for receiving repre-sentations. Benjamin's rigorous historical use of these terms departs sig-nificantly from the Kantian tradition.

18. This passage, along with the passages cited in the following discussion, ap-pears in "Quaderno 16 (Argomenti di cultura—1°)," 1889–1893. The sec-tion is entitled "Oratory, Conversation, Culture" and is a more elaborate version of what appeared in Notebook 1 as "Conversation and Culture." *Se-lections from Cultural Writings* contains a translation of the later version in its entirety (381–385), whereas the shorter first version is included in Gramsci's *Prison Notebooks,* 1: 232–234.

19. This opposition between written and spoken is undoubtedly provoked in part by the immediate historical situation. Hitler, for example, gave the spo-ken word a privileged place in consolidating mass support for the state (and mass media in general were rigorously controlled under the German state): "The power which has always started the greatest religious and political ava-

lanches in history rolling has from time immemorial been the magic power of the spoken word, and that alone. The broad masses of the people can be moved only by the power of speech" (*Mein Kampf* [Boston: Houghton Mifflin Company, 1943], 107, cited in William L. Shirer, *The Rise and Fall of the Third Reich* [New York: Ballantine Books, 1983], 46).

20. Letter from Benjamin to Adorno, 9 December 1938, in *Aesthetics and Politics,* trans. and ed. Ronald Taylor (London: Verso, 1977), 140.

21. *The Economist,* 7 March 1992, 19.

8. Reflections on the Force of the Figure

1. Edward W. Said, "Orientalism Reconsidered," *Cultural Critique* 1 (Fall 1985): 103.

2. Chapter 6 traced the contours of this "human" idea in the figure of the anthropos.

3. Tampering with this configuration poses problems for scholars who have internalized the modern precepts of historical and literary understanding. For example, Said's questioning of this model, which I will deal with in greater detail below, has led to confusion on the part of many of his critics. See Aijaz Ahmad, *In Theory: Classes, Nations, Literatures* (London: Verso, 1992), for a critique that cannot determine whether to qualify Said (and his work) as being too humanist or too antihumanist and therefore claims that he is both and unable to resolve the contradiction between the two (164).

4. This is the formulation of Albert Einstein and Leopold Infeld, *The Evolution of Physics: From Early Concepts to Relativity and Quanta* (New York: Simon and Shuster, 1938), 7. See also the discussion of scientific idealization in chapter 2 above.

5. Said, "Orientalism Reconsidered," 92.

6. Aristotle described the signifying process of personification as a subcategory of metaphor; it involved what he called "setting before the eyes" (*pro ommaton*), *Rhetoric,* III.xi.1–4.

7. Said, "Orientalism Reconsidered," 92.

8. Edward Said, *Orientalism* (New York: Pantheon, 1978), 1.

9. The list of such discussions would be lengthy, and I will limit myself to two paradigmatic references to Nietzsche's unfinished essay in the conceptual context of Said's critical reading: the condemnation paradigm in Ahmad's *In Theory,* 194–197, and Homi Baba's citation en passant of one of Nietzsche's key phrases in *The Location of Culture* (London: Routledge, 1994), 164.

10. Jürgen Habermas, "The Entwinement of Myth and Enlightenment: Re-Reading *Dialectic of Enlightenment*," *New German Critique* 26 (Spring–Summer 1982): 13.

11. Ahmad, *In Theory,* 197.
12. Friedrich Nietzsche, "On Truth and Lie in an Extramoral Sense," in *Philosophy and Truth: Selections from Nietzsche's Notebooks of the Early 1870s,* trans. and ed. Daniel Breazeale (Atlantic Highlands, N.J.: Humanities Press, 1979), 79; German edition: "Ueber Wahrheit und Lüge im aussermoralischen Sinne," *Sämtliche Werke; Kritische Studienausgabe,* vol. 1, ed. Giorgio Colli and Mazzino Montinari (Munich: Walter de Gruyter and Co., 1967–1977), 875. Page references for additional citations appear in the text, with the first indicating the English translation and the second, the German original; English translations are sometimes slightly modified.
13. Dante, *De vulgari eloquentia,* bilingual ed. (Latin-Italian), ed. and trans. Sergio Cecchin (Turin: Tea, 1988), IX.6. Chapter 1 above contains a detailed discussion of other aspects of this passage.
14. Machiavelli, "Che la variazione delle sètte e delle lingue, insieme con l'accidente de' diluvii o della peste, spegne le memorie delle cose" (book 2, chap. 5), *Discorsi sopra la prima Deca di Tito Livio,* vol. 2 of *Le grandi opere politiche,* ed. Gian Mario Anselmi and Carlo Varotti (Turin: Bollati Boringhieri, 1993), 250–251. Machiavelli speculates that the only reason that the linguistic artifacts of classical civilization remained partially extant was because the Christians had no other language to impose and were forced to adopt Latin.
15. Jean-Jacques Rousseau, "Que le p[remi]er langage du être figuré," in *Essai sur l'origine des langues,* ed. Jean Starobinski, vol. 5 of *Oeuvres complètes,* ed. Bernard Gagnebin and Marcel Raymond (Paris: Gallimard, La Pléiade, 1995), 381–382.
16. This passage was a key bone of contention between Derrida's and de Man's conflicting interpretations of Rousseau. See Jacques Derrida, *De la grammatologie* (Paris: Minuit, 1967), 381–397 and Paul de Man, "The Rhetoric of Blindness," *Blindness and Insight* (Minnesota: University of Minnesota Press, 1983), 131–136.
17. See editor Starobinski's comments on this chapter, in Rousseau, *Essai sur l'origine des langues,* 1544–1546.
18. For Aristotle's model of language, the primary substance (*prote ousia*) on which the entire philosophy of language rests is the absolutely particular: "for example, a particular man or a particular horse" (*Categories,* 2a.13–14). Aristotle goes on in *Categories* to draw the logical conclusion that "if these primary substances did not exist, nothing else would exist either" (2b.5–7). How one conceives of that initial experience enables and limits theories of signification, history, and even political action that necessarily depend on it.
19. (84; 881). To a certain extent borrowing Kantian terminology, this passage indicates the transfer ("metaphor") of a perception (*Anschauung,* or "intu-

ition" in English-language Kantian terminology) into a schema. In explaining the coining of *giant*, Rousseau attempts to grasp this visual aspect by relating "passions" to an "idea," which turns out to be erroneously assigned to the expression. For a discussion of figure and *Bild*, particularly in conjunction with Walter Benjamin's use of the latter term, see chapter 3.

20. Benjamin addresses these same questions, using the same conceptual elements and much of the same terminology, in his "Task of the Translator"; see my analysis of this text in chapter 2.

21. (84; 880–881). This passage has been translated many times, but there is little agreement about how to express *Bild* in English. The translation I cite, for example, originally renders the phrase in question as "coins which have lost their embossing"; Walter Kaufmann, whose translation is most often cited and is used by Said and his commentators, prefers "coins which have lost their pictures" ("On Truth and Lie in an Extra-Moral Sense," *The Portable Nietzsche* [New York: Viking Press, 1968], 47); and Paul de Man provides his own somewhat freer translation: "metaphors that have been used up and have lost their imprint and that now operate as mere metal, no longer as coins," *Allegories of Reading: Figural Language in Rousseau, Nietzsche, Rilke, and Proust* (New Haven: Yale University Press, 1979), 111.

22. Paul de Man, "Anthropomorphism and Trope in the Lyric," *The Rhetoric of Romanticism* (New York: Columbia University Press, 1984), 242.

23. Paul de Man, "Pascal's Allegory of Persuasion," *Aesthetic Ideology*, ed. Andrzej Warminski (Minneapolis: University of Minnesota Press, 1996), 51–69. Further references to this essay are to this volume.

24. Given my specific concerns in this chapter, I will not directly reiterate de Man's discussion of the notion of infinity. It should be noted, however, that de Man's contribution to an understanding of infinity's place in the representation of modernity is perhaps the essay's most novel aspect with respect to contemporary theories of language, particularly in conjunction with Cantor's mathematical analysis of infinity and Gödel's concern with contradiction in symbolic logic. As such, it merits a lengthy consideration on its own.

25. Blaise Pascal, "Justice, force," no. 103 of *Pensées*, in *Oeuvres complètes*, ed. Louis Lafuma (Paris: Seuil, 1963), 512. I quote de Man's translation of the fragment, published in "Pascal's Allegory of Persuasion," 67. The earlier Brunschvicg edition of *Pensées*, in which this text is no. 298, offers a slight textual variant that de Man incorporates.

26. Louis Marin, *La critique du discours: Sur la* Logique de Port-Royal *et les* Pensées *de Pascal* (Paris: Minuit, 1975), 383; my translation.

27. *Pensées*, no. 85, in *Oeuvres complètes*, 510; this and subsequent translations of Pascal's texts are mine.

28. Erich Auerbach, "On the Political Theory of Pascal," *Scenes from the Drama of European Literature,* trans. Ralph Mannheim (Minneapolis: University of Minnesota Press, 1959, 1984), 114; German text: Erich Auerbach, "Über Pascals Politische Theorie," *Gesammelte Aufsätze zur romanischen Philologie"* (Bern/Munich: Francke Verlag, 1967), 211; translation slightly modified. Subsequent citations of this text refer to these editions, and page references indicate first the English translation, then the German original.

29. Pascal, "Trois discours sur la condition des grands," in *Oeuvres complètes,* 367.

30. *Pensées,* no. 645, in ibid., 588.

31. Auerbach, "On the Political Theory of Pascal," 117; 214. Translation modified.

32. Pascal, "Trois discours sur la condition des grands," 367.

33. Auerbach, 128; 221. Translation modified.

34. *Pensées,* no. 91, in *Oeuvres complètes,* 510.

35. Antonio Gramsci, "Quaderno 11 (Introduzione allo studio della filosofia)," *Quaderni del carceri,* ed. Valentino Gerratana (Turin: Einaudi, 1975), 1438. Parts of this passage were included in an earlier notebook, which exists in volume 2 of Gramsci's notebooks in English (all the volumes are not yet available); I have therefore adopted that translation, incorporating only Gramsci's later modifications to the passage: *Prison Notebooks,* vol. 2, trans. and ed. Joseph A. Buttigieg (New York: Columbia University Press, 1996), 159.

Index